HEARING THE VOICE OF GOD

Related to Revelation, Conscience, Inspiration, Illumination and Postmodernism

H. D. Williams, M.D., Ph.D.

THE OLD PATHS PUBLICATIONS
142 GOLD FLUME WAY
CLEVELAND, GEORGIA 30528

BIBLE FOR TODAY #3340

> **Disclaimer**
>
> The author of this work has quoted the writers of many articles and books. This does not mean that the author endorses or recommends the works of others. If the author quotes someone, it does not mean that he agrees with all of the author's tenets, statements, concepts, or words, whether in the work quoted or any other work of the author. There has been no attempt to alter the meaning of the quotes; and therefore, some of the quotes are long in order to give the entire sense of the passage.

Copyright © 2008 by H. D. Williams
All Rights Reserved
Printed in the United States of America

Library of Congress Control Number: 2007942449
REL006201: Religion: Biblical Studies - Topical

ISBN 978-0-9801689-0-7

All Scripture quotes are from the King James Bible except those verses compared and then the source is identified.

No part of this work may be reproduced without the expressed consent of the publisher, except for brief quotes, whether by electronic, photocopying, recording, or information storage and retrieval systems.

Address All Inquiries To:
THE OLD PATHS PUBLICATIONS, Inc.
142 Gold Flume Way
Cleveland, Georgia, U.S.A.

Web: www.theoldpathspublications.com
E-mail: TOP@theoldpathspublications.com

BIBLE FOR TODAY #3340
Web: www.biblefortoday.org
E-mail: bft@biblefortoday.org

1.0

C. H. Spurgeon (Prince of Preachers) in 1855 said:

"The Bible…is **God's voice**, not man's; **the words are God's words**, **the words** of the Eternal, the Invisible, the Almighty, the Jehovah of this earth. This Bible is God's Bible, and when I see it, I seem to hear **a voice** springing up from it, saying, "I am the book of God; man, read me. I am God's writing; open my leaf, for I was penned by God; read it, for he is my author, and you will see him visible and manifest everywhere." "*I have written to him the great things of my law*" (Hosea 8:12) (Spurgeon's Sermons, "The Bible," Number 15, SwordSearcher, Ver. 5.2, Broken Arrow, OK.)

Dedication

This work is dedicated to the pastors that God has called to shepherd His people and that have remained faithful to His preserved Words in the *received traditional* Hebrew, Aramaic, and Greek texts and to the accurate and faithful translations of those Words into the languages of the world, especially the English King James Bible. It is hoped that this work will encourage faithful pastors to realize that a dwindling congregation in these last days is not their fault. God loves each of you and your reward is near. The Scriptures declare: *"a short work will the Lord make upon the earth"* (Rom. 9:28). *"And when the chief Shepherd shall appear, ye shall receive a crown of glory that fadeth not away"* (1 Peter 5:4).

This work would not have been possible without my *"help meet"* of forty-six years. She is the wife of my youth who has been by my side without wavering during the bad times as well as the good times. What would I do without her? May the Day Star in her heart bless her mightily, and keep her by my side until He returns!

The significant contribution to this work by Pastor D. A. Waite, Th.D., Ph.D., the Dean John William Burgon of our times, is appreciated very much. Dr. Waite's steadfast stand for God's preserved Words in the *received* Hebrew, Aramaic, and Greek texts behind the King James Bible is well known. His friendship and help to this author over the years is priceless: *"Remembering without ceasing your work of faith, and labour of love, and patience of hope in our Lord Jesus Christ, in the sight of God and our Father"* (1 Thessalonians 1:3).

The assistance of Brothers Tom Eller, R. Ph., and Rob Winograd helped smooth the rough places in this work and this author greatly appreciates their diligence. However, any flaws remain this author's responsibility. May this work assist those led astray from the written Words of God. Its highest goal is:

Sola Dei Gloria! (For God's Glory Alone!)

H. D. Williams, M.D., Ph.D.

FAITH COMETH BY HEARING

There were no bells and whistles
When Christ I did receive
The prick inside my heart
Was not electricity

No quaking of the ground
No moving of the sea
No voices in my head
No visions in my sleep

So what is my assurance
Of a place before His throne
Of knowing life eternal
Where I'll spend my heavenly home

It's really very simple
There's one place you must look
In the pages of the Bible
God's Word, His holy book

No visions or angelic voices
Or parting of the sea
Can match the mighty Words
Settled in eternity

The written Words He hath spoken
In faith that we receive
Are the substance of the faith
In Lord Jesus whom we believe

        Rob Winograd
        September, 2007

CONTENTS AT A GLANCE

TITLE	PAGE
DEDICATION…………………………………………………	5
TABLE OF CONTENTS ………………………………………	7
DEFINITIONS………………………………………………..	17
PREFACE……………………………………………………..	35
CHAPTER 1: INTRODUCTION………………………………	47
CHAPTER 2: THE VOICE OF THE LORD…………………...	83
CHAPTER 3: CONSCIENCE (OUR WITNESS)……………...	120
CHAPTER 4: REVELATION…………………………………	159
CHAPTER 5: INSPIRATION AND ILLUMINATION………..	191
CHAPTER 6: POSTMODERNISM……………………………	213
CHAPTER 7: CONCLUSION…………………………………	273
BIBLIOGRAPHY……………………………………………...	283
ATTACHMENTS……………………………………………..	293
INDEX………………………………………………………..	299
ABOUT THE AUTHOR……………………………………….	307

TABLE OF CONTENTS

TITLE	PAGE
PUBLISHER…………………………………………………...	1
SPURGEON QUOTE…………………………………………..	3
DEDICATION………………………………………………...	5
POEM BY WINOGRAD………………………………………	6
CONTENTS AT A GLANCE…………………………………	7
TABLE OF CONTENTS ……………………………………..	7
ABBREVIATIONS……………………………………………	13
DEFINITIONS………………………………………………..	17
PREFACE……………………………………………………..	35
A Blight…………………………………………………..	35
Postmodernism is Extreme Self-will…………………….	36
Warnings…………………………………………………	37
Postmodernism is From Philosophers and Scholars……	38
An Illustration From Scripture…………………………..	41
The Primary Cause of Postmodernism………………….	44

CHAPTER 1: INTRODUCTION ... 47
- The Problem ... 48
- Abundance Breeds Iniquity ... 48
- Troubling Results ... 49
- The Need ... 50
- The Famine ... 51
- The Essence of Postmodernism ... 52
- Mistakes and Misinterpretations ... 54
- Rejection of Evidence ... 56
- The "Deformation" Versus The "Reformation" ... 58
- Examples ... 59
- Spiritual Failures Caused by Postmodernism ... 62
- The Purpose of This Work ... 64
- Walking by Faith ... 66
- Enormous Confusion About These Issues ... 71
- Misappropriations and Misunderstandings of Terms ... 72
- The Confusion Has Wrought Folly ... 74
- Another Example ... 75
- In Every Generation Human Scholarship and Philosophy Fail ... 80
- The Tenets of Humanistic Philosophy ... 81

CHAPTER 2: THE VOICE OF THE LORD ... 83
- The Importance of Words ... 83
- A Message or The Message ... 86
- The Corrupted Message ... 86
- Authority is Uncertain if the Message is Uncertain ... 87
- Anger, Rebellion, and Depression Linked to Uncertainty ... 88
- Seven Ways "The Voice of the Lord" is Used ... 88
- 1. The Voice of the Lord Used as a Metaphor ... 89
- 2. The Voice of the Lord Used as an Audible Voice ... 91
- 3. The Voice of the Lord Used as Words to Prophets ... 93
  - The Still Small Voice ... 94
  - How The Holy Spirit Teaches ... 96
- 4. The Voice of the Lord Identified With Creation ... 97
- 5. The Voice of the Lord Is Words of the Holy Spirit ... 98
- 6. The Voice of the Lord as a Future Audible Voice ... 100
- 7. The Voice of the Lord is All The Words in the Bible ... 100
- The Guidance of the Holy Spirit ... 105
- The Ante-Nicene Elders Understood ... 107
- Peter Understood ... 110

Job Understood...	111
C. H. Spurgeon Understood...	112
Many Do Not Understand...	112
Many Ancient Hebrews Did Not Understand..............	114
Man's Need to Feel Special..	115

CHAPTER 3: CONSCIENCE (OUR WITNESS)............... 120

A Neglected Doctrine..	120
Our Conscience is Our Witness...................................	123
Our Conscience is an Inherited Faculty of The Mind.....	125
Our Conscience is Not Acquired..................................	126
A Pure Conscience..	128
Our Conscience is Affected by Original Sin................	130
Conscience is Not The Voice of The Lord...................	132
Many Definitions Cause Confusion..............................	133
What is Conscience—From Scripture?........................	138
Scope of The Doctrine of The Conscience..................	139
The Conscience of the Saved......................................	140
The Conscience of the Unsaved..................................	142
Summary of The Doctrine...	143
Ideas Excluded..	144
Ideas Included...	144
A Regenerated Conscience...	146
Conscience is a Goad, Not a Guide............................	146
Warnings..	147
A Weak Conscience and Babes in Christ...................	150
Beware of False Claims, Teachers and 'Prophets'.........	152
Assurance That a Believer is the Child of God............	154

CHAPTER 4: REVELATION.. 159

Revelation Does Not Need Reconstructing................	163
Confusion is Not From God...	165
Early Gnostics Brought Confusion...............................	166
The Doctrine of Revelation...	170
General (Common, Practical) Revelation...................	172
A Blind Watchmaker?...	174
The Unifying Principle...	177
History, Providence, and General Revelation.............	179
Specific Revelation, Including Special Revelation........	180
Cessation of Revelation...	184
Ruckmanites...	186
Other Examples of Confusion and Modern Gnostic......	188

CHAPTER 5: INSPIRATION AND ILLUMINATION.......	191
Inspiration...	191
Theopneustos Means is Given by Inspiration of God.....	191
Pasa Means "All," Not "Every".............................	192
Graphe Means Scripture.......................................	192
The Process of Inspiration...................................	193
The Model for Making Copies..............................	194
The Praise of the Holy Scriptures..........................	198
Alleged Inspiration Problems...............................	200
Illumination..	204
The Cause of Poor Illumination............................	205
Illumination and Conscience................................	206
A Major Cause For Rejection of God's Preserved Received Words..	209
CHAPTER 6: POSTMODERNISM.............................	213
A Concept For Academia or a New Era....................	213
The Definition of Postmodernism..........................	215
Dates...	220
The Search For Truth Without God........................	223
Postmodernism is Here to Stay.............................	224
A Warning to Postmodern Organizations.................	228
Modernism Versus Postmodernism........................	229
Some of the Postulates of Modernism.....................	229
Postmodernism is The Worst Humanistic Philosophy in Man's History...........................	231
Some of the Postulates of Postmodernism.................	233
A Warning to Church Elders................................	235
Some Quotes..	235
Why Are Young People Leaving The Church? A Primary Reason..	236
Four Postmodern Streams....................................	241
Postmodernists Object to Being Challenged to Define Their Beliefs......................................	243
Two Major Divisions of Postmodernism...................	245
The Reason For Rejection of Modernism..................	246
The Postmodern Church.....................................	246
The Roots of the Emerging Church.........................	249
Open and Process Theology.................................	251
The Two Streams in the Emerging Church Movement...	252
What is Their Source of Authority..........................	255
Visual Orientation...	258

Replacement of Orthodox Terminology............	259
A Significant Cause For Failure of Postmodernism.......	262
Shocking New Reports...............................	263
Statistics Support the Harm Postmodernism is Causing..	265
The Bottom Line For The Postmodern Movement........	268
CHAPTER 7: CONCLUSION............................	273
Anchored to The Rock or Geared to The Times...........	274
People Geared to The Times are Not Fit For The Battle..	276
We Will Not Surrender One Page or One Word of Scripture..	278
BIBLIOGRAPHY....................................	283
ATTACHMENTS....................................	293
INDEX...	299
ABOUT THE AUTHOR...............................	307

ABBREVIATIONS

A = Codex Alexandrinus

A.D. = Anno Dei

Apographs = copies of the original manuscripts

ASV = American Standard Version

Autographs = original manuscripts

B = Codex Vaticanus

B.C. = Before Christ

BHS = Biblia Hebraica Stuttgartensia

ca. = circa

CEV = Contemporary English Version

cf = compare

DB = word(s) in Double brackets

DE = dynamic equivalent or equivalence

D.S.S. = Dead Sea Scrolls

e.g. = Latin, exempli gratia = for example

EL = essentially literal

Encarta = Encarta Online Dictionary

etc. = Latin, et cetera = and so forth

ESV = English Standard Version

FE = formal equivalent

FunE = functional equivalent

GTO = Greek Text of Origen

GW = God's Word

i.e. = Latin, id est = that is

ibid = Latin, ibidem = in the same place

Inerrant = containing no mistakes

ISBE = International Standard Bible Encyclopedia

KJB = King James Bible
LB = Living Bible
Lectionaries = a book containing portions of Scripture
Letter = Letter of Aristeas
LXX = Septuagint
MSS = manuscripts
MT = Hebrew Masoretic Text
NASB = New American Standard Version
NCV = New Century Version
NET = New English Translation
NIV = New International Version
NLT = New Living Translation
NRSV = New Revised Standard Version
NT = New Testament
op. cit. = Latin opera citato = in the work previously cited
OT = Old Testament
p., pp = page(s)
Plenary = full, complete, entire
Revision = re-examination for correction; as the revision of a book or writing or of a proof sheet; a revision of statutes.
RSV = Revised Standard Version
RT = Received Texts
TCOP = A book entitled, *The Challenge of Postmodernism*
TEV = Todays English Version
TR = Textus Receptus
TT = Traditional Text
VE = verbal equivalent
VPI = verbal plenary inspiration (inspiration of all the Words of God)
VPP = verbal plenary preservation (preservation of all the Words of God)

VPT = verbal plenary translating

vid. supra = Latin, vide supra = See above or other material in this work

viz. = Latin, videlicet = namely

WH = Westcott and Hort, 1881

DEFINITIONS

Apollinarianism: taught that Jesus had a human body, but that he had only a divine psychological make-up, and was not God.

Charismatic (Movement): is an interfaith movement emphasizing religious experiences such as the second "baptism in the Holy Spirit," accompanied by "speaking in tongues" and miraculous "sign" gifts at the expense of biblical authority and sound biblical interpretation. The movement encourages ecumenism. The movement varies from church to church and denomination to denomination.

Collate: to compare information. Concerning manuscripts (MSS), it means to review several MSS that are essentially the same except for spelling errors and to correct the spelling by reference to the way a word is spelled in most of them. Since MSS from the *Received Text* route are from many geographical areas and are virtually the same, the final collated text's affirmation is by (1) lectionaries, (2) versions, and (3) church pastors' writings, which results in the Traditional Text of the Holy Scriptures. This text is the one present from generation to generation in sanctified churches. It is Beza's Greek text except for a **few** Words found in the other three sources.

Community: a term that postmodernists have personalized in place of "church" (e.g. "our community," "community of faith," or "intergenerational community").

Conscience: a faculty of man placed in the soul of man by God which appropriately determines or judges right or wrong based upon the "law written in [his] heart" (Rom. 2:15) when it is cleansed by the Word of God, and therefore functioning as well as possible in a fallen world. The faculty of the conscience may be seared, defiled, or weak according to Scripture. Therefore, it cannot be relied upon as "*the voice of God*," truth, or an infallible guide.

Confessionalism: dependant on creeds and tradition.

Contemplative Prayer: In the first 16 centuries after Christ, contemplative prayer was communing in prayer while contemplating God's Words. HOWEVER, the meaning has been changed and has been adapted to Eastern meditation or prayer called *centering prayer*, which calls for an "emptying" of the mind and a concentrating on ONE (quote, unquote "sacred") word. "You can find similar practices in Islam, Judaism, Hinduism, Buddhism, Taoism, Nature Religions, and virtually every other living religious tradition. Medical practitioners are even prescribing secular versions of this practice for their patients." [1] It is a dangerous form of meditation or "prayer."

Centering Prayer: See contemplative prayer.

Convergent Church: The following came from the website of an emerging church article: "What is a Convergence Church?"

> "To converge, according to Webster, simply means to move towards one point, to come together or to meet. For far to [sic, too] long the church has been divided and separated from one another... The convergence movement is a coming together of the three major historic branches of the Church, the Sacramental, the Evangelical, and the Charismatic. Each of these expressions of the Church of Jesus Christ have [sic, has] been carefully nurtured by God and greatly used to establish and to expand the [sic] His work on earth... The Convergence Movement has identified the three living

---

[1] Lowell Grisham, "Journeying Toward the Mystery: The Contemplative Practice of Centering Prayer, Step by Step" (http://www.explorefaith.org/prayer/essays/center.html).

streams of the Church and invites God to bring them together as one complete and life-giving river... (Psalm 46:4). The Convergence Movement seeks to blend or merge the essential elements in the Christian faith represented historically in three major streams of thought and practice: the Evangelical, the Charismatic and the Sacramental. These three streams each in their own way have defined the map of Christianity through the ages and will merge like a flood into the future to bring reconciliation and unleash God's powerful purpose for his Church. For the present time, Convergence Churches will be powerful symbols and agents of reconciliation and harmony of God's people."[2] [HDW, spelling, punctuation, and grammatical errors are not mine]

Deconstructionism:

"a textual analysis method; a method of analyzing texts based on the ideas that language is inherently unstable and shifting and that the reader rather than the author is central in determining meaning" (Encarta).

Amazingly, this method started with biblical scholars and philosophers and not with literary scholars!

Dialectical Materialism:

"the Marxian concept of reality in which material things are in the constant process of change, [which is] brought about by the tension between conflicting or interacting forces, elements, or ideas."

Dialectic: is

"debate intended to resolve a conflict between two contradictory or apparently contradictory ideas or elements *logically*, establishing truths on both sides rather than disproving one argument; the methods used in Socratic

---

[2] Quintin D. Moore, Senior Pastor, The Father's House, "What is a Convergence Church?" (http://www.thekingschurch.net/church.pdf, Dec. 2003). Also, see Brian McLaren, "Becoming Convergent." (http://emergent-us.typepad.com/emergentus/files/becoming_emergent.pdf)

philosophy to reveal truth through disputation" (Encarta). (also, see Hegelian philosophy)

Docetism: taught that Jesus was a **created** being, and that He was a god.

Dogmatism:
> "the tendency to express strongly held opinions in a way that suggests they should be accepted without question" (Encarta).

Dynamic Equivalent Translation: substituting or interpreting the meaning or semantics of a word in a written source-language into a written receptor-language without attention to parts of speech, precise meaning, or word order. For example, the word "heart" is substituted for the word "reins." (See *Word-For-Word Translating of the Received Text, Verbal Plenary Translating* by this author.)

Ecumenism:
> "a movement in the Christian Church aiming at unity between different denominations on basic issues" (Encarta)

for the purpose of eventually bringing all religions under one roof, in one "house," and with one ruler, who, incidentally, is seen as the *"false prophet"* in Scripture.

Emerging Church: a church that is utilizing or adapting to some or all of the tenets or concepts of postmodernism to "evangelize," to conduct "worship," and to form an assembly called a "community." The emerging churches assert 'belonging before believing' as opposed to 'believing before belonging.' The movement claims to be moving from "absolute beliefs" to "authentic beliefs." This is simply another adaptation of an assembly of people to another humanistic, philosophical perversion. This is in opposition to an assembly "adapting" to the biblical organization and function of a local church. They claim to be convergent churches, and claim to incorporate styles of worship, which are not offensive to other religions or to the 'seeker.'

Enlightenment, Age of:
"a term used to describe the trends in thought and letters in Europe and the American colonies during the 18th century prior to the French Revolution (1789-1799). The phrase was frequently employed by writers of the period itself, convinced that they were emerging from centuries of darkness and ignorance into a new age enlightened by reason, science, and a respect for humanity. The period is also often referred to as the Age of Reason. The precursors of the Enlightenment can be traced to the 17th century and earlier. They include the philosophical rationalists René Descartes [1596-1650] and Baruch Spinoza [1632-1677], the political philosophers Thomas Hobbes [1588-1679] and John Locke [1632-1704], and various skeptical thinkers in France such as Pierre Bayle [1647-1706]. Equally important, however, were (1) the self-confidence engendered by new discoveries in science—by Nicolaus Copernicus and Galileo, for example—and (2) the spirit of cultural relativism encouraged by the exploration of the non-European world." (Encarta) (my addition, HDW).

Epistemology:
"how we know things or think we know things."[3] "*Epistemology* is the study of knowledge, its scope and limits. As taught within the field of philosophy, it tends to be simply a massaging of verbal definitions, somewhat devoid of any practical tools and suggestions... For most of man's history, the main issue in epistemology was reasoning versus sense perception in acquiring knowledge."[4]

---

[3] D. A. Carson, *Becoming Conversant with The Emerging Church, Understanding a Movement and its Implications* (Zondervan, Grand Rapids, MI, 2005) 27.
[4] Chuck Missler, "The Failure of Empiricism," (*Epistemology, Part 2*, Koinonia House, http://www.khouse.org/articles/2005/563/) accessed 10/20/07.

Epistemologists were opposed by the empiricists, who claimed:

> "the main source and final test of knowledge was sense perception."[5]

Therefore, empiricists believed experimentation, especially through double blind studies, would lead to truth. The failure of all "philosophies" is their *subjectivism*, which is *"after the tradition of men, after the rudiments of the world, and not after Christ"* (Col. 2:8).

Empiricists: see epistemology. Truth exists only through what is revealed by experimentation. It is dependent upon the senses.

Essentialism:
> "the philosophical doctrine that things have an essence or ideal nature that is independent of and prior to their existence" (Encarta).

Humans see only the expression of the "essence." [e.g. in art or in Gnosticism]. Philo (20 B.C.-50 A.D.) facilitated this concept. He taught a number of idyllic intermediate beings, named the pleroma, assisted a created ideal god, called the logos, who generated the visible creation.

Also, *"The Concise Oxford Dictionary of Archaeology*, 1/1/2002 defines essentialism [theologically] as:

> "the idea that there are certain attitudes or emotions that are biologically inherent to human beings in general or to males or females differently. Essentialist claims are often backed up with biological arguments, and are in some cases derived from sociobiology or humanism."

Eutychianism: taught that Jesus' divinity and humanity (nature) were combined into *one* nature. Of course, this would mean Jesus was not exactly man and therefore, He could not serve as the perfect substitute for man. He would be a hybrid.

---

[5] Ibid. (Missler, "The Failure of Empiricism").

Exclusivity: means to be:
> "limited to a group of people, excluding or intending to exclude many from participation or consideration." (Encarta)

Many postmodernists deny the exclusivity of Christianity, and essentially declare that all religions lead to God.

Existentialism: is a philosophical claim that truth is only what you see or what exists. The universe has no other unrevealed existence, intrinsic meaning, or purpose. There is no other existence in dimensions unseen.

Foundationalism: (1) From the Christian's point of view, certain doctrines are foundational and their derivation is from clear statements of Scripture or from systematic study of the Scripture (avoiding figures of speech to establish doctrine). (2) From the humanistic philosopher's point of view, foundationalism is:
> "especially in the tradition of the seventeenth-century French philosopher René Descartes. [He] sought for certitude by contending that there are certain unquestionable truths. These truths serve as the basis of all other knowledge claims, which can be derived from these foundations by **deductive** certainty. Thus, the conclusions are those about which one need, and indeed can, have no doubt."[6]

However, Scriptural truths can only be properly constructed from **inductive** study. Man cannot bring his preconceived notions to Scripture and deductively make facts fit a concept. His construction will be false. This is a significant failure of postmodernists.

Hegelian Philosophy: dialectic discussion, which is:

---

[6] Millard J. Erickson, *The Postmodern World, Discerning the Times and the Spirit of Our Age* (Crossway Books, a division of Good News Publishers, Wheaton, IL, 2002) 88.

> "the process, in Hegelian and Marxist thought, in which two apparently opposed ideas, the thesis and antithesis, become combined in a unified whole, the synthesis." (Encarta)

The process repeats itself in history. In addition, it is:

> "[t]he method used in Socratic philosophy to reveal truth through disputation" (Encarta).

Hermeneutics: for all practical purposes is interpretation of a Biblical passage.

Hermeneutics of Suspicion: This is a mantra of the postmodernist that coincides with their doctrine of deconstructionism. All interpretations are viewed with suspicion and are not to be accepted. They are evaluated only from the speaker or writer's perspective or aim, which are based upon **his** personal and cultural experiences.

Illumination: as defined in this work is:

> "the influence or ministry of the Holy Spirit which enables all who are in a right relation with God to understand the Scriptures. It is obvious that illumination, being the divine unfolding of Scripture already given, does not contemplate the exalted responsibility of adding to those Scriptures; nor does illumination contemplate an inspired and infallible transmission into language of that which the Spirit teaches."

It is not to be confused with:

> "[i]nspiration, by which revelation finds an infallible expression [and] is confounded by both the Romanists and the rationalists."

The Romanists claim that tradition or the "voice" of the church is on equal par with Scripture and may override it if there is a conflict.

> "The rationalist, in pursuit of reason, **confounds illumination**, or the general influence of the Spirit on all

regenerate hearts, **with** the extraordinary achievements of revelation and inspiration."[7]

Illumination is enlightenment of the Words and passages of Scripture as if a light is switched on in a darkened room.

Inscripturated Words: The Words recorded by God's Apostles and prophets in the sixty-six books of the Bible. Not all of the Words spoken by God from heaven or by the Lord Jesus Christ during the first advent are recorded in the Bible. Only the Words that God wanted us to have are inscripturated and preserved. For example, it is very likely that a letter (epistle) to the Corinthian Church was lost (1 Cor. 5:9). Perhaps a letter to the Laodiceans was also lost (Col. 4:16).

Inspiration: theologically: Dr. Thomas Strouse gives a definition, which is concise:

> "Inspiration is the process whereby the Holy Spirit led the writers of scripture to record accurately His very words; the product of this process was the inspired original."[8]

Dr. Lewis Sperry Chafer's definition is not adequate. He says inspiration:

> "is a reference to that controlling influence which God exerted over the human authors (HDW, recorders—God was the author) by whom the Old and New Testaments were written (HDW, recorded). It has to do with the reception of the divine message and the accuracy (HDW, perfection) with which it is transcribed."[9] (HDW, my additions for clarification)

The Words given to the Apostles and prophets to form the message from God were perfect and should not be added to, subtracted from, or

---

[7] Lewis Sperry Chafer, *Systematic Theology*, Vol. 1 (Kregel Publications, Grand Rapids, MI, originally published 1948, 1976) 50-51.
[8] Dr. Thomas Strouse, Dean, Emmanuel Baptist Theological Seminary, "The Translation Model Predicted by Scripture" (http://www.emmanuel-newington.org/seminary/resources/KJV_Model.pdf).
[9] Chafer, op. cit., 61 (Chafer, *Systematic Theology*).

changed. The Words are inerrant and infallible, as to their entire message in all aspects of life (such as science, ethics, morality, history, etc.). The inspired Words were preserved through the centuries as they were copied and therefore, being the same exact Words, are inspired; that is God-breathed.

Knowledge: general awareness or possession of information, facts, ideas, truth, or principles. Recent postmodern philosophers, such as Michael Foucault, insist that:

> "knowledge makes power" is not monodirectional, but rather, "power also produces knowledge."[10]

Therefore, Bart Ehrman, a postmodernist, claims Gnostic books that should have been in the Scripture are not included because the "orthodox" early Christians were in power.

Liberalism: theologically, it is questioning of all the doctrines of the Christian faith, particularly doctrines such as the virgin birth, the resurrection of Jesus Christ, the sinfulness of man, and creation. It insists that the social welfare of man is the supreme goal of man. It promotes universalism and syncretism of the beliefs of all religions. Its basic theology is liberation theology:

> "a movement in Roman Catholic religious teaching that argues that the Church should work actively to combat social, political, and economic oppression" (Encarta).

Logic: western logic is *either/or*, which is broken into rational inductive and deductive logic. Inductive logic is gathering observed facts to produce a universal claim or principle from **observed instances**. Deductive logic begins with a general observation and deducts to instances. Logic uses three important principles: law of identity, law of contradiction (or

---

[10] Erickson, op.cit., 41 (Millard J. Erickson, *The Postmodern World*).

noncontradiction), and law of excluded middle and seeks to eliminate contradictions.¹¹ Eastern logic is *both/and*. It contends that contradictions and paradoxes exist, and rejects a purely rational approach to life. *Both/and* logic is sweeping the West. It amalgamates religions through philosophical tenets. It accounts for the acceptance and the excusing of contradictory life-styles, such as Kabala mixed with Christian tenets, homosexuals and women as ordained Christian pastors, and crosses displayed around the neck of a person who openly fornicates. These are acceptable to most postmodernists. The 'religious' postmodernists require no separation from the persons living lifestyles contradictory to Christianity when they refuse correction—both/and thinking.

Logocentrism: is a term with several meanings. It is:

> "used in postmodernist's writing to criticize what is perceived as an excessive faith in the stability of meanings, or excessive concern with distinctions, or with the validity of inferences, or the careful use of reason, or with other traditional aids to sifting truth from falsity." "The term as used by Jacques Derrida and other exponents of deconstruction designates the desire for a centre or original guarantee of all meanings, which in Derrida's view has characterized Western philosophy since Plato. The Greek word *logos* can just mean 'word', but in philosophy it often denotes an ultimate principle of truth or reason, while in Christian theology it refers to the Word of God as the origin and foundation of all things" (HighBeam Research).¹²

Metanarratives: "all-inclusive [absolute] explanations,"¹³ interpretations, 'the big picture,' or claims for truth. Postmodernists have a profound aversion to metanarratives or absolute propositions. Examples

---

[11] Ibid. 55 (*The Postmodern World*).
[12] HighBeam Research (http://www.highbeam.com/doc/1O56-logocentrism.html).
[13] Erickson, op. cit, 45 (*The Postmodern World*).

would be: 'reality is the nature of the mind;' or 'materialism' or 'natural forces' are the driving forces, which is the claim of communism's dialectical materialism; or Christianity's metanarratives such as an 'unlimited omniscient, omnipotent, omnipresent God.'[14] Some postmodernists have applied this 'construction' to any concept of "God;" and so, for example, they claim God cannot be, for example, the following: both merciful and just, or allow 'free-will' and be omniscient at the same time. The "constructive" postmodernists (those who claim to pick only the 'good' out of postmodernism) do not seem to realize that rejection of metanarratives, such as the Bible as absolute authority, will lead to subjective experiences and opinions as authority. Authenticity cannot be established by subjectivism, which results in an unlimited number of 'truths' (almost as numerous as the number of people). The desire by postmodernists for authenticity cannot be achieved by rejection of the metanarrative called the Bible [the preserved, inerrant, infallible, inspired *received absolute* Words promised by God (Psa. 12:6-7, Mat. 5:17-18, 24:35, etc., etc., etc.)]. Also, large cohesive theories or passages thought to explain reality, existence, the universe, God, truth and similar concepts. For example, science, religion, and the Bible are metanarratives. Some authors speak of the topics of systematic theology are metanarratives. Postmodernists disdain metanarratives.

Marxism: applied Hegelian philosophy (see above) to economics, which asserts society progresses from rich and poor to a society where neither rich nor poor exist; and which desires to enslave the entire world under those in power.

Meaning:

---

[14] Ibid. 45 (Erickson, *The Postmodern World).*

"what something signifies or indicates; psychological or moral sense, purpose or significance; what a word, sign, or symbol means." (Encarta).

Postmodernists do not believe a definite meaning derives from some fixed meaning in a given text, but the "interpretive community" or person decides the meaning.[15] Therefore, dynamic equivalent translating is acceptable.

Mysticism:
"belief in intuitive spiritual revelation; in religion the belief that personal communication or union with the divine is achieved through intuition, faith, ecstasy, or sudden insight rather than through rational thought (Encarta)."

Narrator: a postmodern name for 'pastor.' Also, the role of pastor for many postmodern churches is "pastor as storyteller."[16]

Neo-Evangelicalism:
"is the philosophical movement which subjects cooperation in ministry to social and spiritual need rather than biblical authority. It endeavors to infiltrate society with a respectable gospel through emphasizing toleration and theological pragmatism. It seeks to present a united voice in evangelicalism by bringing together theological liberals and conservative evangelicals in cooperative efforts and movements."[17]

Neo-Orthodoxy:
"is the movement which, while affirming the transcendence of God, the finiteness and sinfulness of man, and the necessity of supernatural divine revelation of truth; seriously departs from orthodoxy, redefines biblical terminology, accepts the

---

[15] Ibid. 52 (Erickson, *The Postmodern World*).
[16] Carson, op. cit., 23 (*Becoming Conversant with the Emerging Church*).
[17] http://www.svchapel.org/Assets/Docs/DoctrinalStatement.pdf

views of destructive higher criticism, denies the inerrancy of the Scriptures as historic revelation, accepts religious experience as the criterion of truth, and abandons other important truths of the Christian faith."[18]

Plenary: all the words in a text; full, unlimited; no words excluded.

Pluralism: either (1) empirical pluralism, the diversity reflected in "*out of every kindred, and tongue, and people, and nation*" (Rev. 5:9) and "*men, out of every nation under heaven*" (Acts 2:5), or (2):

> "philosophical pluralism, the stance that asserts that no single outlook can be the explanatory system or view of reality that accounts for all of life."[19]

Number two is the hallmark of a postmodernist.

Postmodernism: although there are many variations and significant overlapping, three basic views are noted. (1) Postmodernism is (a) an attitude of uncertainty about most things and (b) applicable truth is derived from a person's community (subjectivism), (2) Postmodernism is extreme selfism (subjectivism) and uncertainty about everything. Although there may be absolute truth, man cannot know it. (3) Postmodernism is the belief that there is no absolute truth. Subsequently, metanarratives are rejected (i.e. God, Bible, ideas, materialism, etc.). Only the individual can determine truth for himself from his experiences of reality. All three positions are humanistic and result in rejection of absolute truth, particularly the Bible.

Pragmatism:

> "a philosophical view that a theory or concept should be evaluated in terms of how it works and its consequences as the standard for action and thought" (Encarta).

---

[18] http://www.svchapel.org/Assets/Docs/DoctrinalStatement.pdf
[19] Carson, op. cit., 31 (*Becoming Conversant with the Emerging Church*).

In other words, the outcome determines truth.

Premodern: prior to the onset of modernism, which is usually set in the seventeenth century; but this work defines modernism as beginning with the opposition to the dark ages that began in the late fifteenth century when the "Morning Star" of the Reformation, John Wycliffe, began his godly work against Roman Catholicism.

Relativism:
> "it is the theory that denies absolutism and insists that morality and religion are relative to the people who embrace them. Lest Christians think none of this applies to them, [Brian] McLaren, [a postmodernist], draws attention to the ethnic cleansing of the Old Testament, to David's many wives, to injunctions against wearing gold rings."[20]

However, this fails to account for God's dispensational ways of dealing with man. His commandments are not relative, but absolute from age to age, from faith to faith, from dispensation to dispensation. God is the ultimate authority, which man has refused.

Reality: based on fact, observation, or experience and so undisputed; used to emphasize the accuracy or appropriateness of a particular thing; essential, that is of basic, essential, or critical importance. For the Christian, reality is based on the essentiality of Scripture, the revelation of Jesus Christ, who represents God and all His attributes. For the secularists, reality may be unseen, but it is represented by the material universe; or reality is only the material universe.

Reductionism:
> "is a theory that asserts that the nature of complex things is reduced to the nature of sums of simpler or more

---

[20] Carson, op. cit., 31 (*Becoming Conversant with the Emerging Church*).

fundamental things. This can be said of objects, phenomena, explanations, theories, and meanings." (Wikipedia).

For example, postmodernism's reduction of modernism is often distorted to the point of perceiving it as 'confessional Christianity' (i.e. based on confessional creeds or fixed denominational beliefs rather than the Bible) and rational without any emotion (i.e. cold). Some postmodernists reject this definition and claim they desire to return to tradition and confessional Christianity. Of course, ultimately, this means a return to a form of sacramentalism.

Renaissance: the end of the middle ages, therefore
> "the period in European history from about the 14th through 16th centuries regarded as marking the end of the Middle Ages and featuring major cultural and artistic change" or "the cultural and religious spirit that characterized the Renaissance, including the decline of Gothic architecture, the revival of classical culture, the beginnings of modern science, and geographical exploration" (Encarta).

Revelation: is the revealing of truth.

Subjectivism: "emphasis on personal feelings or responses as opposed to external facts or evidence;" or a philosophical theory "stating that people can only have knowledge of what they experience directly;" or a philosophical theory "stating that the only valid moral standard is the one imposed by somebody's **own conscience**, and therefore that society's moral codes are invalid." (Encarta). This is the great fallacy of all philosophy, but particularly postmodernism, although most postmodernists would deny this claim, and assert they believe in 'community' above individuals. However, the postmodernists neglect "birds of a feather flock together."

Theophany: the pre-incarnate appearance of God in the Old Testament, which is frequently called "*the angel of the Lord.*"

Transcendentalism: "philosophy emphasizing reasoning **or** the divine" In regard to reasoning: a philosophical "system of philosophy, especially that of Kant, that regards the processes of reasoning as the key to knowledge of reality;" **or** in regard to the divine, a philosophical "system of philosophy, especially that associated with Ralph Waldo Emerson and other New England writers, that emphasizes intuition or the divine" (Encarta). The divine is mystical, not a person, the Lord Jesus Christ, as revealed in a Holy Bible.

Truth: (1) As defined by Christianity, Truth is the Lord Jesus Christ and the Words He gave for inscripturation (Jn. 14:6, 17:17). To the secularist, the philosophical definition of truth has changed many times during the centuries and reflects Pontius Pilates' question of the Lord Jesus Christ: "What is truth?" (Jn. 18:38). For example, some have declared truth is (2) ideas, which reflect material external reality, or (3) ideas reflect a greater reality, such as the Greek "pleroma." But throughout history, the secular ideas of a "reflective" reality have changed from age to age. (4) A third concept declares truth cannot be known, and only the philosophy of pragmatism is valid. (5) Lastly,

> "truth is **not** simply something that exists independently of the knower, so that whoever discovers it is in possession of the truth. Rather, what one knows and believes to be true is a product of one's historical and cultural situation."[21]

This is the most important concept of truth to the postmodernist. (6) There are other ideas about truth that are too numerous to mention here.

---

[21] Erickson, op. cit., 42 (*The Postmodern World*).

PREFACE

A Blight

Many recent books have appeared in the market place concerning the hearing of God's voice. Most of the books are not exegetical works, a careful study and interpretation of Biblical texts to arrive at proper conclusions and applications. Statements by godly church elders of sanctified churches concerning this historical issue are not included in many of the works. As a result, a number of them have reached endpoints that conflict with proper and careful hermeneutics, the interpretation of the passages pertinent to the topic of hearing God's voice. A misunderstanding of Biblical figures of speech, such as metaphors, similes, and other *"similitudes"* or types related to this theme, is influencing interpretations by many authors. Many of the errors relate to the Biblical use of the following terms: *"the voice of the Lord,"* *"revelation," "conscience," "inspiration,"* and *"illumination."* The confusion created by the misunderstanding and poor exegesis of the Scriptures concerning these doctrines is amplified by the extreme godless human philosophy of *"the last days"* called postmodernism and by *"perilous times"* (2 Tim. 3:1-2). The blight of postmodernism is causing the Words of God to be viewed with disdain, analyzed with doubt, studied with uncertainty, corrupted at will, interpreted liberally, and rejected as Truth.

This work will be a *"hard"* look at these issues (Deut. 17:8, Psa. 63:8, Pro. 13:15, Jer. 32:17). The Lord told us that when things pertaining to judgment are *"hard,"* He would provide a place for us to go (Deut. 17:8). That place today is His preserved Words (Mat. 4:4, 24:35). There is nothing too *"hard"* to be solved by the Lord God (Jer. 32:17). Let us call upon Him in prayer as we traverse His Words back and forth; perhaps He will be gracious to us as we attempt to wrestle with these issues. This work is not a casual examination of the issues.

The Holy Spirit, speaking through Paul, warned us that *"in the latter times some shall depart from the faith, giving heed to seducing spirits, and doctrines of devils; Speaking lies in hypocrisy; having their* **conscience** *seared with a hot iron;"* (1 Tim. 4:1-2). The factors mentioned above are significantly contributing to the rejection of God's received, preserved, inspired, inerrant, infallible Hebrew, Aramaic, and Greek Words, and their accurate and faithful translation into various languages of the world (e.g. the accurate and faithful KJB). However, God will preserve His Words for ever, in spite of the attack and corruption by many men influenced by humanistic philosophy (Psa. 12:6-7, Psa. 117, Mat. 24:35, Col. 2:8, and many other verses).

Postmodernism is Extreme Self-Will

Postmodernism is not just *"every man doing what is right in his own eyes"* (Judg. 17:6, 21:25). It is far worse. It is **extreme self-will**. Postmodernism is a progression of iniquity to the point of rejecting **all** truth, especially foundational Truth, which is the Holy Scriptures. There has been a particularly sustained, unrelenting attack on the Words of God in the last several centuries. Men of faith everywhere are lamenting: *"If the foundations be destroyed, what can the righteous do?"* (Psalms 11:3). Nevertheless, faithful believers know that His Words will last *"for ever"* as He promised.

However, the assault on His Words is an overwhelming tidal flood that is washing upon the shores of every nation. During the dispensations of law and of grace, until the present days, men knew preserved, **external** truth existed, but they thought that they could get away with *"doing what is right in [their] own eyes"* (Judg. 21:25, 2 Tim. 3:1-2). For example, in the dispensation of law, as the Israelites grew more wicked, they hid their idols in their rooms (Eze. 8:12) or escaped to the "groves" to commit evil with like-minded wicked men (Judg. 3:7). They thought God did not see them. Nevertheless, He is an omnipotent, omniscient, omnipresent God.

In these last days, the postmodernist chips away at these three cardinal and foundational truths about God, omniscience, omnipotence, and omnipresence by putting forth 'new' concocted theologies called process, open, and dipolar theology. The tenets of these theologies are not derived by systematic examination of the preserved Scriptures guided by the Holy Spirit. Rather, they are postulates constructed from a few passages of Scripture.

Furthermore, postmodernists use many of the passages from corrupted 'new' versions of the 'bible' to formulate these 'new' theologies. Exegetical manipulation and interpretations to match cultural influences dominate the 'new' translations *"through philosophy and vain deceit, after the tradition of men, after the rudiments of the world, and not after Christ."* (Colossians 2:8). The technique of dynamic equivalent translating is the excuse the postmodernist offers.

Now, men everywhere *openly* defy the Scriptures, and abhor the authority of the righteous commandments from a Holy God. The first part of Colossians 2:8 comes to mind as a significant warning of the days in which we now live: *"Beware lest any man spoil you."*

Warnings

At the beginning of the church age, Jude warned us that *"certain men crept in unawares, who were before of old ordained to this condemnation, ungodly men, turning the grace of our God into lasciviousness."* In these last days, the insidious encroachment of self-willed men touting postmodern philosophy creep into institutions of higher learning, churches, and our homes. Without a doubt, they are turning *"the grace of God into"* self-willed lusts that undermine our churches and culture. In these last days, the result of their unholy desires are no less damaging than the men who "crept in unawares" into the early church.

Jesus warned that **self-willed** men who *"prophesied in [His] name"* would not *"enter into the kingdom of heaven"* (Mat. 7:21-23). These men do not *"the will of [His] father which is in Heaven,"* but their own self-will and gainsaying (Gr. αντιλεγω = speak against). They speak against clear Scriptural doctrines (Jude 1:10-11). Jesus called it iniquity.

The Old Testament frequently warns man to beware of "self." Isaiah clearly warns us of self-will, calling it iniquity. Isaiah said, *"All we like sheep have gone astray; we have turned every one to* **his own way***; and the LORD hath laid on him the* **iniquity** *of us all"* (Isaiah 53:6). How can they escape the fires of hell when His precious Words are trampled in the mud of human philosophy? How can they escape the fires of hell when God's precious gift of salvation is so openly rejected for *"another gospel"*?

Postmodernism is from Philosophers and Scholars

In these last days of **extreme self-will**, of **denial of truth**, and of **uncertainty** about everything, the tenets of postmodernism are sweeping the world like a horrible storm. They have rapidly filtered down from the scholars and philosophers into our educational institutions over the last six to seven decades through the new technologies and mass media, such as the internet and satellite communication.

The method mirrors the insidious secretive process by which the false Greek text was "cast upon the world" by Brooke Foss Westcott (1828-1903) and Fenton John Anthony Hort (1828-1892) and friends.[22] This infection spreads by the students of these ungodly men to the common man in the pew and on the street, just like the disease of postmodernism.

Now, men everywhere believe their own conscience and thoughts are *"the voice of the Lord"* illuminating and enlightening them to truth without regard to God's **specific, special,** and **inspired** Words. This is not a new problem. Man has always desired to live through sight and not by faith. Idols were the answer for many men through the ages. Now man's own imagination and thoughts are upon a throne of divinity.

Spiritual things are always a last resort for man. The Apostle John addressed the question of how to know you are a child of God through spiritual things (e.g. 1 John) and not through the five senses. An audible voice is deferring to one of the five senses, hearing. The ancient and modern Gnostics and charismatics often claim that hearing the audible voice of God is a necessary requirement to confirm that a believer is a child of God. First John is a great book to refute these ideas and for *"babes"* seeking maturity in the things of God. The inscripturated phrase *"hear my voice"* used by God is a metaphor to discern spiritually His message through very precise Words.

John Wesley (1703-1791) reported on *"vain men"* misunderstanding their imaginations and thoughts as the *"voice of God."* He said:

> "How many vain men, not understanding what they spake, neither whereof they affirmed, have wrested this Scripture [Rom. 8:16] to the great loss if not the destruction of their souls! How many have mistaken the **voice** of their

---

[22] H. D. Williams, M. D., Ph.D., *The Lie That Changed The Modern World* (Bible For Today Press, Collingswood, NJ, 2004) 57

own imagination for this witness of the Spirit of God, and thence idly presumed they were the children of God while they were doing the works of the devil! But with what difficulty are they convinced thereof, especially if they have drank deep into that spirit of error! All endeavors to bring them to the knowledge of themselves they will then account fighting against God; and that vehemence and impetuosity of spirit which they call *"contending earnestly for the faith,"* sets them so far above all the usual methods of conviction that we may well say, *"With men it is impossible."*[23]

Rt. Rev. Edward Harold Browne, D.D., writing in 1878, said:

"In all ages of the Church we find frequent tendencies to mysticism. The desire for a kind of ecstatic vision of things Divine, of abstraction from the external world, and an absorbed contemplation of the Deity, is natural to enthusiastic temperaments, and is not uncommon in time of dogmatic controversy. The state so sought after seems to offer a refuge...Those who have taken this line...look for constant revelations from the Divine to the human intelligence. The mystic is transported out of self, and aims at frequent supernatural communion with God. To such a person the condition of the devout soul is a condition of constant inspiration. It is very true that the Holy Spirit is ever present with the Church, ever dwells in the souls of Christians, is our teacher and guide in all things, is every ready to enlighten our understandings, as well as to convert our hearts. But this truth of Scripture, pressed to the extent of mysticism, breaks down the boundary between the inspiration of Prophets or Apostles, and the enlightenment of the Christian soul."[24]

More recently, *"vain men"* are "convinced" that **"revelation"** is a man's thoughts garnered by his personal **experience**. Subsequently, man has decided that there is **no external truth**. They believe truth is

---

[23] John Wesley, "The Witness of The Spirit-Discourse" (*Great Preaching, Swordsearcher,* Ver. 5.1.1.1).

[24] Rt. Rev. Edward Harold Browne, D. D., *The Inspiration of Holy Scripture* (S. W. Green Printers, T. Whittaker, 2 Bible House, New York, NY, 1878, originally printed in a series of Theological Essays entitled, "Aids to Faith")14-15.

internal in man, and it is specific to the individual and his experiences. The postmodernists are particularly antagonistic to the pure, preserved, perfect, *received,* **external** written Words of God, the **traditional** Bible of Christianity. This work hopes to shed light on these subjects. Hopefully, it will be of some use, and hopefully to God's glory. It is with these thoughts in mind that this author leaves this brief abstract of the work with an example from Scripture that offers some insight into the misunderstanding, misinterpretations, mis-exegesis, and mis-illumination so common in these last days because men have misunderstood *"the voice of the Lord."*

An Illustration From Scripture

In the book of 1 Kings, we find an interesting text that we will use for identifying types applicable to these thoughts. They also illustrate and offer insight into the process of illumination or enlightenment. Many students of God's Words misunderstand the types. Please note the words bolded in the following discourse.

In 1 Kings 19:10-13, most individuals frequently quote verse twelve to defend their claims of hearing the audible *"voice of the Lord."*

> *And after the earthquake a fire; but the LORD was not in the fire: and after the fire* ***a still small voice****. 1 Kings 19:12*

God's revelation to His **prophet**, Elijah, began with God's command to *"stand upon the mount."* A mount is made of **"rock."** Elijah was to be prepared to hear. Later, Elijah is in a cave <u>in</u> the **"rock"** (ver. 13). Believers are in the **"Rock"** (Deut. 32:4, Eph. 1:10). God passed by the entrance of the cave followed by a strong wind, an earthquake, and a fire. God was *not* in the wind, earthquake, or fire. He did ***not*** speak out of the three loud natural disasters. It would have been necessary for Him to speak loudly. It would have been spectacular. If God spoke audibly to anyone today, it would be dramatic. God got Elijah's attention by a **"still small voice,"** which was not a **voice** with discernable words (see the Hebrew root words behind "still" and "small"). The *voice* was *indiscernible*, but Elijah knew it was time for God to speak to him through **revelation**. He was a **prophet** of God. The indiscernible, still, small *voice* in the dark cave was the beginning of the ***illumination*** or **enlightenment** of Elijah, but Elijah had to go to the **"opening"** or entrance of the cave to **clearly** hear (the Words of) the audible "*voice*" of the Lord. As a prophet of God, he was qualified to hear the audible voice of God. Nevertheless, he needed to come out of the *darkness* of the cave into the *light* (1 Jn. 1:5-6, 2:8, Rev. 16:10).

For believers in the age of grace, we need to come out of darkness into His glorious light (Psa. 36:9, 97:11). We need to stand in the mount, **in** the "*Rock.*" When our foundation is the "Rock," it is there that we can clearly **see, read, and spiritually hear** the *received* Words of *revelation* given by *inspiration* to His *prophets* and *Apostles* to record. These inscripturated Words are *light* (Psa. 43:3, 119:130) and are a light to our path (Psa. 119:105). We have those Words. However, we must come to the point of *opening* His Words to "hear" them just as Elijah came to the *opening* of the cave. The Holy Spirit will illuminate the Words when we **open** our Bible, read, and study the Words, daily. He will place a beam of light on the Words with the calm, silent **"*voice of illumination*"** so that they are clearly seen and spiritually discerned without the need of audible words.

Dr. John Walvoord, writing about the illumination of God's Words in Scripture without hearing the audible voice of God, said:

"A third phase of revelation has to do with the illumination of the inspired Word, making it known to man, applying it to specific problems."[25] "God is able, however, to speak to the heart of man with such reality that the effect is produced **without** the need of actual [audible] words. Such is the experience of the Christian who is frequently taught by the Holy Spirit **the truths of God**, and yet the Christian would have difficulty finding words to express all that the Spirit had made known."[26] [HDW, my emphasis and addition for clarity].

The "truths of God" are found in Scripture (Jn. 17:17). The Words of Scripture are those given by Him who declared, *"I am the light,"* three times in Scripture.

*"Then spake Jesus again unto them, saying, **I am the light** of the world: he that followeth me shall not walk in darkness, but shall have the light of life" (John 8:12). "**I am come a light** into the world, that whosoever believeth on me should not abide in darkness" (John 12:46). "As long as I am in the world, **I am the light** of the world" (John 9:5, cf. Psa. 36:9).*

When Jesus talked to His Apostles in the Upper Room the night before His crucifixion, He assured them that they would *receive* **all** His Words (Jn. 14:23, 26, 16:13, 17:8, 17). They would be guided into all truth (Jn. 16:13); the Words which are light and provide *"light"* (Psa. 119:130); God's Words of special revelation. The Holy Spirit illuminates them. They provoke our heart, mind, and conscience in order to grow in His knowledge and wisdom. Every believer hungers for the knowledge of God. We will only grow with confidence if we study His written Words and commit as many as possible to memory. Only the written Words assure us

---

[25] John F. Walvoord, "The Work of the Holy Spirit in the Old Testament," (Bibliotheca Sacra, Vol. 97, Dallas Theological Seminary, 1940, Logos, 2002) 294
[26] Ibid. 315 (Walvoord, "The Work of the Holy Spirit in the Old Testament").

of **any** Truth. Enlightenment or illumination of His Words will be lacking if a believer is backslidden or of the flesh.

Our enemy, Satan, would love everyone to believe that his own *"conscience"* is *"the voice of the Lord,"* as a license to remain in an immature or backslidden condition. As we shall see, hearing the audible *"voice of God"* is a delusion encouraged by the present day tenets of postmodernism, and it is giving heed to seducing spirits and doctrines of devils.

The Primary Cause of Postmodernism is Destruction of the Foundations

"If the foundations be destroyed, what can the righteous do?" (Psalms 11:3)

Although the subjectivism of postmodernism is a major cause for the spreading phenomenon of allegedly "hearing the audible voice of God," it is not the primary cause. Subjectivism has been a problem since the Garden. With the arrival of postmodernism, the real problem is the belief that there is **no** external truth; truth is absolutely relative to the individual and his experiences, i.e. extreme selfism and subjectivism to the exclusion of all external truth; and so, uncertainty about EVERYTHING else. The **primary** development causing people to turn from the sufficiency of the Bible to subjectivism is the horrendous attack on the *received* Scriptures over the last 140 yrs (i.e., since Westcott and Hort). Therefore, the consensus of the populace is that we do not know for sure that we have the Words of God; there is no sure foundation for the majority of people. Subsequently, they have determined that it is better to turn to the "voice" in their head (i.e., their thoughts and conscience) for 'truth' and for direction in life. Although the attack on God's Words began in the Garden, Satan has stepped up his attack as we approach the end of this dispensation, hoping to destroy confidence in the precious Words *received* and preserved. Our enemy knows his time is short.

In addition, listening for an audible voice, which is separate from our own thoughts, will place a person under the spell or influence of devils. Their function is to cause as many believers as possible to turn from God's preserved, inspired, life-giving Words. The purpose of devils is to prevent unbelievers from spiritually hearing God's Words, because "*faith cometh by hearing, and hearing by* **the word of God**" (Rom. 10:17). The Words point to the Lord Jesus Christ, our Redeemer, Great God, and Saviour.

Please do not neglect the footnotes in this work. They include a great amount of information that will help those who are seeking truth, answers, and hope.

H. D. Williams, M.D., Ph.D.

CHAPTER 1

INTRODUCTION

TO HEARING THE VOICE OF GOD
Related to Revelation, Conscience, Inspiration, Illumination, and Postmodernism

*And they heard **the voice of the LORD God** walking in the garden in the cool of the day: (Genesis 3:8a) "now therefore hearken thou unto **the voice of the words of the LORD**." (1 Samuel 15:1b, cf. Dan. 10:6) And I heard **a great voice** out of heaven saying…Write: for these **words** are true and faithful. (Revelation 21:3a,5d)*

This author approaches these subjects with great trepidation. Pastors, teachers, missionaries, commentaries, or books on systematic theology rarely expound the topics of *"conscience"* and *"the voice of the Lord."* One feels like he is 'treading where angels fear to tread.' Why? The terms "God spoke to me," or "God told me," or "I heard His voice," or similar phrases are frequently heard in conversations with individuals, heard on television, or promulgated in written materials. Many people believe that they are literally hearing an audible *"voice of the Lord."*[27] Others believe their conscience, angelic visions, and similar occurrences are *"the voice of the Lord"* or revelations.

---

[27] Henry and Richard Blackaby, *Hearing God's Voice* (Broadman and Holman Publishers, Nashville, TN, 2002). Throughout this book, the authors claim hearing an audible voice, and the authors confuse examples of illumination with revelation and ultimately inspiration.

The Problem

In a postmodern world, specific Words do not form doctrines or truths. The postmodernists claim not all the Words from God were preserved; only a message, concept, thought, or idea is available.[28] Subsequently, freedom from absolute authority rules the day. Obviously, any construction of truth by man under these circumstances is possible. Any malevolence becomes likely. For example, gender-neutral "bibles," ecumenism, neo-evangelical perversions, liberal humanistic philosophies, and many heretical doctrines arise. Their 'communities' mix their practice of religion with influences from Eastern Buddhism, Hinduism, Islam, and other forms of paganism. They defend their right to amalgamate doctrines and beliefs as acceptable and true. These things are accelerating the conversion to a postmodern culture that approves **any** evil. One wonders what will be the next perversion to arrive on the scene.

Abundance Breeds Iniquity

In many cultures, the advance of technology coupled with postmodern beliefs has assisted in the overthrow of Biblical moral and doctrinal stands. As a result, many people have concluded or surmised that success is equivalent to materialism and power. Prosperity, pride, and pleasure have caused men to deny the need for God and His Words. God accused Jerusalem in Judah of the same problem.

---

[28] Pastor D. A. Waite, *Defending the King James Bible, A Fourfold Superiority: Texts, Translators, Technique, Theology, God's Words Kept Intact in English* (Bible For Today Press, Collingswood, NJ, Eighth Printing, 2002) 1-250. Also see, J. A. Moorman, *Early Manuscripts, Church Fathers, and the Authorized Version* (Bible For Today Press, Collingswood, NJ, 2005) 9-36, 119-312. Also, see Dr. Don Jasmin, "Essential Books on Dispensationalism" (*The Fundamental Digest*, Vo. 16, Number 3, June-July, 2007) 9.

> *"Behold, this was the iniquity of thy sister Sodom, pride, fulness of bread, and abundance of idleness was in her and in her daughters, neither did she strengthen the hand of the poor and needy" (Ezekiel 16:49)*

Therefore, most people today measure accomplishment by net-worth or authority.

Even churches are measuring success by the extent of material success, the number of tithing members of a church, political power, and similar features. These markers are not God's idea of success. These things do not produce joy. God measures success by a person having faith in His Son, which ultimately produces the fruit of the Spirit in an individual (Phil. 1:6, Gal. 5:22-23).

Examine the number of wealthy or powerful people who commit suicide, take drugs, or seek sexual outlets to escape the false happiness of these deceitful lures. For still others, the guilt caused by abandonment of Biblical morals, doctrines, and precepts is not a problem because their consciences are seared by sin (1 Tim. 4:2). Current examples of people exhibiting completely, cauterized, scarred consciences would be terrorists who kill innocent people, including children, deluded men who murder, and pedophiles without a twinge of guilt.[29] All of these factors in a postmodern setting lead many to believe God's Words are lost, corrupted, or failing, which induces them to be uncertain about everything.

Troubling Results

The troubling results of these fallacious beliefs and positions are: **(1)** Some individuals in this postmodern milieu have eaten the forbidden

---

[29] The Islamic children sent as suicide bombers in Palestine (http://www.zionist.com/2007/08/22/more-palestinian-children-sacrificed-to-allah).

fruit in the Garden and have fallen for the lie of the wicked one that they *"shall be as gods, knowing good and evil"* (Gen. 2:17, 3:5). When they discover that they are no more "respected" than any other individual, bitterness and depression often ensues (Acts 8:23, 10:34, Rom. 3:12-17).

(2) Others have become "little Christs" in the worst sense of the meaning. They believe that they are hearing the audible *"voice of the Lord"* in their minds. They believe that they receive *inspired* revelations, which are nothing more than their own imaginations and thoughts amplified by our enemy, that old serpent the devil (Gen. 3:1, Acts 5:3-4).

(3) Still others are deluded because evil men and demons *"crept in unawares"* and led them astray (Acts 8:19-23, Jude 1:4). When they discover they have been fed false doctrines and lies, they very often turn from Christianity altogether (Jn. 8:44).

(4) Many individuals are emotionally hurting. They have become disillusioned with life as they discover the resources in a materialistic and technologically dominated society do not meet their needs.

The Need

Most of these people are in need of proper exegesis:

(1) of the *received,* preserved, Biblical Truth and its authority from inspired Words safeguarded by an Almighty God in Hebrew, Aramaic, and Greek; and

(2) from faithful and accurate translations into their language-group (e.g. the King James Bible).

(3) They need to be indwelt, regenerated, sealed, baptized, and filled by the Holy Spirit. When they have not grieved or quenched Him, enlightenment will come to them like *"the day dawn, and the day star arise in [their] hearts"* (2 Pe. 1:19).

The Famine

However, there is an early famine in the land for God's precise, preserved, special, specific, healing, and life-changing Words. Interpretations by man, which are often flawed, perverted, and based on corrupted texts, are peddled as the Words of God. For example, compare these translations of 2 Cor. 2:17:

> KJB: *"For we are not as many, which **corrupt the word of God**: but as of sincerity, but as of God, in the sight of God speak we in Christ." 2 Corinthians 2:17*

> NIV: *"Unlike so many, we do not **peddle the word of God for profit**. On the contrary, in Christ we speak before God with sincerity, like men sent from God." 2 Corinthians 2:17*

> NKJV: *"For we are not, as so many, **peddling the word of God**; but as of sincerity, but as from God, we speak in the sight of God in Christ." 2 Corinthians 2:17*

The KJB translation is correct because the Greek word translated corrupt is a present, active participle meaning corrupt, derived from a noun meaning huckster or peddler.[30] The NIV and NKJV miss the true

---

[30] Barnes Notes: *"Which corrupt the word of God.* Margin, "deal deceitfully with." The word here used (καπηλευοντες) occurs nowhere else in the New Testament, and does not occur in the Septuagint (LXX). The word is derived from καπηλος, which signifies, properly, a huckster, or a *retailer of wine*; a petty chapman; who buys up articles for the purpose of selling them again. it also means sometimes a vintner, or an innkeeper. The proper idea is that of a small dealer, and especially in wine. Such persons were notorious, as they, are now, for diluting their wines with water, (comp. Sept. in Isa. i. 22;) and for compounding wines of other substances than the juice of the grape, for purposes of gain. Wine, of all substances in trade, perhaps, affords the greatest facilities for such dishonest tricks; and accordingly the dealers in that article have generally been most distinguished for fraudulent practices and corrupt and diluted mixtures, hence the word comes to

sense of the underlying Greek word. The passage strictly means many *corrupt*. The meaning originates from the noun, peddler, who is often a huckster that corrupts things such as accurate weight measurements for gain or adulterates a liquid product by diluting it for profit. However, the words, for profit, are not in the original text. The fact that the Words of God are corrupted is the most important concept, which only the KJB accurately reflects. The translations that are wrong help produce a famine for Gods Words. This is similar to food that provides no nutrition such as sugar, which provides energy but not the nutritional elements necessary to sustain life.

The confusion resulting from widely varying "bibles" or translations has caused more and more people to doubt that an omnipotent, omniscience, and omnipresent God exists and that His Words are preserved. Therefore, people have turned to **their inner** thoughts, imaginations, and dreams as "truth" for the conduct of their lives.

The Essence of Postmodernism

This is the essence of the postmodern generation. The postmodernist believes there is **no *external* absolute written truth** and **nothing** is known **with certainty**. Subsequently, God is allowing a

---

denote to adulterate, to corrupt, etc. **It is here applied to those who adulterated or corrupted the pure word of God in any way, and for any purpose.** It probably has particular reference to those who did it either by Judaizing opinions, or by the mixtures of a false and deceitful philosophy. The latter mode would be likely to prevail among the subtle and philosophizing Greeks. It is in such ways that the gospel has been usually corrupted." Vines Words also lists the meaning of the Greek word as "corrupt, corrupted, adulterate, etc.

Chapter 1–Introduction

famine of His Words to begin[31] and our children are exhibiting severe educational deficiencies,[32] criminal activity in gangs,[33] and hedonism.[34] These overwhelming tragedies, deficiencies, and character failures are exactly what happened to the nation Israel for ignoring and not obeying God's specific and protective Words.

---

[31] Max W. Mader, "A Famine of the Word of God." Mader said: "I used to wonder how come the Bible predicted a famine in the last days for the **Words of the Lord**, when there are still millions of **"Bibles"** being printed every year. Are not Christian shops, churches and homes bursting with Bible translations and paraphrases to suit every taste? What does this prophecy mean? [Amos 8:11] I wonder no longer, because now I know that the predicted famine of the **Word of God** has already begun. The **Real Bible** is fast disappearing from Christian churches and homes. To be sure there are scores of modern translations available: but the **Real Word of God,** the **King James Bible,** is comparatively hard to find and seldom used. Soon it will be as scarce as is bread during a literal famine." (http://avoiceinthewilderness.org/snotes/sermon83.html)

[32] John M. Bridgeland, John J. Dilulio, Jr., Karen Burke Morrison, "The Silent Epidemic, Perspectives of High School Dropouts, A Report by Civic Enterprises with Peter D. Hart Research Associates" (Bill and Melinda Gates Foundation, March, 2006).

[33] Gang activity is on the increase in every part of America. One city reports:, "Stockton, with approximately 150 gangs and a soaring crime rate…" and crimes are soaring secondary to gangs. (http://findarticles.com/p/articles/mi_qa3985/is_200109/ai_n8955222). Arizona reports: "Although juvenile gangs have existed in the United States for decades, gangs today are much more violent, criminally oriented, and better armed than in the past and require more determined and extensive response from public safety officials." (http://www.jrsa.org/pubs/reports/sjsreport/arizona.html). "The proliferation of youth gangs since 1980 has fueled the public's fear and magnified possible misconceptions about youth gangs. To address the mounting concern about youth gangs, the Office of Juvenile Justice and Delinquency Prevention's (OJJDP's) Youth Gang Series delves into many of the key issues related to youth gangs." (http://www.ncjrs.gov/html/ojjdp/2000_9_2/intro.html).

[34] Mike Shelstrate, "Rampant Hedonism, The Destruction of America" (Rense.Com, http://www.rense.com/general34/ramg.htm). Accessed Oct., 2007.

> *"Behold, the days come, saith the Lord GOD, that I will send **a famine in the land**, not a famine of bread, nor a thirst for water, but of hearing **the words of the LORD**" (Amos 8:11). "My people are destroyed for lack of knowledge: because **thou hast rejected knowledge**, I will also reject thee, that thou shalt be no priest to me: seeing thou hast forgotten the law of thy God, **I will also forget thy children**" (Hosea 4:6). "For men shall be lovers of their own selves,..."Traitors, heady, highminded, **lovers of pleasures** [hedonistic] more than lovers of God;" (2 Timothy 3:2a, 4). [HDW, my addition]*

Although we live in the age of grace, it is time for men to hear our Lord's statement: *"If ye love me, keep my commandments"* (John 14:15, cf. 14:23). The hyper-dispensationalists claims of legalism or of assertions that the verses, such as John 14:15, are addressed to the nation Israel only are false.[35] Verses such as John 14:15 are scattered throughout Scripture and the hyper-dispensationalists arguments cannot be sustained (cf. Rom. 13:9, 2 Cor. 5:14-15, Gal. 5:13, 1 Jn. 2:5, 5:2, etc.).

Mistakes and Mis-interpretations

The mistakes of Israel outlined in the Old Testament were for the church to observe and learn from to keep from making the same blunders (1 Cor. 10:6). However, churches, institutions, nations, believers, parachurch organizations, Bible schools, seminaries, and families are being misled by seeking wisdom in all the wrong places, by depending on wealth and materialism to sustain them, and by worshipping idols, athletes, and *"their own selves"* (2 Tim. 3:1-2).

Many believers, much less unbelievers, disregard God's preserved Words, and turn their attention instead to (mis)interpretations and

---

[35] This author believes in seven dispensations. He does not accept Covenant Theology; and he believes Israel and the church are separate entities throughout the Scriptures.

(mis)translations of His Words by scholars who claim they have found the Words of God. In addition, too many prefer to listen to the deceivers on television and to those who are deluded that cross their paths instead of listening to His preserved, perfect Words (Psa. 12:6-7, 18:30, 19:7, Mat. 24:35, Mk. 13:31, Lk. 21:33, etc.).

When this author first became a believer and trusted in the Lord Jesus Christ, he rarely heard others claiming they heard the "clear voice of God" telling them His will or revealing prophetic events. It seems in the last few years, the clamor of people professing to hear God's audible voice has grown to a loud uncertain trumpet (1 Cor. 14:8). They are not trying to express the illumination of God's Words by the Holy Spirit, or enlightenment of His will for their lives through His precious Words, or the prompting of a sanctified believer's good conscience "*bearing [them] witness in the Holy Spirit*" to the "*law written in their hearts*" (Rom 2:15, 9:1). They truly believe **their** thoughts are "*the voice of the Lord.*"

This postmodern phenomenon is very significant. As men and women have turned from the **external**, preserved, inspired, inerrant, infallible written Words of God to guide them, God has turned them over to their own lusts (Rom. 1:24). They will not endure sound doctrine (2 Tim. 4:3). As we shall see, this phenomenon is a sign of the last days, and it is a witness to the philosophical catastrophe of postmodernism. Postmodernism did not cause this seduction. This author believes the Lord has allowed these changes to occur because men have turned to themselves for truth. False teachers, "so-called" prophets, and deceivers are seducing them. The Lord said:

> "*For false Christs and false prophets shall rise, and shall shew signs and wonders, to seduce, if it were possible, even the elect*" (Mk. 13:22).

These heresies are allowed by God in order to try believers. Paul said:

> *"For there must be also heresies among you, that they which are approved may be made manifest among you" (1 Corinthians 11:19).*

Rejection of Evidence

Postmodernism (extreme selfism and uncertainty about every expression) has accelerated the rejection of the *historical* and *providential* evidence for God's preserved Words to the jot and tittle. It is a phenomenon that must be reckoned with by all of those who love Him and His Words. The postmodernists have *"cast away"* His Words.

> *"They have cast away the law of the LORD of hosts, and despised the word of the Holy One of Israel" (Isa. 5:24c).*

The postmodernists give absolutely no consideration to the doctrines of preservation, inspiration, inerrancy, and infallibility found in the Scriptures. These doctrines are basic to the proper functioning of a Christian church and to the proper life-style of immersed believers. The rejection of these basic doctrines by most individuals and churches in these last days has produced a plethora of postmodern church practices that defy clear Scriptural commandments and precepts.

Furthermore, the postmodern churches *emerging* from the results of postmodern philosophy enjoin a concept called the *convergent* church. They claim their practice and application of doctrine in the Bible is the realization of the converging of premodern, modern, and postmodern cultures and philosophies. However, their primary underlying "convergent" theme in emerging churches is deconstructionism. A deconstructionist reduces biblical hermeneutics to accepting any interpretation by any individual as a possibility *for them*. They proclaim every position is correct because every person's experience and culture is always different.

Therefore, essentially any application and practice of any interpretation as doctrine must be allowed for in worship, evangelizing, and service. Subsequently, anyone can speak in a service; plays and other performances such as dancing are allowed; bands with a rock beat are welcomed; incense is frequently burned, votive candles prevail; the need for separation from apostasy and heresy is denied; traditionalism or sacramentalism from almost any denomination or religion, slightly modified, is permissible; evangelizing becomes primarily a "relationship"; etc. One has to wonder how much of a relationship Philip had with the Ethiopian eunuch in the desert or with Simon before witnessing to them, and there are many other similar instances in Scripture (Acts 8:9ff, 8:26ff).

Clearly, there is rejection of many Scriptural commandments and doctrines. They are ignored because no metanarrative will be accepted by the postmodernist, including the inspired preserved, *received* Bible that is *absolute*. It can only be absolute if preserved perfectly, which it is; but the modernists and postmodernists have rejected the Scriptural declarations about inspiration and preservation plus the evidence from history and providence. This author believes the Bible is the supreme 'metanarrative,' supreme authority, and supreme contract from God. God allows postmodernists or anyone to reject this truth revealed in His Words. This is similar to an automobile driver who can "reject" speed limit signs, but eventually he will face the local law enforcement officials. Although our gracious God, the Supreme Judge, allows a period of time intended for repentance, the time will come when He will judge everyone by His precise Contract (Jn. 12:47-48).

> "The second half of our Bible is set off from the first half by calling the former "the Old Testament" and the latter "The New Testament." While the term testament can mean "a will," it is more correctly understood in this context in the sense of "a covenant" or "a contract."[36]

Manipulation of God's Truth, His Contract, in any way by deconstructionism will not stand before heaven's court in that day.

The "Deformation" Versus The "Reformation"

Just as assuredly as the *"Reformation"* took millions out of the clutches of Rome, the *"Deformation"* (called "Deconstructionism" by postmodernists, see footnote 44) will bring millions back under the banner of the harlot church. God in fulfillment of the Revelation of Jesus Christ (Revelation, chapters 17-18) is allowing this. Acceptance of weeping icons of Mary as evidence of God's presence; seeing manifestations of channeled beings;[37] and the alleged receiving of audible Words from God are occurrences which are helping to desensitize and repel a generation of deceived seekers from **completed revelation**, which is found in the sixty-six books of the *received* Bible (Jn. 17:8).

This generation will gladly accept the ecumenical church of the soon to come world government and leader and they will welcome the "new" bible of the one world order, which will laud the classic tenets of postmodernism—uncertainty and extreme selfism. Surely, the wording of the "new" bible will allow uncertainty about everything EXCEPT the

---

[36] *The King James Study Bible*, "Introduction to the New Testament" (Thomas Nelson Publishers, Nashville, TN, 1988) 1399.
[37] Dave Hunt, *Occult Invasion, The Subtle Seduction of the World and Church* (Harvest House Publishers, Eugene, Oregon, 1998) many pages, see the index.

authority of the coming one-world political Antichrist and religious false prophet leaders. The desensitized people in the days of the Antichrist will stand in line to receive the mark of the beast. They will be **uncertain** that God's warnings about the mark apply to them (Rev. 14:11).

Examples

A few months ago, a real estate sales representative visited our property, which is for sale. In the course of showing the property, our conversation turned to the Lord Jesus Christ and the Scriptures. He informed me that he was "a prophet" and that the Lord told him that:

> "an awful terrorist attack was going to occur in Miami very soon (i.e. several weeks, HDW), with something as serious as a suitcase atomic bomb, and thousands of people would be leaving Florida to buy land in Georgia."

Shortly after this incident, Trinity Broadcasting Network (TBN) presented a group of seven "pastors, evangelists, and prophets" giving their testimony. One evangelist reported that he could frequently see "giant angels" protecting his meetings and ministering to the attendees. He said, *"They are present today."* Another person, a lady, could see different colors above the heads of those in the audience, and the colors represented problems the person was having. On another program, Pastor Mark Chirrona reported, *"angels are speaking to me."*[38] He encouraged the audience to be listening for them. Other "so-called" male and female preachers are encouraging believers to hear God's (audible) voice or to speak in "the language of angels" (i.e. speak in tongues). They imply that if a believer does not hear His voice speaking to them and they do not

---

[38] This author recorded on a DVD a significant amount of the program where these 'things' happened.

speak in tongues, then they are not walking with the Lord and they are "grieving" the Holy Spirit.[39] A pastor of an independent nondenominational church we visited told this author and his wife to return to an evening service to learn why we should speak in tongues.

Other current prominent evangelical leaders such as Henry Blackaby, Wayne Gruden, Jack Deere, and many others are promoting and encouraging people to listen for God's voice, whether it is by intuition, hunches, promptings, or an audible voice.[40] They claim, like the charismatics who speak in tongues, that there is a learning curve. For example:

> "Wayne Grudem, a highly regarded theologian who nevertheless is a wholesale believer in extra-biblical revelations of many kinds, answers:
> > "Did the revelation seem like something from the Holy Spirit; did it seem to be similar to other experiences of the Holy Spirit which he had known previously in worship. Beyond this it is difficult to specify much further, except to say that over time a congregation would probably become more adept at making

---

[39] Henry and Richard Blackaby, *Hearing God's Voice* (Broadman and Holman Publishers, Nashville, TN, 2002) and Henry Blackaby's *Experiencing God* are filled with admonitions to believers that if they are not hearing the audible voice of the Lord then they are not sanctified. For a good critique of Blackaby's *Experiencing God,* see http://www.svchapel.org/Resources/articles/read_articles.asp?ID=54 .

[40] Pastor Gary E. Gilley, Ph.D., *Is That You Lord? Hearing the Voice of the Lord, A Biblical Perspective* (Evangelical Press, Darlington, England, or Webster, NY, 2007) 25-30. Dr. Gilley has a good Scriptural review in his book concerning these issues. It would be a good book for someone's library, although I am disappointed that he quotes the NASB on rare occasions in the book. His book is primarily about knowing the will of God, although he does address some causes such as subjectivism and its evolution to the postmodern concept. He exalts the Bible, but the question for him is: "If the Bible is a contract or covenant given by God with precise words, how can we be certain of the words, if they are only in the "original" manuscripts?"

evaluation… and become more adept at recognizing a genuine revelation from the Holy Spirit and distinguishing it from their own thoughts."[41]

Dr. Gary E. Gilley reports in his book that the autumn 2005 catalogue of *Quaker Books* has the following promotion:

"Quaker spiritual authority lies not in belief systems—in creeds—but in direct communication between individual Friends and the Divine Spirit. All other forms of authority, 'be they written words [including Scripture, I would presume] steeple–house or a clerical hierarchy', cannot replace this direct communion."

We must clearly state that this belief is not Scriptural. Even guidance for key persons in the Scriptures by "direct communion" is rarely given by an audible voice of the Lord. Most of their lives were lived by written Scriptural principles. Dr. Gilley states:

"Even guidance given to the key characters of Scripture was rare and reserved for a handful of decisions. God spoke most often in biblical times through the prophets, yet even major prophets could go years without a word from the Lord. Many others who walked powerfully with God and accomplished much for his glory never once heard from God, to our knowledge. I think of Nehemiah, Ezra, Esther, Ruth, David's mighty men and thousands of others—the list is almost endless. As a matter of fact, the vast majority of the godly found in Scripture never personally heard from God concerning their individual lives and decisions. The ones of which we are aware were the exceptions, not the rule."[42]

---

[41] Ibid. 30 (Gilley, *Is that You Lord?*).
[42] Ibid. 38 (Gilley, *Is that You Lord?*).

What role has the Scripture, if God is "giving instructions on every consequential issue, we have to wonder what role Scripture plays?"[43]

Spiritual Failures Caused by Postmodernism

Hearing an audible *"voice of the Lord,"* seeing or hearing (giant) angels, speaking in tongues, laughing in the Spirit (the Toronto Movement or Blessing), performing fake healings, distributing prayer bracelets and "cloths" for a donation, holy anointing oil and other incredible delusions and occult manifestations are all signs of postmodernism. A world is being led astray by deconstructionism,[44] poor

---

[43] Ibid. 70 (Gilley, *Is that You Lord?*).
[44] Leland Ryken, "The Bible as Literature, Part 1: "Words of Delight": The Bible as Literature" (Bibliotheca Sacra Volume 147, Dallas Theological Seminary, 1990; Logos, 2002) p. 6. and Paul J. Achtemeier, Harper's Bible Dictionary (Harper & Row, Publishers ; Society of Biblical Literature: 1st ed. San Francisco : Harper & Row, 1985) p. 570. Paul J. Achtemeier said: "**Deconstructionism** is a postmodern exegetical approach to literature, especially the Bible, which linguistically breaks down a passage to the point that the words can be made to say "anything" the reader or exegete wants it to say" (i.e. a passage is "new" to every reader). Achtemeier also said: "**Deconstruction** is a philosophy that has barely begun to make an impact on the literary study of the it. It maintains that the text can only be perceived by a reader who brings an array of personal associations and interpretive strategies to the act of reading. Consequently, every reading of a text creates, so to speak, a new text, and no text can exist except in a one-time, more or less idiosyncratic version. Because each re-creation of the text is different, the act of deciding the meaning of the text must continually be held in abeyance or deferred. To fix a reading of a text would be to falsify the text's nature as open and indeterminate. Talk about uncertainty—well here it is." Leland Ryken said: "To those who have inquired into literary approaches to the Bible, other obstacles appear formidable. One is the sheer confusion of techniques that fall under the rubric of "literary criticism." Unfortunately that discipline is in disarray; in fact it is an embarrassment to one who is part of that discipline. The prevailing

exegesis of the Scriptures (exegetical manipulation), greed, selfism, doubt, and corrupted versions. These spiritual failures may be attributed to sin and a *"weak, seared, or defiled"* faculty of the mind, *"the conscience"* (Rom. 2:15, 1 Cor. 8:7, 10, 1 Tim. 4:2). J. Oswald Sanders (1917-1992) of the China Inland Mission, said:

> "Ignorance of the function of the **conscience** [from Scripture] and of the divine provision for its healthy exercise leads to **serious spiritual disorders**."[45] [HDW, my addition and emphasis]

The lack of knowledge of the proper and right Words of God causes a weak conscience (see below). The traps devised by deceitful men cause scripturally uneducated people to fall into many pits. The eventual

---

fashions in literary criticism are ideologically based. Unfortunately those ideologies are generally uncongenial to evangelical Christians. They include philosophic nihilism or skepticism, Marxism, and militant feminism. Iconoclasm toward traditional interpretations of literary texts dominates published scholarship, with the methods of deconstruction serving as the handy demolition tool for those who disdain the truth and beauty that readers have found in literature through the ages. The chaotic state of current literary criticism should not prevent biblical expositors from approaching the Bible as literature. For one thing biblical scholars at large are as guilty as literary critics are of practices that are uncongenial to an evangelical viewpoint. In the standard journals on biblical scholarship there is the same range of belief and unbelief, the same preponderance of hostility to an evangelical view of the Bible, and the same incidence of specialized vocabulary and esoteric methods encountered in literary journals. In both cases reliable guides are needed to help weed out the aberrations, but it is unwarranted to refuse to enter the field simply because there is much that is uncongenial. Some of the destructive current trends in literary criticism began with biblical scholars and philosophers, not with literary scholars."

[45] J. Oswald Sanders, *A Spiritual Guide*, p. 57 as quoted by Roy B. Zuck, "The Doctrine of the Conscience" (*Bibliotheca Sacra*, Vol. 126, Dallas Theological Seminary, 1969) 329.

spiritual disorders, guilt, and shame brought on by falling into their traps are devastating for people.

Sanders also points out the serious problem of the condemning conscience in people who sincerely desire to do the will of God. He said:

> "Many sensitive Christians have limped through life because of a morbid and weak conscience whose condemning voice allowed them no respite. Their sincerity and desire to do the will of God only accentuated the problem and caused them to live in a state of perpetual self-accusation. Delivery from this unhappy state is possible through the apprehension and appropriation of the teaching of Scripture on the subject."[46]

Therefore, the "sensitive Christian" delves deeper into many of the excesses of postmodernism, hoping to find the answer to or excuse for their guilt and shame; searching every 'new' version of the Bible that appears on the scene to try to ease their pain. Meanwhile, the perverters for gain feed their frenzy by releasing a 'new' version every six months in English,[47] which amounts to deconstructionism (see footnote 44), to fit their *seared* consciences. Postmodernism will fail also as modernism's false philosophies failed.

The Purpose of This Work

The purpose of this work is:

(1) to review *"the voice of the Lord"* in the Scriptures and in the few exegetical works of godly men who have reported on this issue and

---

[46] Ibid. 369 (Zuck).
[47] Laurence M. Vance, Ph.D., "The Holman Christian Standard Bible (HCSB), The Southern Baptist Bible" (http://www.av1611.org/vance/hcsb.html). Dr. Vance said: "Does a new generation arise every six months? That is how often a new English Bible version comes out."

(2) to review the major points and issues associated with *"conscience," "revelation,"* and *"illumination" or "enlightenment,"* which are causing confusion for many people. In most instances, as we shall see, *"the voice of the Lord"* refers to the inscripturated Words of God, written for man. Mankind is expected to "turn"[48] their heart, mind, conscience, and souls to the *"jot [and] tittle"* (Mat. 5:17-18) of God's Words. The *"jot and tittle"* make up the phonemes or **certain** sounds of *"the voice of the Lord"* from Genesis to Revelation (1 Cor. 14:8). In this dispensation by His grace for their protection, God wants believers to *"hear, hearken, and do"* His commandments, precepts, statutes, and laws, which are written and preserved in "the" special Book (Ex. 15:26, Jn 3:29, Jn. 10:4-5, 10:27, 18:37).

His commandments, precepts, statutes, and laws are the *"the voice of the **words** of the Lord"* (1 Sam. 15:1, cf. Deut. 4:12, 36, Dan. 10:6). All of the "letters" of every inscripturated Word in each part of the canon of Scripture is our bread (Mat. 4:4). The bread of life is the Word(s) of Life. Our bread is also *"the voice of the Lord,"* who walked in the Garden (Gen. 3:8). He is *"the living bread which came down from heaven"* (Jn. 6:51). The *"voice of the Lord"* is one of many metaphors for the Word(s) of God and for the Lord Jesus Christ, who was made flesh (Gen. 3:8, John 1:1, 14). The Lord Jesus Christ's "voice" is a metaphor for the gospel appeal to lost man (Rev. 3:20) and for his sheep to follow Him (Jn. 10:27) in the way (Jn. 14:6), where they will find green pastures (Psa. 23:2, Jn. 10:9).

(3) Finally, this work will examine postmodernism's rejection of *certainty* (which has contributed to the confusion about *"the voice of the*

---

[48] The concepts of turning and seeking his face, hearing and hearkening are related to reading and understanding the Words of God's voice given to the prophets and Apostles by revelation. Anyone can hear better by "turning" toward the speaker.

Lord, the *"conscience," "revelation," "inspiration," "illumination"* and many, many other things). Certain truth for the postmodernist is pragmatic truth; i.e. that which works and is convenient to "self." We call people who use pragmatic truth, mosaics. They choose 'truth' that suits them, which, of course, their conscience would endorse.

Walking By Faith

If we were able to detect God through our fleshly senses of seeing, tasting, touching, and hearing, we would not be living by faith, but by *"sight."* The Scriptural concept of faith includes *"walk[ing] by faith, not by sight"* (2 Cor. 5:7) and it is *"the evidence of things not seen"* by the physical senses. The Scriptures plainly teach:

> *"Now faith is the substance of things hoped for, the evidence of things **not seen**" (Hebrews 11:1, cf. Rom. 8:24, 2 Cor. 4:18). "But without faith it is impossible to please him: for he that cometh to God must believe that he is, and that he is a rewarder of them that diligently seek him" (Hebrews 11:6). "So then faith cometh by hearing, and hearing by the word of God" (Romans 10:17).*

In the majority of instances **in Scripture** where *"the voice"* refers to an audible voice, God is speaking to his prophets and Apostles to present revelations (e.g. Gen. 8:15, 24:7, Ex. 6:13, 2 Cor 13:3, Acts 8:6, etc.). Paul said: *"Since ye seek a proof of Christ **speaking in me**."* *"Christ speaking in me"* is the evidence of an Apostle, which is confirmed by the signs of an Apostle (2 Cor. 12:12, 1 Thess. 2:13). On **rare** occasions, person(s) other than the prophets and Apostles in Scripture heard the audible voice of God (e.g. Hagar, Gen. 21:17; Manoah and his wife, Judges 13; Jesus baptism and just before His crucifixion, Mat. 3:17, Jn. 12:28-30; etc.). Furthermore, the nation Israel at Mt. Sinai heard His voice with great fear when God revealed His plans and expectations for the future of His people.

The third person of the Trinity, God the Holy Spirit, is the agent Who empowers us to live a sanctified life according to the inscripturated Words. He prompts and empowers us to spiritually hear the inscripturated Words *"behind thee, saying, This is the way, walk ye in it, when ye turn to the right hand, and when ye turn to the left"* away from the Lord's commandments (Isaiah 30:21, Deut. 5:32, 17:20). The Lord gives believers that spiritual ability to know when they are turning away by utilizing *"the candle of the Lord"* (Pro. 20:27) and the *"voice"* of our conscience (see below) that testifies to *"the work of the law written in our hearts"* (Rom. 2:15). The conscience, which is a faculty of the mind created within "every" man by God,[49] can be influenced by the Words of God, by our parents, by the local church, by teachers, by society, and by our "selves." What takes precedent and influences the conscience the most depends on one's *"first love"* (Rev. 2:4), which should be the Saviour and His Words (Ex. 20:6, Jn. 14:15, 21, 23). Those preserved Words are nearby for anyone who desires them because of His love.

> *"But what saith it [the righteousness of faith]? The word is nigh thee, even in thy mouth, and in thy heart: that is, the word of faith, which we preach;" (Romans 10:8) [HDW, my addition for clarity].*

The conscience is sanctified and cleansed with the washing of water by the Word illuminated by the Holy Spirit (Eph. 5:26). However,

---

[49] This author is aware that many students of God's Words believe that the conscience is a faculty in the heart within the spirit of man. The "heart" in Scripture is such a broad topic that it can at times be associated as part of the mind within the soul. Since verbal thoughts originate in the mind, and the spirit of man in the unbeliever is not quickened, it seems better to place the conscience in the soul of man where the mind is located.

Pastor D. A. Waite, Th.D., Ph.D., reminds us that we must study the Words to know them:

> "You cannot depend upon a 'conscience'... Conscience means knowing within ourselves. God has given us a conscience **if we know and study the Words of God.** When we sin, our conscience says this is wrong. This is true if we have a conscience that is functioning. If a conscience is seared with a hot iron, sin has no affect. To believers, when God the Holy Spirit is living in our bodies, we have a conscience."[50] [HDW, my emphasis]

God's love and mercy allows a believer to discern and understand God's protective written Words in the dispensation of grace (Eph. 1:10, 3:2, Pro. 9:10). In the believer, the Holy Spirit *illuminates* the "Words." The illumination brings spiritual understanding. The delusion of and need to hear the audible voice of the Lord is evidence of a *weak* or *defiled* conscience in a believer who is struggling with assurance [1 Jn. 3:19-20 (note: *"heart"* in these verses pertains to the conscience, and *"things"* to the Scripture), 1 Cor. 8:7].

When the Scriptures were complete, the audible voice of the Lord ceased. It was no longer needed. The *"perfect" "voice of the words of the Lord"* was now available on earth. As we shall see, God the Holy Spirit only *"speaks whatsoever he shall hear"* from the Lord Jesus Christ and the Father to the Apostles and prophets (Jn. 16:13). The Lord Jesus Christ said: *"Believest thou not that I am in the Father, and the Father in me?* ***the words*** *that I speak unto you I speak not of myself: but the Father that dwelleth in me, he doeth the works."* (John 14:10, cf. Jn. 7:16-17). The Trinity agrees on the Words. The Lord our God is one God; they are in complete unity (Deut. 6:4, Mk. 12:32, Rom. 3:30, 1 Cor. 8:6). The

---

[50] Pastor D. A. Waite, *Romans: Preaching Verse by Verse* (Bible For Today Press, Collingswood, NJ, 2005) 63.

Words given to and recorded by the Apostles and prophets are precise, special, and agreed upon by the Trinity.

The present claim by many to hear the audible voice of the Lord is contrary to the progressive revelation of Scripture through dispensations,[51] and the cessation of gifts when the Scriptures were complete (see below). In addition, hearing an alleged audible *"voice of the Lord"* would make anyone susceptible to the *"wiles of the devil."* We have *"a more sure word,"* than hearing an audible voice. It is the written testimony of the prophets and Apostles (2 Pe. 1:19-21) to the Words given to them for us. One day everyone will hear the *"voice"* of the **written** Words whether they want to or not. Rebellion, mysticism, spiritism, and every philosophy or belief that directs people away from the "Book" will cease. The Lord said:

> *"And in that day shall the deaf* **hear the words of the book***, and the eyes of the blind shall see out of obscurity, and out of darkness" (Isaiah 29:18).*
>
> *"For the terrible one is brought to nought, and the scorner is consumed, and all that watch for iniquity are cut off: That make a man* **an offender for a word***, and lay a snare for him that reproveth in the gate, and turn aside the just for a thing of nought" (Isaiah 29:20-21)*
>
> *"They also that erred in spirit shall come to understanding, and they that murmured shall learn* **doctrine***" (Isaiah 29:24).*
>
> *"Woe to the rebellious children, saith the LORD, that take counsel, but not of me; and that cover with a covering, but not of my spirit, that they may add sin to sin:"(Isaiah 30:1)*

---

[51] Charles Ryrie, *Dispensationalism Today* (Moody Press, Chicago, 1965) 33-36.

> "Now go, write it before them in a table, and note it in a book, that it may be for the time to come for ever and ever:" (Isaiah 30:8)
>
> "Wherefore thus saith the Holy One of Israel, Because ye despise **this word**, and trust in oppression and perverseness, and stay thereon:" (Isaiah 30:12)
> "And **thine ears shall hear a word** behind thee, saying, This is the way, walk ye in it, when ye turn to the right hand, and when ye turn to the left." (Isaiah 30:21)

The Scriptures outline the function of the Holy Spirit. For the believer, He indwells, regenerates (quickens), baptizes, fills the sanctified, provides power to *"mortify the deeds of the body"* (flesh), *"beareth witness with our spirit that we are the children of God"* and illuminates (enlightens) God's Words (Rom. 8:13, 16). The way the Holy Spirit *"beareth witness"* is by the fruit of the Spirit (Rom. 8:23). Galatians 5:22-23 outlines *"the fruit of the Spirit."* No man on earth will have this fruit if he is not quickened.

In addition, 1 John outlines the way a believer can know that he is a child of God (1 Jn. 5:13). There is no mention by the Apostle John of believers hearing an audible voice of God to bear witness of salvation. It bears repeating:

> "We have also a more sure word of prophecy; whereunto ye do well that ye take heed, as unto a light that shineth in a dark place, until the day dawn, and the day star arise in your hearts:" (2 Peter 1:19)

God gave the Words by His prophets and Apostles, which are surer than any claims by man. He preserves them for us (Psa.12:6-7). They are the Words with a *"voice"* that we hear behind us *"saying, This is the way, walk ye in it"* that are in a Book (Isa. 30:21). They are specific, precise Words with a message. *"[T]his word"* you are not to despise (see the verses from Isaiah above).

Enormous Confusion About These Issues

There seems to be enormous confusion today about the way the Holy Spirit *guides* and *illuminates* our understanding of the inspired, inerrant, infallible, preserved Scriptures (Jn. 16:13). The confusion has been generated in part by a very poor understanding of *"the voice of the Lord," "conscience," "revelation," "inspiration," and "illumination"*[52] and by exaltation of "self" in a postmodern world. For example, some assume and believe that our *"conscience"* is *"the voice of God"* speaking to us.[53] Others report that a movie or DVD about the Scriptures has as much authority as the *received,* inspired, written Words in the Bible (see chapter six and visual orientation).[54] Still others proclaim the "church"

---

[52] Lewis Sperry Chafer, "Revelation" (*Bibliotheca Sacra*, Vol. 94, Dallas Theological Seminary, 1937) 264-280. Dr. Chafer discusses the misunderstanding of the terms revelation, inspiration, and illumination in a series on Bibliology.

[53] Roger Douglass Congdon, "The Doctrine of Conscience" (*Bibliotheca Sacra*, Vol. 103, Dallas Theological Seminary, 1946) 69. Dr. Congdon said: "'Conscience is the voice of God in us.' This is a popular saying without Biblical foundation." Also, see Roy B. Zuck, "The Doctrine of Conscience" (*Bibliotheca Sacra*, Vol. 126, Dallas Theological Seminary, 1969) 331. Dr. Zuck said: "Others have held that the conscience is the voice of God in man, the personal presence and influence of God Himself." Of course, these beliefs are false.

[54] Arthur W. Hunt III, *The Vanishing Word, The Veneration of Visual Imagery in the Postmodern World* (Crossway Books, Wheaton, IL, 2003) 207. Dr. Hunt reports: "Lately the [American Bible] Society has been asking the question, 'How can the message of the Holy Scriptures be faithfully translated and communicated from one medium to another?' Or to put it another way, is it possible to make a video version of the Bible that has as much authority as a print version of the Bible? This is a rather

has as much authority as the written Words of God (e.g. Roman Catholicism, postmodern emerging church). It bears repeating that the confusion makes us susceptible to *"the wiles of the devil"* (Eph. 6:11). In addition, we must recognize that many "pulpiteers" are deceivers for *"gain"* (1 Tim 6:5) and:

> *"they vex you with their wiles, wherewith they have beguiled you in the matter of Peor, and in the matter of Cozbi, the daughter of a prince of Midian, their sister, which was slain in the day of the plague for Peor's sake" (Numbers 25:18).*

Misappropriation and Misunderstanding of Terms

The misappropriation and misunderstanding of the above terms has had a significant bearing on the following:

(1) the rejection or ignoring of Biblical Truth, which is the specific preserved, *received* inerrant Words in Hebrew, Aramaic, and Greek,

(2) the rejection of the Lord Jesus Christ as Truth Incarnate (Jn. 14:6, 17:17, cf. 1 Kg. 17:24),

(3) the modern day phenomena and plethora of "books" claiming to be *"the"* Bible, as if they were every Word of God (e.g. NIV, GNB, LW, NASB, NKJV, NLT, ESV, RSV, and dozens more). Please see *"Word-For-Word Translating of the Received Texts, Verbal Plenary Translating"* by this author.

(4) the explosive growth of charismatic beliefs[55] producing:

---

interesting question, which the Society has answered in the affirmative."
[55] David Cloud, "Charismatic Movement Continuing To Spread Among Southern Baptists" (FBIS, Way of Life, Friday Church News, 5/11/07, wayoflife.org)

Chapter 1–Introduction

(a) healing services on demand (making God a "doc" in the box or on a puppet string),

(b) acceptance of glossolalia (speaking in tongues),

(c) claims that God is speaking *audibly* to the modern-day, man-in-the-pew prophet and,

(d) the claim of new revelations to prophets such as Joseph Smith,[56] Mary Baker Glover Eddy,[57] and Ellen G. White,[58] which has resulted in:

- **alleged** *additional* **inspired**, written Scripture and,
- **alleged** *new* prophecies and revelations,

(5) the rejection of modern philosophy and the subsequent substitution of postmodern philosophy,[59] which has resulted in the rejection of reason:

> "as here considered, indicates the intellectual and moral faculties of man exercised in the pursuit of truth" [60]

---

[56] The Mormons have many websites such as, http://www.josephsmith.net/portal/site/JosephSmith, that claim Joseph Smith is a "prophet, seer, and revelator like Moses."

[57] Harold O. J. Brown, *Heresies, Heresy and Orthodoxy In The History of the Church* (Hendrickson Publishers, Peabody, MA, 1988) 44, 49, 74. Dr. Brown said: "The 'Christian Science' of Mary Baker Eddy (1821-1910) is a modern variety of Gnosticism...which not merely offers a "gnosis" that it holds superior to the mere knowledge of the Bible, but revives a number of specifically Gnostic ideas....and they go beyond Monanus in that their fresh revelations substantially modify the teaching of the Bible itself." Also see, Walter Martin, *The Kingdom of the Cults* (Ravi Zacharias, General Editor, Bethany House Publishers, Bloomington MI, 2003) 150-162.

[58] Walter Rea, "Seventh Day Adventist, They Alone View Ellen G. White as Inspired" (http://www.bible.ca/7-WhiteInspire.htm) Rea said: "However, now that it is an absolute proven fact that White plagiarized 80-90% of her "inspired writings, including almost all her visions, modern SDA leaders, are quickly watering down the churches historic stand on White's inspiration."

[59] Zane Hodges, "Post-Evangelicalism Confronts The Postmodern Age, A Review of The Challenge of Postmodernism" (The Journal of the Grace Evangelical Society, The Grace Evangelical Society, Vol. 9, 1996) 7.

(6) the assertion that ancient Gnostic writings are as important to truth as the Scriptures[61] and,

(7) the exponential acceleration of universalism and ecumenism.[62]

The Confusion Has "Wrought Folly"
As Opposed to *"What Hath God Wrought!"*
(i.e. His Words) Num. 23:23,[63] cf. Jos. 7:15]

"God is not the author of confusion" (1 Cor. 14:33). The confusion surrounding these issues has led many to folly, and many to believe:

(1) that the Scripture is not complete because:

(a) God continues to speak through current or modern-day prophets who are able to give additional revelations;

(b) the Words of God may be eclectically put together by adding to, subtracting from, or changing the Words to make them "better." **Alternatively,** they claim the Words may be changed in light of the relatively recent discovery of MSS in garbage

---

[60] Chafer, op. cit., 264, ("Revelation").

[61] Bart Ehrman, *Lost Scriptures, Books that Did Not Make It into the New Testament* (Oxford University Press, New York, NY, 2003)1-5. Also, see Bart Ehrman, *Lost Christianities, The Battle for Scripture and the Faiths We Never Knew* (Oxford University Press, New York, NY, 2003) ix.

[62] David Cloud, "Paradise Gathering: Another Ecumenical Rock & Roll Fest" (FBIS, Way of Life, Friday Church News, 6/09/07, www.wayoflife.org). Also, see "500 Churches and 67 Denominations Participate in Franklin Graham Norfolk Festival," Friday Church News Notes, May 25, 2007, www.wayoflife.org fbns@wayoflife.org, 866-295-4143). Also, see "The Ecumenical Thrust of the National Day of Prayer" (Friday Church News Notes, May 11, 2007. Also, see "Chuck Colson and Rome" Updated April 18, 2007 (first published October 14, 2002) (David Cloud, Fundamental Baptist Information Service, P.O. Box 610368, Port Huron, MI 48061, 866-295-4143, (www.wayoflife.org, fbns@wayoflife.org).

[63] Albert Barnes, *Notes on the Old Testament, Explanatory and Practical*, (SwordSearcher, Ver. 5.1.1.1, Broken Arrow, OK, originally published 1832-1872, 2007) Nu. 23:23

dumps, graves, or back rooms that are **considered** by some to be the oldest and best. **On the other hand,** they also claim when additional MSS are found the Words should be changed by reconstructing of the text, even though we have no originals to determine if any change is legitimate.[64]

(c) some segments of the *powerful* Christian community have selected some writings while rejecting other Christian writings because they do not fit into the scheme of those in control or in authority.[65] Thus, they claim the canon of Scripture is a fabricated product from political struggles and it is open for the addition or removal of books (see footnote 61, Ehrman for references).

(2) that dynamic equivalent translations (man's interpretations) are better than formal equivalent, verbal translations (Word-for-Word translations).[66]

The results of the disagreements over these issues, which are sometimes caustic and were previously accompanied by murder, have precipitated *great* confusion and bewilderment for the masses. The

---

[64] Phil Comfort, *Encountering The Manuscripts, An Introduction to New Testament Paleography and Textual Criticism* (Broadman and Holman Publishers, Nashville, TN, 2005) vii-viii. This book and many others indicate "scholars" are searching for manuscripts to correct the Received Text in favor of the Critical Text (reconstructed). For example, Dr. Comfort in his book, *Essential Guide to Bible Versions,* (Tyndale House Publishers, Inc., Wheaton, IL, 2000) on page 254, continues to espouse the ending of Mark 16 at verse 8 is best, when Dean John Burgon **proved** that verses 9-20 were originally present in his book, *The Last Twelve Verses of Mark, Vindicated Against Recent Critical Objections & Established* (Dean Burgon Society, Collingswood, NJ, originally published 1871, republished 2nd printing, May, 2002).
[65] Ehrman, op. cit.
[66] H. D. Williams, M.D., Ph.D., *Word-For-Word Translating of the Received Texts, Verbal Plenary Translating* (Bible For Today Press, Collingswood, NJ, 2007) 1-32.

uncertainty surrounding these issues has led some to believe absolute *truth* cannot be known. Rather, they believe the pronouncements and influence of many scholars who assert that:

(1) evidence for a current inerrant, infallible, inspired, preserved Bible is tenuous at best, and

(2) only the *original* "manuscripts" called autographs are inerrant and inspired.[67]

Another Example

Dr. Mal Couch said:

> "It must be remembered that when we speak of inspiration and inerrancy, we're referring to <u>the original autographs</u>, or initial writings of the apostles, not later copies. There are copy errors that are continually being corrected even now, two thousand years after the times of the New Testament. Finally, In believing that the Bible is inspired and inerrant we hold that God divinely guided the apostles and prophets to write down exactly what He wanted, and that the Scriptures are [HDW, note the present tense] totally without error and accurate [HDW, how can they be without "error" **presently** if our "copies" have errors and we do not have the originals?]. Evangelicals have historically held to this view, and it is often stated as a belief in verbal (the **very words**, not just thoughts and ideas), plenary (equally in every part of the Scriptures) inspiration. It should be stated, though, that only the original documents (…referred to as autographs) are free from error." [HDW, my emphasis and comments]

---

[67] Floyd Nolen Jones, Th.D. Ph.D., *Which Version Is The Bible* (Kings World Press, Goodyear, AZ, 2006) 186-189. Dr. Nolan gives the most likely origin of "providential restoration" and Benjamin B. "Warfield's solution was to shift his doctrine of inerrancy to include **only** the original autographia; no longer holding to the belief in the inerrancy of the Bible…the Traditional Text." See p. 189. Benjamin Breckinridge Warfield (1851-1921) was a professor at Princeton.

Dr. Couch and others need to answer this question. "If the Scriptures were *only* without error in the original writings and we do not have the originals, how can we ever be one hundred percent (100%) certain "that God divinely guided the apostles and prophets to write down exactly what He wanted, and that the Scriptures **are** totally without error and accurate"? Furthermore, **without the originals** are you certain the Words were divinely protected? We cannot, at least not without the understanding that believers must accept by faith (Heb. 11:6) that the **easily collated**[68] copies of the providentially guided *Received* Texts (MSS) **are** as perfect as the originals and that they conform to our Lord's promise:

> *"Heaven and earth shall pass away, but my words shall not pass away." (Matthew 24:35, Mk. 13:31, Lk. 21:33)*

Therefore, some of us currently, and many saints in the past, believe that the Hebrew, Aramaic, and Greek **Words** behind the King James Bible are perfect, just as God promised. An example that those in the past believed in the perfect preservation of God's Words through the ages is found in *The Westminster Confession of Faith* (1646, note the date is after the original KJB of 1611), which clearly states:

> "The Old Testament in Hebrew...and the New Testament in Greek...being immediately inspired by God, and, **by His singular care and providence, kept pure in all ages,** are therefore authentical; so as, in all controversies of religion, the Church is finally to appeal unto them."[69]

---

[68] Dean John William Burgon, *The Causes of Corruption of the Traditional Text* (The Dean Burgon Society, Collingswood, NJ, 1998) 16.
[69] Dr. Jeffery Khoo, Dean, Far Eastern Bible College, *The Burning Bush, Vol. 12, Number 2, July 2006,* p. 77. As quoted in the *Burning Bush.*

Incredibly, many seminary and Bible school teachers, like Dr. Couch, do not believe that God has done as He promised. Therefore, they go to great *exegetical manipulation* of the Scripture to expunge God's promises of preservation.[70]

If individuals cannot trust God's promise to preserve every one of His Words, how can they reach a saving knowledge; a knowledge that **must be** retained (1 Cor. 15:2) of Christ's virgin birth, death, and burial *"for our sins"* (1 Cor. 15:3-4), and the miraculous resurrection in three days (1 Cor. 15:4) ***"according to the Scriptures"***? Just as surely as these things happened and many other miraculous revealed *"things,"* God has preserved His Words to the *"jot and tittle"*! It does not matter what the doubt producing "scholars" pronounce from their ivory "idol-producing" towers. These are cardinal doctrines. Can cardinal doctrines be separated one from another? Can a believer decide which doctrines he believes if they are literally stated in His inspired Words? Is he permitted to choose which Words are inspired, holy, pure, perfect, and inerrant? *"I trow (think) not"*(Lk. 17:9).

If there are errors in our current "copies" of the Traditonal/Received Texts (the Hebrew Masoretic text and the Greek Received Text), then how can we claim "verbal (the **very words**, not just thoughts and ideas), plenary (equal in every part of Scriptures) inspiration?" (see Dr. Couch's quote above). If we believe there are errors, then we could not make these claims, because some of the Words may be from man's invention by changing, adding, or subtracting words, whether by innocent error or on purpose. The claim of *verbal plenary* inspiration overshadowed by unequivocal "errors" becomes duplicity in disguise and

---

[70] James B. Williams, General Editor, Randolph Shaylor, Managing Editor, *God's Words In Our Hands, The Bible Preserved For Us* (Ambassador Emerald International, Greenville, SC, 2003) 86-111. Many classical verses such as Psa. 12:6-7, 119:89, 1 Pe. 1:23-25, etc. are exegetically manipulated.

causes confusion for believers. **If** we stand upon the **Words** being preserved, in the historical *Received Texts'* route copies called apographs, which demonstrate God's *"right hand"* at work, **then** we can properly and logically claim verbal plenary inspiration, preservation, inerrancy, and infallibility. If Dr. Couch is referring to printing and orthographic errors only, which are easily corrected,[71] then his statement may be satisfactory because **man** has never produced a "perfect" product without linguistic or mechanical errors, especially from handwritten copies or a printing press.

Furthermore, the *critical text* manuscripts currently favored by scholars (particularly B and Aleph) that underlie the "new" versions are so corrupt that *collation* of them is impossible. Whereas, the *Received Texts* have few differences compared to the thousands in B and Aleph, and the *received* MSS can be easily collated (see the definitions at the beginning of this work). Dean Burgon has clearly demonstrated these facts in his many books.[72] By virtue of the nature of the corrupted *critical text* MSS, readings must be **selected** rather than collated. This is eclecticism. The confusion created has contributed to "turning" from God's preserved Words. Freedom from the *absolute* Words of God has contributed to the *uncertainty* sweeping the world and to the spread of suppositions, delusions, theories as truth, and lies by the modern mass media. Thus, the postmodernists' ilk is duplicated and reinforced ad nausea to an unsuspecting world by every media mechanism possible.

Who would not like to imagine the visible churches around the world uniting around the providentially preserved *received* Words of God

---

[71] Dean John William Burgon, *The Causes of Corruption of the Traditional Text, Vol. II* (Dean Burgon Society Press, Collingswood, NJ, originally published 1896, 1998) 16.
[72] Dean John William Burgon, (see) *Revision Revised,* and *The Traditional Text of the Holy Gospels,* and *The Causes of Corruption,* and *Inspiration and Interpretation,* and *The Last Twelve Verses of Mark.* All of these are available through The Dean Burgon Society or Bible For Today, Collingswood, NJ.

promised by the Scriptures? How different this world would be! Rather, men would prefer to unite around **their** philosophies.

In Every Generation Humanistic Scholarship and Philosophy Fail

Humanistic scholarship fails to demonstrate the ability to improve spiritual "life" through reason, science, philosophy, and materialism in every generation. The modern age failed spiritually because so much faith was placed in these factors. Some people are mourning the failure of the modern age secondary to the misplaced faith. Furthermore, postmodern individuals have decided that truth is relative to **each** individual at any point in time because of the failure of modernism. Therefore, according to the postmodernists, what may be true today for an individual will not necessarily be true tomorrow, and may never be true for anyone else. According to this scheme, truth has nothing to do with societal beliefs, a set of morals, or a specific system of beliefs such as Christianity, Islam, Buddhism, Hinduism, Shamanism, or New Ageism. They have concluded that truth has to be individualized for each person, while others have concluded that there is **no** such thing as truth. Postmodernists believe the immaterial conscience, mind, or human spirit determines what is "right" for each individual. Therefore, a belief system such as Christianity:

> "may be true for some people, in some places, and at some times, but it is not true for all people, in all places, and at all times. It is relatively true, not absolutely or universally true."[73]

---

[73] H. D. Williams, M.D., Ph. D., *The Lie That Changed The Modern World* (The Bible For Today Press, Collingswood, NJ, 2004) 366.

They no longer accept even the possibility of the universality of any one-belief system that would be good for the world. However, they may accept universal governmental rule as a necessity, but only under the following circumstances:

(1) the judicial system established would have to accept a wide variety of excuses from individuals for failing to conform to the universal laws (e.g. alternative life styles instead of homosexuals, abortion instead of murder, kleptomania instead of stealing, etc.) and,

(2) the judicial laws of the society would have to be liberal and would have to accept any pagan worship and belief, but reject any belief system that proclaims "one" way to God, heaven, and eternal life (Jn. 14:6).

The tenets discussed above are the hallmark of *postmodernism* and a later chapter will expand on them.

The Tenets of Humanistic Philosophy

God knew what the aspects of every philosophy throughout history would be. Therefore, He had the four tenets of all humanistic philosophy recorded for us in the book of Genesis. The progenitor is the devil. At least three of the four tenets can be found in all the philosophies of man throughout the ages, but particularly in the philosophy of men in the last days (Col. 2:8), postmodernism.

(1) Yea, hath God said. (Genesis 3:1)
(2) Ye shall not surely die. (Genesis 3:4, such as in Hinduism's reincarnation, the "soul sleep" of atheists and Seven Day Adventists)
(3) Ye shall be as gods. (Genesis 3:5)
(4) Ye shall know good and evil. (Gen. 3:5)

This preliminary discussion was a long introduction preceding the following sections. However, it was necessary to establish the importance of the topics to follow.

CHAPTER 2

"THE VOICE OF THE LORD"

An Examination of the Biblical Definition

The Importance of Words

In this chapter, we will examine the term, *"the voice of the Lord,"* followed by "conscience," "revelation," "inspiration," "illumination," and postmodernism in later chapters of this work. Obviously, a voice consists of words made by air expelled over the vocal apparatus (larynx), lips, and tongue. God expects everyone to "hear" His Words in His recorded message. Each Word is made up of syllables consisting of *"jots and tittles"* of Hebrew and Aramaic Words or parts of Greek Words (Mat. 5:17-18, Rev. 22:19). Change any of the syllables, or fail to pronounce properly the Words, and the message created by the vocalization process will change. Moses had a problem with pronunciation or stuttering (Ex. 6:30). Therefore, God allowed his brother to act as his voice (Ex. 7:1).

God despises those who claim their lips and tongue are free to form words without regard to Him (Psa. 12:4). David rejoiced that the Lord kept him from the destroyer by the Words from His lips (Psa. 17:4). God has promised not to "break" or "alter" the Words that go out from His lips (Psa 89:34). They will always be present for us to utilize (Psa. 119:89, Mat. 4:4, 24:35, 1 Pe. 1:23-25).

Most reasonable people know the reason God's Words cannot be added to, subtracted from, or changed. His Words form a "legal" contract with man (see below) and they are the "testament" of our Lord (Heb. 7:21, 9:15-16). Nevertheless, in the postmodern world, people frown upon organizing precepts, postulates, propositions, or facts to formulate a truth by use of the Words of God. Metanarratives that do not take into account individuals experiences and feelings are not utilized.

The postmodernists want freedom from the message of a Holy God (Psa. 2:1-3). For example, they will not accept the conclusions of systematic theology about an omniscient, omnipresent, omnipotent God. Systematic theology is foundationalism, which the postmodernists refuse to accept because of their silly doctrines of deconstructionism and disdain for metanarratives employed by them. But, God expects us to come and reason with Him (Isa. 1:18). Many doctrines are truths formed by precept upon precept (Isa. 28:9-10).

God's message is made up of Words that are fixed, permanent, preserved, inerrant, and inspired, which bind men to a standard, which form a covenant with God, which are a testament (last-will) for our Lord, and which cannot be changed. The **Words** form the contract and message. They are a permanent contract that cannot be changed! Dr. Leland Ryken said,

> "There is no meaning without **words**. If we change the **words**, we change the meaning."[74] [HDW, my emphasis]

Martin Luther recognized the importance of words, and therefore having all the God-breathed Words, saying in response to John 6:63:

> "Christ did not say of His thoughts, but of **His words**, that they are spirit and life." [HDW, my emphasis]

---

[74] H. D. Williams, M.D., Ph.D., *Word-For-Word Translating of the Received Texts, Verbal Plenary Translating* (Bible For Today Press, Collingswood, NJ, 2007) 95-96.

And God Himself said:

> *"And the LORD said unto Moses, Write thou these **words**: for **after the tenor of these words** I have made **a covenant** with thee and with Israel." (Exodus 34:27)*

In other words, God said the *"Words"* form the message (*"tenor of these words"*). The precise *"Words,"* which cannot be added to, subtracted from, or changed, make *"a covenant"* (see Deut. 4:2, Prov. 30:5-6, Rev. 22:18-19). A covenant, "[i]n its broadest usage, means any contract."[75] The Words of the Bible are a contract. The Words of the Bible are a testament (last-will). The Bible is God's contract or covenant with man given through the testimony of a sovereign God. A testament (i.e. OT and NT) is God's will, which has been sealed and delivered by His Son and signed with His Son's blood. Man, especially in light of the gift of His Son, cannot change it.

In modern law books, contracts and covenants are documents that cannot be changed except by the agreement of at least two parties or a sovereign person concerning a last will or testament. In the case of a testament, the last-will is fixed upon the death of the testator, and may not be changed by the surviving party or parties (Heb. 9:15-16). Christ is the testator of the will of God. Since Christ's death on the Cross is an event planned in eternity past by God, His death was a sure thing (Rev. 13:8). Therefore, His last-will and testament (the Bible) was "fixed" before the foundation of the world. This is exactly what the Scripture tells us: *"For ever, O LORD, thy word is settled in heaven"* (Psalms 119:89). The Words were fixed, permanent, and *"for ever...settled"* in heaven prior to the foundation of the earth.

---

[75] Henry Campbell Black, M. A., *Black's Law Dictionary, Definitions of the Terms and Phrases of American and English Jurisprudence, Ancient and Modern* (West Publishing Company, St. Paul, MN, 5th Editon, 1979) 327.

The Scriptures make certain that we understand a voice is most importantly **Words** that bring a message by saying to us in several places, *"the voice of the **words**"* (Deut. 4:12), *"the voice of your **words**"* (Deut. 5:28), *"these **words** the Lord spake...with a great voice"* (Deut. 5:22, *"and when I heard the voice of his **words**"* (Dan. 10:9).

A Message or The Message

If the above comments are clearly understood, then a believer could substitute "message" for voice in many places where it occurs in the original text and the King James Bible. For example, *"the voice of the words of the Lord"* can be interpreted or understood to mean 'the *message* of the Words of the Lord.' Similarly, *"the voice of the Lord"* means '**the message** of the Lord;' but a student of God's Words must always bear in mind that very specific, precise, inspired, preserved, inerrant Words form the message. It is not a non-specific message; it is not a message formed without careful attention to the *"jot and tittles."* The word, *"message,"* occurs seven times in the King James Bible.

The Corrupted Message

Two significant false claims in this age corrupt this important concept. First, modernistic textual criticism influences many "teachers" so much that they believe *uncertain* words form "a preserved message" from God. Second, a very poor, popular, dynamic equivalent translation called *"The Message"* is presently on the market around the world. For these reasons, this author and many others are now reluctant even to use the word, *"message,"* for fear students may **not** garner that the true meaning of *"the message"* in the preserved Scriptures is reliant on the precise Words of God.

Furthermore, the word, "*voice*," carries a significant connotation to words formed from the vocalization process, which includes the "lips." This is an important concept in Scripture (e.g., Pro. 8:6, Isa. 28:11, etc.). The Scriptures are Words from the lips of God. The Words are not uncertain and the message they form is not uncertain.

Authority is Uncertain
If "the Message" is Uncertain

The individual who believes any of the Words or the message *received* from the Lord are **uncertain** is operating under the devices of the wicked one (Gen. 3:1 Mat. 13:19). Eventually, it guarantees that uncertainty will bring opportunity to escape the **authority** of the Words in His Covenant. God wants everyone to know for certain His Words, saying:

> "*Have not I written to thee excellent things in counsels and knowledge, That I might make thee know the **certainty of the words of truth**; that thou mightest answer the words of truth to them that send unto thee?*"(Proverbs 22:20-21)

Every possible device is used to cause damage to the certain message, *"the words of truth."* Since fallen man cannot gain freedom from "The Message" that cannot be changed, he is frustrated and combative. He is like a small child whose arms are held or bound at his side against his will. The child screams stomps his feet, and writhes in a fit of anger against the authority of restraint. Rebellion is anger turned into revolt against authority; it is the sin of witchcraft (1 Sam. 15:23). The postmodern age is in rebellion against a fixed Contract that God will not change and has preserved. Grace and faith in His Son's Words govern His agreement with man. Most men do not want to hear that they must have faith in *"the voice (message) of the words of God"* recorded precisely *"for ever."* For most individuals, it is frightening or frustrating to the point of producing anger and rebellion. However, hearing *"the voice of the words of the Lord"* and coming under God's authority produces the only true freedom in life.

Anger, Rebellion, and Depression Linked to Uncertainty

Individuals, who have been rebellious and angry at God and subsequently come to an understanding of their error, will often become depressed. Depression is *'anger at self'* turned inward. True freedom and release from these scourges on mankind, anger, rebellion, and depression, come from understanding and appropriating God's love and forgiveness for any individual by the method that God presents in His Words (Gal. 1:6-12, 1 Jn. 1:9). God created the earth for man's enjoyment and left careful instructions for its inhabitants intended for their well-being and salvation from sin. One of the keys to understanding God is insight into how He uses *"the voice of the Lord"* or '**the message of the Lord**' in the Words that He gave us for our benefit.

Seven Ways
"The Voice of The Lord" is Used

Hopefully, this work will (1) *"answer the words of truth to them"* who are seeking truth concerning *"the voice of the Lord," "conscience," "revelation," "inspiration,"* and *"illumination,"* and (2) describe how man has drifted so far from *"the way."* Sometimes, man needs assurance that He is a child of God. If man does not understand the ways of God, he reverts to the senses, such as hearing or seeing, to convince himself and others that he is a child of God. Sometimes, charlatans use references to the senses in order to entice babes in Christ to open their wallets. They claim, "God told me..." or "I had a vision...," which implies a special relationship to God that should be honored by giving the imposters money.

Understanding how *"the voice of the Lord"* and the other terms above are used in Scripture will help many believers avoid falling into a pit, will keep many children of God *"in the way,"* and will give assurance to many who have been troubled by false teachers. Hearing an audible voice or seeing spirits is not the way of the Lord in the age of grace. The context of the phrase *"the voice of the Lord"* occurs seven different ways in Scripture:

1. *"The Voice of the Lord"* Used as a Metaphor

The *"voice of the Lord"* occurs as a metaphor for:
(**a**) a person who is the *"Word of God."*

> *"And they heard **the voice of the LORD God** walking in the garden in the cool of the day...(Genesis 3:8). In the beginning was the Word, and the Word was with God, and the Word was God. (John 1:1). And **the Word was made flesh**, and dwelt among us, (and we beheld his glory, the glory as of the only begotten of the Father,) full of grace and truth." (John 1:14)*

The same *"voice of the Lord God"* walking in the Garden is the *"voice"* Saul heard at his conversion on the road to Damascus. Paul (Saul's name after conversion) said that Ananias, a disciple of the Lord in Damascus, *"Came unto me, and stood, and said unto me, Brother Saul, receive thy sight. And the same hour I looked up upon him. And he said, The God of our fathers hath chosen thee, that thou shouldest know his* *will, and **see** that **Just One**, and shouldest **hear the voice of his mouth**"* (Acts 22:13-14). The *"Just One"* is none other than the risen Lord Jesus Christ. He is *"the voice of God."* He is the Word of God (Jn. 1:1-2, 14).

One of the most amazing events in the Bible occurred in the Upper Room between "the voice of the Lord" and God the Father. Jesus prayed to His Father the evening prior to His crucifixion while the disciples listened to this "High Holy Prayer." What a privilege it is for us to stand on Holy Ground and listen:

> *"For I have given unto them **the words** which thou gavest me; and they have received them, and have known surely that I came out from thee, and they have believed that thou didst send me" (John 17:8).*

Jesus said the Words given to the Apostles and prophets would be recorded for believers to have and follow during the centuries following the Apostolic Age. In other words, Jesus prayed for you and me, saying:

> *"Neither pray I for these alone, but for them also which shall believe on me through **their word**;" (John 17:20).*

The Comforter, whom the Father and Jesus sent, would guide the Apostles and prophets into *"all truth"* (Jn. 16:13), teach them *"all things,"* and *"bring all things to [their] remembrance"* (Jn 14:26). That is, the Words, so that those who followed them in the generations to come might *"believe on [the Lord Jesus Christ] through **their word[s]**"* (Jn. 17:20) given to them by the Holy Spirit (Jn. 14:16, 16:13) and dutifully recorded.

(b) The second use of the *"voice of the Lord"* as a metaphor is for **all** of God's Words at any point in time in progressive revelation (i.e. the seven dispensations), whether recorded or not recorded, until the Scriptures were complete (e.g. Deut. 13:18, Jer. 3:25). For example, at the time of the giving of the law, Moses gave the nation of Israel **all** the Words of the voice of the Lord but they were not yet recorded (Ex. 15:26, 24:3, Deut. 15:5, Ex. 17:14, 34:27). They were later recorded and became God's inscripturated Words, called commandments, the law, statutes, covenant, or ordinances (e.g. 2 Kgs. 17:34, 35, 37, 38). They were the ceremonial and civil law for the nation Israel. God revealed and Moses recorded precise Words in the five books known as the Pentateuch (Ex 24:4, Nu. 33:2, Deut. 31:9).

2. *"The Voice of The Lord"* Used as an Audible Voice

The *"voice of the Lord"* spoke also as an audible voice *"**from heaven**"* until the Scripture was complete (1 Cor. 13:8-10):

(a) He spoke to His prophets from heaven, which means He is the invisible Spirit that speaks and that is present in dimensions that are beyond our understanding of space, time, and matter. The Words may or may **not** have been recorded or inscripturated.

> *"And when Moses was gone into the tabernacle of the congregation to speak with him, then he heard **the voice** of one speaking unto him from off the mercy seat that was upon the ark of testimony, from between the two cherubims: and he spake unto him" (Numbers 7:89). "To him that rideth upon the heavens of heavens, which were of old; lo, he doth send out **his voice**, and that **a mighty voice**" (Psalms 68:33). "Did ever people hear **the voice of God** speaking out of the midst of the fire, as thou hast heard, and live?" (Deuteronomy 4:33). "**Out of heaven** he made thee to hear **his voice**, that he might instruct thee: and upon earth he shewed thee his great fire; and thou heardest his words out of the midst of the fire" (Deuteronomy 4:36).*

(b) The *"voice of the Lord"* from heaven on certain occasions is the voice of the Father, who is spirit, heard by some that affirmed the Son, His baptism, and His transfiguration on the Mount (Mat. 3:17, 17:5, Jn. 12:28-29)

(c) The voice that spoke in Hebrew to Paul on his way to Damascus was the Lord Jesus Christ. (Mat. 3:7, 17:5, 2 Pe. 1:17, Acts. 26:14)

A *"face to face"* meeting with God implies a turning of the head toward Him in order to hear Him distinctly. Occasionally, He appeared as a theophany, which still necessitated turning toward the Lord of hosts. For example, when Jacob wrestled with the angel of the Lord, which was a theophany, it was described as a *"face to face"* meeting with God. (Gen. 32:30, cf. Judg. 6:22). He had to turn toward the audible *"voice of the Lord,"* a theophany (Deut. 5:4). We know that the people did not literally see God, because even Moses requested to see God, but he was only allowed to see His "*back parts*" and not His face (Ex. 33:18-22). Seeking God's presence or seeking God's face is an admonition for us to turn our heads toward Him. We hear best as humans by turning our heads and ears toward a voice. We cannot **read** or *"hear" "the voice of the words of the Lord"* on a printed page without turning our heads toward the Words. The commandment to *"seek his face"* is to read and meditate on His Words daily with prayer (Psa. 105:4). This will lead to fellowship with the Lord by illumination of the Words recorded by the Old and New Testament Apostles and prophets, resulting in great joy (1 Jn. 1, especially verse 4).

3. *"The Voice of The Lord"* Used as Words to Prophets

The *"voice of the Lord"* is also the Words given to the Old Testament prophets **and recorded**. His voice speaks to us **through** the Words given to them and recorded, and man is expected to hear them.

> *"And thou shalt return and obey **the voice of the LORD**, and do all his commandments which I command thee this day" (Deuteronomy 30:8). "And the LORD appeared again in Shiloh: for the LORD revealed himself to Samuel in Shiloh by the word of the LORD" (1 Samuel 3:21). "Samuel also said unto Saul, The LORD sent me to anoint thee to be king over his people, over Israel: now therefore hearken thou unto **the voice of the words of the LORD**" (1 Samuel 15:1). "But **Jeremiah said**, They shall not deliver thee. Obey, I beseech thee, **the voice of the LORD, which I speak unto thee:** so it shall be well unto thee, and thy soul shall live" (Jeremiah 38:20). "And the people said unto Joshua, The LORD our God will we serve, and his voice will we obey" (Joshua 24:24).*

Any Words spoken to the prophets by God were *"revelation,"* and the Words may or may ***not*** have been inscripturated (written in a manuscript that would become part of the Bible). For example, when the Lord spoke to God's prophet, Samuel, giving him revelations about Saul, the precise Words given to Samuel were not recorded. We do not know every Word that was spoken to Samuel by God, but some of them were recorded. In many cases, they were recorded by the prophet or by his amanuensis. For example, 1 Samuel 10:1-8 clearly reveals future events received by revelation from the Lord by Samuel concerning Saul, but the precise Words from the Lord were not recorded. The precise Words of the Lord to the couple on the road to Emmaus were not recorded (Lk. 24:13ff).

In this section, we are interested in the recorded Words. The Words of the voice of the Lord to His prophets **that were inscripturated** are often preceded by *"thus saith the Lord," "the Lord said," "the Lord spake," "according to the word of the Lord,"* and many similar expressions, which occur thousands of times in Scripture. At times, the Lord demanded that *"**all**"* the Words were to be inscripturated (e.g. Jer. 30:2).

An example of the authority and procedure for receiving God's Words is demonstrated in the way Aaron became the prophet for Moses. Moses acted typically as "God" to Aaron (Ex. 4:16). Moses spoke *"face to face"* with Aaron. God audibly spoke *"face to face"* with Moses and it was such a significant event that it was recorded (Ex. 33:11, Deut. 34:10). The 'congregation' of the nation Israel is considered to have spoken with God *"face to face,"* but Moses had to stand between them and God to receive and then deliver the Words to the nation (Deut. 5:4). Why? For the common man, the experience of hearing the audible *"voice of the Lord"* is too frightening to hear or receive. The claim of the common man that he is hearing the audible voice of the Lord is ludicrous. Therefore, the Words of God were repeated by the prophet to the people (Ex. 20:19). Furthermore, we believe the Words recorded in heaven and given to God's prophets and Apostles were inscripturated so that man would have no excuse for disobedience (Ex. 17:14, 24:4, 7, 12, 34:27, Psa. 119:89).

The Still Small Voice

God spoke to the prophet Elijah as a *"still small voice"* after He passed by and did not speak out of the strong wind, the earthquake, or the fire (1 Kg. 19:12). Dr. John Gill (1690-1771) has suggested a typology in reference to the *"still small voice."* He said that:

> "...all this may be considered as showing the difference between the two dispensations of law and Gospel; the law is a voice of terrible words, and was given amidst a tempest of wind, thunder, and lightning, attended with an earthquake, Heb 12:18, but the Gospel is a gentle voice of love, grace, and mercy, of peace, pardon, righteousness, and salvation by Christ; and may also point at the order and manner of the Lord's dealings with the souls of men, who usually by the law breaks the rocky hearts of men in pieces, shakes their consciences, and fills their minds with a sense of fiery wrath and indignation they deserve, and then speaks comfortably to them, speaks peace and pardon through **the ministration of the Gospel** by his Spirit; blessed are the people that hear this **still, small, gentle voice**, the joyful sound, Ps 89:15.[76]

Please note that Dr. Gill is referring to the inscripturated Words of the law and of grace as *"the still small, gentle voice."*

It is significant that the *"still small voice"* was not audible (understandable) until Elijah went to the *"entering"* (opening) of the cave (1 Kg. 19:13) and into the light where he could discriminate the Words of God's *"voice."* For the believer today, we must "open" the Words of God inscripturated by His Apostles and prophets (i.e. read the Bible) to *"hear"* the Words of His voice.

The significant point is that it is the written Words of God, which preserve for us the Gospel, by which the pastor, evangelist, missionary, teacher, or witness brings the message. The Holy Spirit reproves:

> *"the world of sin, and of righteousness, and of judgment: Of sin, because they believe not on me; Of righteousness, because I go to my Father, and ye see me no more; Of judgment, because the prince of this world is judged." (John 16:8-11)*

---

[76] Dr. John Gill, *Exposition of the Old and New Testaments, Exposition of the Whole Bible* (SwordSearcher, Ver. 5.1.1.1, 2007, Broken Arrow, OK) 1 Kg. 19:12.

The Holy Spirit does this by glorifying the Lord Jesus Christ's work (Jn. 16:14) by and through illuminating truth, which is *"all"* the inscripturated Words of *"the voice of God"* recorded by the Apostles and prophets of God (Deut. 4:33, Jn. 16:13). The Lord Jesus Christ promised His Apostles and prophets that the Spirit of Truth, who is the Holy Spirit, would guide them into *"all truth,"* which they recorded for us (Jn. 16:13, 2 Tim. 3:14-16, 1 Pe. 1:18-25, 2 Pe. 1:19-21). Belief comes by hearing the "voice" in the recorded Words of God (Rom 10:17).

How The Holy Spirit Teaches

It is important to understand that God spoke in perfect, pure Words to His Apostles and prophets (Psa. 12:6-7). For the Christian seeking *illumination* of the written Words of God in the canon of Scripture, God can teach the heart of man without the need of actual audible Words. Dr. John Walvoord, writing about revelation, the illumination of God's Words in Scripture, and the need by some for an audible voice, said:

> "A third phase of revelation has to do with the illumination of the inspired Word, making it known to man, applying it to specific problems."[77] "God is able, however, to speak to the heart of man with such reality that the effect is produced **without** the need of actual [audible] words. Such is the experience of the Christian who is frequently taught by the Holy Spirit **the truths of God**, and yet the Christian would have difficulty finding words to express all that the Spirit had made known."[78] [HDW, my emphasis and addition for clarity].

---

[77] John F. Walvoord, "The Work of the Holy Spirit in the Old Testament," (Bibliotheca Sacra, Vol. 97, Dallas Theological Seminary, 1940, Logos, 2002) 294

[78] Ibid. 315 (Walvoord, "The Work of the Holy Spirit in the Old Testament").

The "truths of God" are found in the Scripture (Jn. 17:17).

4. *"The Voice of The Lord"* Identified with Creation

The *"voice of the Lord"* is also identified with creation and nature such as in thunder and lightning (Job 28:26). The reason for this is to present the Lord's voice as a type, which is meant to give a 'picture' of the creative power, glory, majesty, and strength of the Words given by His voice. The *"voice of the Lord"* occurs seven (7) times in the following Psalm. Seven is the number in Scripture for spiritual perfection or completeness.

> *"Give unto the LORD, O ye mighty, give unto the LORD **glory** and **strength**. Give unto the LORD the glory due unto his name; worship the LORD in the beauty of holiness. The voice of the LORD is upon the waters: the God of glory thundereth: the LORD is upon many waters. The voice of the LORD is **powerful**; the voice of the LORD is full of **majesty**. The voice of the LORD breaketh the cedars; yea, the LORD breaketh the cedars of Lebanon. He maketh them also to skip like a calf; Lebanon and Sirion like a young unicorn. The voice of the LORD divideth the flames of fire. The voice of the LORD shaketh the wilderness; the LORD shaketh the wilderness of Kadesh. The voice of the LORD maketh the hinds to calve, and discovereth the forests: and in his temple doth every one speak of his glory. The LORD sitteth upon the flood; yea, the LORD sitteth King for ever. The LORD will give strength unto his people; the LORD will bless his people with peace" (Psalms 29:1-11).* "Hear attentively the noise of his voice, and the sound that goeth out of his mouth. He directeth it under the whole heaven, and his lightning unto the ends of the earth. After it a voice roareth: he thundereth with the voice of his excellency; and he will not stay them when his voice is heard. God thundereth marvellously with his voice; great things doeth he, which we cannot comprehend" (Job 37:2-5). "The LORD

also thundered in the heavens, and the Highest gave his voice; hail stones and coals of fire" Psalms 18:13).

The Lord *"hath made the earth by his power, he hath established the world by his wisdom, and he hath stretched out the heaven by his understanding. When he uttereth his voice, there is a multitude of waters in the heavens; and he causeth the vapours to ascend from the ends of the earth: he maketh lightnings with rain, and bringeth forth the wind out of his treasures"* (Jeremiah 51:15-16).

Carl Armerding, commenting on Psalm 29, said:

> "In the Old Testament, the word which is most frequently translated *power* is the Hebrew koach. In Psalm 29, **the great "Psalm of the Voice of the Lord" (and, therefore, the psalm of the Word of God)**, verse 4 states: "The voice of the LORD is powerful; the voice of the LORD is full of majesty."
> God's Word, therefore, is said to be filled with power, in both the Old and New Testaments, and by each of the major words which are used to convey the different connotations of the concept of power."[79]

Paul makes use of God's creation in Psalm 19 as a type of the power of the voice of the Lord in the gospel (Rom. 10:17-18).

5. *"The Voice of The Lord"* Is Words of The Holy Spirit

The *"voice of the Lord"* is also the Words spoken or given by the Holy Spirit. The Holy Spirit guided the Apostles and prophets to remember the Words that Jesus spoke (Jn. 14:26) and the Holy Spirit also guided them into *"all truth"* without drawing attention to Himself. Most

---

[79] Carl Armerding, "The Power of the Word" (*Bibliotheca Sacra,* Volume 116. Dallas Theological Seminary, 1959 Logos, 2002) 116:53.

of the Words were to be recorded (Jn. 16:13), but some were not, such as the Words of the Holy Spirit warning the wise men not to return to King Herod (Mat. 2:12).

The Holy Spirit pleads with us to hear *"the voice of the Lord"* in the Lord's inscripturated Words, saying:

> *"Wherefore (as the Holy Ghost saith, **Today if ye will hear his voice**, Harden not your hearts, ...Take heed, brethren, lest there be in any of you an evil heart of unbelief, in departing from the living God. But exhort one another daily, while it is called Today; lest any of you be hardened through the deceitfulness of sin. For we are made partakers of Christ, if we hold the beginning of our confidence stedfast unto the end; While it is said, **Today if ye will hear his voice**, harden not your hearts,..." (Hebrews 3:7-8a, 12-15b; cf. Psa. 95).*

Please note that the Words He wants *"ye"* to hear are quotes of Words **already** inscripturated (e.g., Words found in Psa. 95:8, Deut. 4:36).

Robert Murray McCheyne (1813-1843) preached a great message on "Grieve Not The Holy Spirit" and said:

> "**The office of the Spirit is to glorify the work of Christ**. 'He shall glorify me: for he shall receive of mine, and shall shew it unto you. All things that the Father hath are mine: therefore said I, that he shall take of mine, and shall shew it unto you' (John 16:14-15). This is the office of the Spirit. He delights not to show himself, but Christ. When three thousand were converted on that day of Pentecost, it was the Spirit that did it; he showed them divine excellency of the work of Christ. And why does he this? Because it gives glory to God in the highest, peace on earth, and goodwill to men. **But sometimes a believer looks away from the work of Christ to the work of the Spirit in him**, and begins to rest on that as the ground of peace. Now this grieves the Spirit. If he were a selfish Spirit, he would rejoice at this: but he is not a selfish Spirit, therefore, nothing grieves him so much as

this. 'Grieve not the Holy Spirit of God, whereby ye are sealed unto the day of redemption.'"[80] (HDW, my emphasis).

The Holy Spirit also spoke audibly to God's prophets and Apostles. For example, the Holy Spirit wanted Paul and Barnabas separated from the work in the church at Antioch for missions, and He spoke audibly to the church (Acts 13:2). He warned Paul not to go into *"Phrygia and the region of Galatia"* and *"Bithynia."* He caused Paul to see a vision in the night that directed the missionaries into Macedonia (Acts 16:6-10). All of these things occurred before the cessation of certain gifts and the completion of Scripture (1 Cor. 12-14). This period of time when the Holy Spirit spoke was a great time of transition between two dispensations—the dispensations of Law and of Grace.

6. *"The Voice of The Lord"* as a Future Audible Voice

The *"voice of the Lord"* will also be the *"voice"* heard at the resurrection of the saints and at the Great White Throne Judgment. The Lord Jesus Christ, the Lamb of God, is the judge that will decide who will participate in each of the resurrections (Jn. 10:16, 27, 11:25, 1 Thess. 4:16) and at the judgment seats (Jn. 5:22, Rom 14:10, Rev. 20:11).

7. *"The Voice of The Lord"* is All The Words in The Bible

The *"voice of the Lord"* is also **all** of the inscripturated Words from Genesis 1:1 to Revelation 22:21 given to the prophets and Apostles to record. There is little doubt about the definition of an Apostle (Acts 1:21-

---

[80] Robert Murray McCheyne, "Grieve Not The Holy Spirit" (*Great Preaching*, SwordSearcher, Ver. 5.1.1.1, Broken Arrow, OK) Introduction.

22). The definition of a prophet is commonly divided into two concepts. (1) A prophet is one who **foretells** God's Truths about the future; or (2) a prophet is often designated as one who preaches or **forthtells** the Truth. Prophets often had both responsibilities. The responsibility to record God's inspired Words is one of the responsibilities of some of God's prophets (2 Pe. 1:21). Some prophets or seers of God such as Gad, Nathan, and the "*old prophet*" did not write any Scripture. This author considers any recorder of the inscripturated, inspired Words of God in the sixty-six books of the Bible, as a prophet. For example, the writers of Ruth, 1 and 2 Kings, Job, Mark, Luke, Jude, and all the other sixty-six books were recorded by "prophets;" they were all guided by the process of inspiration.

"*The voice of the Lord*" for the "usual" believer through the ages is the **inscripturated Words,** which are those recorded for us in the sixty-six books.[81] This is in apposition to God's prophets, Apostles, and a few selected individuals mentioned in Scripture who actually heard the audible voice of God. For example, in the Old Testament, the Lord repeatedly mentions that the people did not "*obey [His] voice,*" which He describes as "*the words of [His] voice,[His] statutes, [His] commandments, [His] voice*", and "*[His] laws.*" The prophet Daniel records for us a clear passage in Daniel 9:10-13 where he identifies written Words as "*the voice of the Lord our God,*" "*the law,*" and "*thy truth,*" given by "*the prophets:*"

> "*Neither have we obeyed **the voice of the LORD our God**, to walk in his laws, **which he set before us by his servants the prophets**. Yea, all Israel have transgressed thy law, even by departing, that they might not **obey thy voice**; therefore the curse is poured upon us, and the oath*

---

[81] Gilley, op. cit., Chapter 7, pp. 69-76 (*Is That You Lord?*). This is a good survey of relevant Scripture for someone who is still not convinced that God's voice for this generation (dispensation) is the Bible. Has not God done enough for this dispensation through grace and His Words?

> *that is **written** in the law of Moses the servant of God, because we have sinned against him. And he hath **confirmed his words**, which he spake against us, and against our judges that judged us, by bringing upon us a great evil: for under the whole heaven hath not been done as hath been done upon Jerusalem. As **it is written** in the law of Moses, all this evil is come upon us: yet made we not our prayer before the LORD our God, that we might turn from our iniquities, and understand **thy truth**." (Daniel 9:10-13)*

When Daniel said: *"which he set before us,"* he meant that God literally placed His recorded Words by His prophets before the nation Israel.

Please note that **all** inscripturated Words are considered *"the voice of the Lord;"* even the horrible letter written by David to have Uriah killed (2 Sam. 11:12-15). They are God's inscripturated Words used for our admonition and for our salvation.[82] They are for our joy and for our judgment. They are for our guidance and for our discipline. They are the very Words of Life.

The Lord speaking through Paul wants us to understand that all of the inscripturated Words are God-breathed. Using a very technical term, θεοπνευστος, the Lord said:

> *"**All** scripture is given by inspiration of God (θεοπνευστος), and is profitable for doctrine, for reproof, for correction, for instruction in righteousness:"(2 Timothy 3:16)*

Theopneustos (θεοπνευστος) means God-breathed. It is an anthropomorphism. Anthropomorphically, breathing consists of two phases: inhaling and exhaling. If someone inhales, he must exhale. As

---

[82] Salvation in all three of its aspects: (1) moment of being born-again, justification, (2) sanctification, and finally, (3) glorification when we go to be with the Lord.

God exhaled, he gave the prophets and Apostles Words *"for ever settled"* formed by His lips, which were recorded for us. One might say that the Words the Trinity inspired and agreed upon are the Words expired by the Father, the Son, and the Holy Spirit and recorded by the receivers of the inspired Words. They are *"for ever settled in heaven"* and we can say that they will be available *"for ever"* on earth (Psa. 119:89, Mat. 24:35, Mk. 13:31, Lk. 21:33).

Many expositors have done an excellent job explaining this very important verse and its context (2 Tim. 3:16). It refers to all of the *received* precious, prepared, preserved, inspired, inerrant, infallible Words given to us in the canon of Scripture. They have been guarded by the institutions ordained by God, which are the nation Israel and the sanctified churches (Rom. 3:1-2, 1 Tim. 3:15). The Holy Spirit attends the preservation of the Words as He guided God's institutions by illumination. His *"peculiar"* people in those institutions during the dispensation of the Law and of Grace have watched over the Words, which have been placed into sixty-six books called the canon of Scripture (Deut. 14:2, 1 Pe. 2:9).

The Scriptures do **not** indicate that God spoke or speaks to *each* individual audibly; rather that He speaks through the "**the voice of the words** *of the Lord,*" the inscripturated Words. Throughout history, He rarely spoke audibly to an individual who was not a prophet or an Apostle. In the past, when He has spoken at special times through His servants the angels, by dreams, by visions, by an audible voice, *"by his servants the prophets"* and *"apostles"* (2 Pe. 3:2), the instances were circumstantially related to a change in dispensations. The changes were in the *"fullness of time,"* when progressive revelation was important and when it was necessary to protect His incarnate Son (e.g. Mat. 2:13). Progressive revelation was important until *"the perfect[83] is come"* (1 Cor. 13:10). Presently, the Father, the Lord Jesus Christ, and the Holy Spirit guide by the written Words of God. They convict, reprove, rebuke, and admonish our heart, mind, and souls to recognize and understand the Truth through illumination of the perfect Words. This is not an accomplishment through our senses. Our actions demonstrate our understanding and recognition of Truth. Our obedience is a result of reading, hearing, and **doing** His commandments.

The few men in history, other than His limited number of Apostles and prophets, who have had the privilege to hear the audible voice of the Lord, have testified of the awesome experience (Ex. 20:19, Mat. 3:17, Acts 9:7, Jn. 12:28-29). Although the Lord is no respecter of persons, He has *not* spoken audibly to the overwhelming majority of believers throughout history to direct them into His will. This is in stark contrast to the many who claim "He spoke to or told me..." The Lord expects us to know His written Words, which are His commands, statutes, laws, and will for our lives.[84] Anything we do, say, or think contrary to His written Testimony or Covenant is not His will. The written *"voice of the words of the Lord"* will *"guide"* us (Psa, 48:14, 25:9). For example, God does not speak to us to tell us what color of socks to wear. However, if we put on a pair of socks with evil words on them, like I was once given as a joke, it would be contrary to the written Words of God (Psa. 36:4, 37:27,

---

[83] The word "perfect" is neuter in the Greek. Many exegetes have attributed this passage to the second coming of Christ, but the word would be masculine if that were the case and the sentence structure would be different. In addition, Paul often uses the word *"perfect"* to reference the Scriptures in his epistles.

[84] His will is for us to know His Son (Jn. 3:16), repent, and follow Him by obedience to His Words by faith. *"Faith cometh by hearing and hearing by the word of God"* (Rom 10:17). The New Testament has multiple commands for this dispensation; for example, all of the Ten Commandments but one are repeated, administration and organization of the church is clearly given, etc.

Rom. 12:21, Phil. 4:8-9 [85]). We would not be set aside to God. We would not be "doing" according to His will to be "*holy for I am holy*" (1 Pe. 1:16). The word, holy, means to be sanctified or set aside to God and separated from habitual sinners. If God's will is for you to perform a special service for Him, such as being a missionary, pastor, or teacher, he will create such a strong desire in your heart that it can not be resisted (e.g. Jer. 20:9). Knowing God's will is not hearing an audible voice. The Holy Spirit guides us by God's recorded will and through a right attitude, godly counsel, and providence.

The Guidance of the Holy Spirit

Albert Barnes gives a very good description for us concerning how God guides in his comments on Psalm 25:9. He said:

> "The meek will he guide - The humble, the teachable, the prayerful, the gentle of spirit - those who are willing to learn. A proud person who supposes that he already knows enough cannot be taught; a haughty person who has no respect for others, cannot learn of them; a person who is willing to believe nothing cannot be instructed. The first requisite, therefore, in the work of religion, as in respect to all kinds of knowledge, is a meek and docile spirit. See Mt 18:3. In judgment - In a right judgment or estimate of things. It is not merely in the administration of justice, or in doing "right," but it is in judging of truth; of duty; of the value of objects; of the right way to live; of all upon which the mind can be called to exercise judgment, or to come to a decision. And the meek will he teach his way - The way in which he would have them to go. The "methods" by which God does this are: (1) By His word or law,

---

[85] The word evil in Hebrew רע (ra) occurs 623 times. It carries a sense of mischief, wrong, calamity, etc. Evil occurs 119 times in the New Testament and is a translation of the Greek words, κακος (kakos) and πονηρος (poneros), which have similar meanings to the Hebrew. Pornography is derived from poneros.

> (a) laying down there the principles which are to guide human conduct, and
> (b) in numerous cases furnishing specific rules for directing our conduct in the relations of life;
>
> (2) by His Spirit,
> > (a) disposing the mind to candor,
> > (b) enlightening it to see the truth, and
> > (c) making it honest and sincere in its inquiries;
>
> (3) by His providence - often indicating, in an unexpected manner, to those who are sincere in their inquiries after truth and duty, what He would have them to do; and
>
> (4) by the advice and counsel of those who have experience - the aged and the wise - those who have themselves been placed in similar circumstances, or who have passed through the same perplexities and embarrassments.
>
> By all these methods a person who goes to God in humble prayer, and with a proper sense of dependence, may trust that he will be guided aright; and it is not probable that a case could occur in which one who should honestly seek for guidance by these helps, might not feel assured that God would lead him aright. Having used these means, a person may feel assured that God will not leave him to error."[86]

Please note that Barnes does not mention hearing an audible voice. It is very sad that so many teachers of God's Words have misled so many hurting individuals to believe that they can expect to hear the audible voice of God.[87] When they mistake their conscience as the voice of God, and things go awry, they are left in confusion, which often turns to anger at God.

---

[86] Albert Barnes, *Notes on the Old Testament, Explanatory and Practical* (SwordSearcher, Ver. 5.1.1.1, 2007, originally published, 1832-1872) comments on Psa. 25:9.

[87] Henry and Richard Blackaby, *Hearing God's Voice* (Broadman & Holman Publishers, Nashville, TN, 2002). This book and many of the other books by the internationally known Blackabys make the claim God's audible voice can be heard by believers.

The Ante-Nicene Elders Understood

The Ante-Nicene (prior to 325 A.D.) church elders understood that the Scripture is *"the voice of God."* For example, Clement of Alexandria (c. 150-217 A.D.), although he was a Gnostic, understood this important principle. He said in a passage titled, *Scripture, The Criterion by which Heresy and Truth Are Distinguished*:

> "He, then, who of himself believes **the Scripture and voice of the Lord,** which by the Lord acts to the benefiting of men, is rightly [regarded] faithful. Certainly we use it as a criterion in the discovery of things. What is subjected to criticism is not believed till it is so subjected; so that what needs criticism cannot be a first principle. Therefore, as is reasonable, grasping by faith the indemonstrable first principle, and receiving in abundance, from the first principle itself, demonstrations in reference to the first principle, we are **by the voice of the Lord trained up to the knowledge of the truth.**
> For we may not give our adhesion to men on a bare statement by them, who might equally state the opposite. But if it is not enough merely to state the opinion, but if what is stated must be confirmed, we do not wait for the testimony of men, **but we establish the matter that is in question by the voice of the Lord, which is the surest of all demonstrations,** or rather is the only demonstration; in which knowledge those who have merely tasted the Scriptures are believers; while those who, having advanced further, and become correct expounders of the truth, are Gnostics. Since also, in what pertains to life, craftsmen are superior to ordinary people, and model what is beyond common notions; so, consequently, we also, giving a complete exhibition of the Scriptures from the Scriptures themselves, from fa th persuade by demonstration."[88] (cf. 2 Pe. 1:17-21). (HDW, my emphasis)

---

[88] Alexander Roberts; Donaldson, James ; Coxe, A. Cleveland: The Ante-Nicene Fathers Vol. II : Translations of the Writings of the Fathers Down to A.D. 325, Clement of Alexandria, "The Stromata" (Miscellanies), Book VII, Chapter XVI (Oak Harbor : Logos Research Systems, 1997) 551.

Irenaeus (12-190 A.D.)[89] was a disciple of Polycarp (c.69- c.155), who was mentored by the Apostle John. Polycarp sent him to the area of Lyons, France as a missionary/elder/bishop/pastor. Three of his books are preserved for us. They are a treasure for the church. The books are in one work called, *Against Heresies*.

Dr. John O. Hosler, Senior Pastor, Napier Parkview Baptist Church, quotes Irenaeus in the preface of a book, *Is That You Lord? Hearing The Voice of the Lord, A Biblical Perspective* by Dr. Gary Gilley:

> "It is within the power of all, therefore, in every Church, who may wish to see truth, to contemplate clearly the tradition of the apostles manifested throughout the whole world; and we are in a position to reckon up those who were by the apostles instituted bishops in the Churches, and [to demonstrate] the succession of these men to our own times; those who neither taught nor knew of anything like what these [heretics] rave about. For if the apostles had known hidden mysteries, which they were in the habit of imparting to 'the perfect' apart and privily from the rest, they would have delivered them especially to those to whom they were also committing the churches themselves."[90]

Dr. Hosler continues by saying:

> "Irenaeus learned the *sole authority of the apostolic tradition* [what Gary Gilley would refer to as the 'sole authority of the Scriptures;] from none other than Polycarp when he wrote:
>
> > "But Polycarp also was not only instructed by apostles, and conversed with many who had seen Christ, but was also, by apostles in Asia, appointed bishop of the Church in Smyrna, whom I also saw in my early youth, for he tarried [on earth] a very long time, and when a very old man, gloriously and most

---

[89] Please see the attachment to this work concerning Irenaeus.
[90] Gilley, op. cit., 10-11. (Dr. Hosler is quoting from *Against Heresies*, Book III, Chapter iii.3)

> nobly suffering martyrdom, departed this life, having always taught the things which he had learned from the apostles, and which the Church has handed down, and which alone are true. To these things the Asiatic Churches testify, as do also those men who have succeeded Polycarp down to the present time—a man who was of much greater weight, and a more steadfast witness of the truth than Valentinus, and Marcion, and the rest of the heretics. He it was who, coming to Rome in the time of Anicetus, caused many to turn away from the afore-said heretics to the Church of God, proclaiming that he had received this one and sole truth from the apostles...

> "Let this book teach us what Irenaeus knew—namely that New Testament truth from God is a closed system to which nothing can be added and is present with us today in the Scriptures alone. Irenaeus said,

> "Since, therefore, the tradition from the apostles does thus exist in the Church, and is permanent among us, let us revert to the Scriptural proof furnished by those apostles who did also write the Gospel, in which they recorded the doctrine regarding God, pointing out that our Lord Jesus Christ is the truth, and that no lie is in Him."[91]

There is no doubt where apostolic-appointed pastors and their disciples believed the *"voice of the Lord"* is heard and found; it was in the written Words recorded by the Apostles and prophets. There is no claim that the *"voice of the Lord"* is an audible voice during that period, except by heretics. Surely, this suggests something powerful to those who claim extra-biblical revelations from God such as hunches, promptings, an

---

[91] Gilley, op. cit., 11-12 (Dr. Hosler quoted Irenaeus from *Against Heresies*, Book III, Chapter iii.4, and Book III, Chapter v.1 respectively). Irenaeus is one of my favorite pastors in the first generation after the Apostolic Age. I congratulate Dr. Hosler for finding these apropos quotes.

audible voice, and similar claims—the written revelation in the sixty-six books is the place to turn for the will of God and for direction in life.

Tertullian (150-215 A.D.) said:

> "Now, what is "the dead" but the flesh? And **what is "the voice of God" but the Word**? And what is the Word but the Spirit?"[92] "So much has been settled by **the voice of God**; such is **the contract** with everything which is born:"[93] (HDW, please see the footnote, my emphasis)

Lactantius (c 240-320 A.D.) said:

> "Our expressions, although they are mingled with the air, and fade away, yet generally remain comprised in letters; **how much more must we believe that the voice of God both remains for ever**, and is accompanied with perception and power, which it has **derived from God the Father**, as a stream from its fountain!" [94] (HDW, my emphasis).

Peter Understood

Lastly, we have "a more sure word of prophecy" (2 Pe. 1:19), **His written Words**, than "<u>this voice</u> which came from heaven [that Peter, James, and John] heard, when we were with him in the holy mount." (2 Pe. 1:18, see Mat. 17:1ff). Because, "[k]nowing this first, that no prophecy of the scripture is of any private interpretation. For the prophecy came not in old time by the will of man: but holy men of God spake as they were moved by the Holy Ghost." (2 Peter 1:20-21). These verses are one of the

---

[92] Roberts et al, op. cit, Vol III, 572.
[93] Ibid. Vol. III, 227. Tertullian was implying that the Scripture is a legal "contract." The words of a legal contract between parties may not be changed except by approval of both parties. God said His Words in His contract are "for ever" and that they may not be changed (Deut. 4:2, Pro. 30:5-6, Rev. 22:28-19).
[94] Ibid. Vol VII, 107.

greatest affirmations of the God-breathed inscripturated Words, which came not by the private interpretation ("sayings" or "words") of any man, but by the Father, the Lord Jesus Christ, and the Holy Spirit. In addition, God tells us that He "hast magnified [His written] word above all [His] name." (Psalms 138:2, HDW, my additions). Let all of us trust in the inscripturated Words of "the voice of the Lord," who walked in the Garden. Let us not be swayed by the modernist and postmodernist claiming to have heard an audible "voice of the Lord." As the Apostle Peter told us, we have "a more sure word." We can hold it in our hands and keep it in our hearts; that is the greatest assurance in this wicked, sinful world.

Job Understood

Job clearly understood that God's voice is **in** His written Words. Job said the following, **before** God spoke to him *audibly* out of *"the whirlwind"* (Job 38:1):

> *"Neither have I gone back from **the commandment of his lips**; I have esteemed **the words of his mouth** more than my necessary food" (Job 23:12, cf. 18:23-24, 22:22, 24:13, 32:8, 33:14, Mat. 4:4).*

It is believed by this author that Job was a contemporary of Moses and had access to the commandments of God recorded by Moses at Mount Sinai. For example, (1) Job desired his words to be recorded in rock like God's Decalogue (Job 19:24). (2) *"The names of his friends, the*

Temanite and the Shuhite, and the mention of the Sabeans, indicate the Idumean parts of Northern Arabia as the scene of the history." [95]

Moses was commanded to write all the Words from God's lips (Ex 17:14, 24:4, 34:27, Deut. 31:9, etc.), and Job must have known them in light of His comment(s) in the verses mentioned above (Job. 23:12, etc.). He apparently had not learned God's *"commandment"* from seeing Him or from an audible voice of God (Job 42:5, 38:1, 40:6). Finally, Job saw the whirlwind from which God spoke. No man can see God and live. Men and women in the Bible saw either visions or the Angel of the Lord.

C. H. Spurgeon Understood

Spurgeon, the Prince of Preachers, said:

> "The Bible...is **God's voice**, not man's; **the words are God's words, the words** of the Eternal, the Invisible, the Almighty, the Jehovah of this earth. This Bible is God's Bible, and when I see it, I seem to hear **a voice** springing up from it, saying, "I am the book of God; man, read me. I am God's writing; open my leaf, for I was penned by God; read it, for he is my author, and you will see him visible and manifest everywhere." "I have written to him the great things of my law, but they were counted as a strange thing." (Hosea 8:12).."[96]

Many Do Not Understand

In these last days because of the exaltation of "self" (2 Tim. 3:1-5), the individual seeks an inner audible voice as proof of how special they

---

[95] Professor H. S. Osborn, LL.D., *A Classic Book of Biblical History and Geography* (SwordSearcher, Ver. 5.1.1.1, Originally published, 1890, 2007) Job.

[96] C. H. Spurgeon, "The Bible—Sermon 15" (*The Spurgeon Sermon Collection*, The Master Christian Library, Ages Software, 2000) 102-103.

are and as assurance of their salvation. This need has been influenced greatly by postmodern philosophy (Col 2:8), which is the culmination of the influence of the eclecticism of world religions, ecumenism, and devils (see below).

As a result of this insidious philosophy of man creeping into every aspect of the lives of men, it is no surprise that Jack Deere, author of *Surprised by the Voice of God* and former professor at Dallas Theological Seminary, fails to understand the inscripturated inspired *"voice of the words of the Lord."* He does *not* believe that Biblical miracles and signs were for the purpose of authentication at special times in history. J. Lanier Burns reports on this misunderstanding by Deere, saying:

> "This is Deere's second "surprise" volume. It follows his *Surprised by the Power of the Spirit* (see Robert A. Pyne's review in *Bibliotheca Sacra* 152 [April-June 1994]: 233-34). The author's basic point, as before, is that "no biblical arguments are adequate to support cessationism (HDW, meaning some gifts ceased), and experience demonstrates that the miraculous and prophetic gifts are being given today." *Surprised by the Voice of God* is a sequel in argument, style, and tone, so in one sense it is not a "surprise" but a continuing argument for a modern form of charismatic Christianity. Juxtaposing his former views as a professor at Dallas Seminary with his discovery of "life-changing realities," **he now seeks to show how God speaks apart from the Bible** but never in contradiction to it."[97]

Deere fails to understand that we must *"live by faith,"* and not by sight (Rom. 1:17). He believes that the Biblical miracles performed by the Lord Jesus Christ and the Apostles can happen today for the ordinary man-on-the-street believer. Burns correctly states

---

[97] J. Lanier Burns, "Book Reviews" (Bibliotheca Sacra Volume 154. Dallas Theological Seminary, 1997; Logos, 2002) 373.

"A number of miraculous episodes in the Bible validated God's abiding truths for that audience—and for believers today. A miracle that authenticated God's truths in the first century is as relevant today as it was then. Believers can trust the Bible as God's proven Word, even as they pray for His guidance and miraculous provisions for their present needs." [98]

Many Ancient Hebrews Did Not Understand

The desire of the early Hebrews to "hear" the audible *"voice of the Lord"* was very strong. During the inter-testament period (between completion of the Old Testament canon and beginning of the New Testament canon), the Rabbis had to *"oppose it"* and to insist on the *"the supremacy and the sufficiency of the written law"* (see the next quote):

"The rabbis held that bath qol (HDW, Hebrew, bath qol, according to the Rabbis, = daughter of the voice = divine voice to the prophets without visual manifestations of a person) had been an occasional means of Divine communication throughout the whole history of Israel and that since the cessation of the prophetic gift it was the sole means of Divine revelation. It is noteworthy that the rabbinical conception of [bath qol] sprang up in the period of the decline of Old Testament prophecy and flourished in the period of extreme traditionalism. Where the gift of prophecy was clearly lacking — perhaps even because of this lack — there grew up an **inordinate desire for special Divine manifestations**. Often a voice from heaven was looked for to clear up matters of doubt and even to decide between conflicting interpretations of the law. So strong had this tendency become that Rabbi Joshua (circa 100 AD) felt it to be necessary to oppose it and to insist upon **the supremacy and the sufficiency of the written law.** It is clear that we have here to do with a conception of the nature and means of Divine revelation that is distinctly inferior to the Biblical view. For even in the Biblical passages where mention is made of the voice from heaven, all that is really essential to

---

[98] Ibid. 374 (Burns).

the revelation is already present...without the audible voice."[99] (HDW, my emphasis and comments)

Therefore, we see that the desire to hear the divine audible *"voice of the Lord"* is not new, **but** it has taken on a different aspect in these last days. In modern and now postmodern times, the man on the street desires to hear the audible *"voice of God"* so strongly that he believes the voice of man's *conscience*, or even his thoughts, or even another voice from demons, hallucinations, or mental illness heard in his mind is *"the voice of the Lord."* He often believes that the voice he hears in his mind is *revealing* special guidance and revelation.

Man's Need to Feel "Special"

Man's need to feel "special" in these last days is most likely a consequence of rampant sin that results in guilt and shame in a world gone "wild." Some seek *relief* from sin through ways spurred on by the prince of this world that are not Biblical. The simple answer to all of these shortcomings is for man to believe with simplicity the written *"voice of the Lord"* and to go boldly to the throne of grace (Heb. 4:16), remembering:

> *"If we confess our sins, he is faithful and just to forgive us our sins, and to cleanse us from all unrighteousness" (1 John 1:9).*

The *"voice of the Lord"* is *"the voice"* Dean Burgon mentions in a passage that is used as an oath and is affirmed annually by the Board of Directors and faculty of Far Eastern Bible College. Dean Burgon said:

> "the Bible is none other than **the voice** of Him that sitteth upon the throne. Every book of it, every chapter of it, every

---

[99] International Standard Bible Encyclopedia, "Bath Kol," 222-223.

verse of it, every word of it, every syllable of it, every letter of it, is direct utterance of the Most High. The Bible is none other than the Word of God, not some part of it more, some part of it less, but all alike the utterance of Him that sitteth upon the throne, faultless, unerring, supreme."[100] (HDW, my emphasis)

A Gideon member recently informed this author via email that Dr. Henry Blackaby was the featured speaker at the 2007 Gideon International Convention held in Atlanta in mid July. The Gideon related that Dr. Blackaby had written a book, "*Hearing the Voice of God.*" At the Gideon meeting and in his book, Dr. Blackaby declared that every believer should hear the audible voice of God. The concerned Gideon informed me of a letter he sent to Gideon headquarters which states in part:

"I also **absolutely reject** Dr. Blackaby's philosophy which says that we can hear the audible voice of God, as he tried to set forth in his talks, and which his book "Hearing God's Voice" teaches."[101]

This author obtained Dr. Blackaby's book, "*Hearing the Voice of God.*" He states:

"Modern Christians sometimes struggle because they must relate to an invisible God. They do not hear his audible voice. They do not feel his physical touch... Some people contend that God no longer speaks to people beyond what he has already said in Scripture... We contend that God does speak to his people."[102]

---

[100] Jeffery Khoo, "FEBC Faculty United on Verbal Plenary Preservation (VPP)" (*The Burning Bush,* Vol. 13, Nu. 2, July, 2007) 66.
[101] Excerpt from a personal email to this author.
[102] Henry and Richard Blackaby, *Hearing God's Voice* (Broadman & Holman Publishers, Nashville, TN, 2002) pp. 16-17. The Blackabys quote Scripture from the NASB, HCSB, and the NIV.

Chapter 2–The Voice of the Lord

Pastor Gary E. Gilley, Th.D. from Cambridge graduate school, writes about Henry and Richard Blackabys' new book, *Hearing God's Voice*, saying:

> "Hearing God's Voice, is virtually a rehash of Dr. Blackaby's earlier work "Experiencing God". The thesis of both books (as well as his entire ministry) is "God created us for fellowship with him and He desires an intimate, personal relationship with us, SO HE WILL SPEAK TO US." (page 15.). This man and his sons have done more to promote subjective, mystical (nonclassical) Christian living than any other modern noncharismatic leader. While the charismatics all elevate subjective experiences above what God has said in his Word, the Blackabys do this by a combination of out-of-context Scriptures, personal experiences, historical illustrations and authoritative assertions that lack any solid biblical base. It is a lethal combination and especially lethal to their readers and hearers who are sadly taken in by this false understanding of God's voice. Perhaps the most disturbing aspect found in "Hearing God's Voice" is the elevation of supposed "revelations" from God to the status of Scripture. When challenged, those taking the Blackaby's position always act shocked when accused of this crime. Even though they say revelation is revelation, no matter what the form, noncessationists (i.e., those who believe God speaks audibly to His people today apart from the Bible) usually deny that their "revelations" are on a par with Scripture. But in his book, on several occasions, they actually capitalized the word "Word" when referring to their individual messages from the Lord (pages 9, 52, 173). Even more of a concern to me is that we are instructed to write down God's "new" words to us so that they can be referred to later (so-called journaling) (pages 227, 229, 230, 236 and 241). This understanding they try to promote in their teaching is that personal revelation is equal to Scripture and is most articulated in this statement in their book on page 230 "Whenever God speaks, his Word becomes a north star for your life. It doesn't change. It is sure. As you accumulate a record of God speaking to you over the years, you will have a clear picture of where God has led you. This will give you powerful assurance as God continues to lead you in the

> *future" (p 230). [THIS IS ABSOLUTE NONSENSE BY THE BLACKABYS!]*
>
> *The Blackabys are ascribing the attributes of the inscripturated Word to the supposed private revelations received by individuals. If we now write these "words" from God in a book and use them as guides for our lives, HAVE WE NOT ELEVATED THEM TO THE LEVEL OF SCRIPTURE? Why not then distribute these "guides" along with the Bible? But the Blackabys are simply being consistent as they did in their book "Experiencing God" which says if God speaks audibly and individually to us apart from the Bible, what He says must carry the same authority and significance of Scripture. Dr. Blackaby's vain philosophy does not deceive the true child of God and he is typical of people who the Apostle Paul warned about when God inspired Him to pen these words in Colossians 2:8 "Beware lest any man spoil you through philosophy and vain deceit, after the tradition of men, after the rudiments of the world, and not after Christ!"*[103] *[HDW, my emphasis and addition]*

This author could not have said it better! Other dangerous books, which are top sellers, and brought to the attention of the readers, are *"Conversations with God"* and *"Conversations with God for Teens."* The author of these works writes answers to questions from teens, but his answers are masqueraded as if they are *"the voice of the Lord."* Some report that Scripture is used incorrectly or not at all, even though it is called *"the voice of the Lord."* Multiple internet sites suggest that there is much to avoid in these books because they are not biblical.

---

[103] Pastor Gary E. Gilley, Th.D., from Cambridge graduate school, writes about the Blackaby's mistakes often. Although this quote is an excerpt from a personal email to this author, see:
http://www.svchapel.org/Resources/BookReviews/book_reviews.asp?ID=300, where the part of the quote in this work may be found; also see,
http://www.svchapel.org/Resources/BookReviews/book_reviews.asp?ID=195,
http://www.svchapel.org/Resources/articles/read_articles.asp?ID=54

There is another dangerous book related to the voice of the Lord and postmodernism. Dr. Cloud said:

> "Brian McLaren's 'A New Kind of Christianity' is a dangerous book that ridicules staunchly Biblical, fundamentalist position on every hand. It slanderously labels such a position as Phariseeism and likens it to medieval Roman Catholicism...though purporting to represent a more intellectual approach to Christianity, the book is filled with strawman arguments, shallow reasoning, and Scripture taken wildly out of context. It teaches that the Bible is not the infallible Word of God and that all doctrines and theologies are non-absolute, that we need to approach the Bible 'on less defined terms' (p. 56). It teaches that the Bible alone should not be our authority, but that the Bible should be only one of many authorities, such as tradition, reason, exemplary people and institutions one has come to trust, and spiritual experience (pp. 54, 55). It teaches that it is wrong and Pharisaical to look upon the Bible as 'God's encyclopedia, God's rule book, God's answer book' (p. 52). It teaches that the authority of the Bible is not in its text itself but in a mystical level above and beyond the text (p. 51). It teaches..."[104]

This quote will set the stage for the discussion concerning postmodernism in chapter 6 of this work. The "guru" of the postmodern emerging church is Brian McLaren. McLaren is typical of the postmodernists who exalt their thoughts and conscience to equality with Scripture. Far too often in these last days, man claims his thoughts arising from the influence of his conscience are *"the voice of the Lord!"*

So, what is the *conscience*?

---

[104] David Cloud, "Beware of Brian McLaren and 'A New Kind of Christian'" (*Fundamental Baptist Information Service*, Way of Life Information Services, Port Huron, MI, first published Jan. 26, 2006).

CHAPTER 3

CONSCIENCE
(OUR WITNESS)

"For when the Gentiles, which have not the law, do by nature the things contained in the law, these, having not the law, are a law unto themselves: Which shew the work of the law written in their hearts, their **conscience** *also bearing witness, and their thoughts the mean while accusing or else excusing one another" (Romans 2:14-15).*

A Neglected Doctrine

This term, the *"conscience,"* is our next consideration among the terms: *"the voice of the Lord," "conscience," "revelation," "inspiration,"* and *"illumination"* causing confusion in the latter days. Postmodernism amplifies the confusion. These factors cause many aberrant behaviors and claims.

The *"conscience"* is one of the most misunderstood and neglected concepts in the Bible. Roy B. Zuck said:

> "A study of the conscience is perhaps one of the most neglected aspects in biblical anthropology and psychology. Comparatively few systematic theologies even make mention of it. And how many sermons on the subject of the conscience can the reader recall having heard?"[105]

A researcher has reported that he could not find any reference to conscience in all Christian writings prior to four hundred (400) A.D. The first to use the term was Chrysostom (c. 347-407 A.D.) who said the

---

[105] Zuck, op. cit., 369 (Bibliotheca Sacra, Vol. 126).

conscience *"with the created universe as (sic, is) a means of knowledge of God."*[106] From Augustine (354-430 A.D.) to the Reformation, little is mentioned about conscience. During the Reformation, the definition of conscience varied widely. Martin Luther (1483-1546) said at the Diet of Worms:

> "I am convinced by the passages of Scripture, which I have cited, and my conscience is bound by the word of God. I cannot and will not recant anything; since it is insecure and dangerous to act against conscience."[107]

Congdon concluded that:

> "Luther's idea of conscience was that it was a consciousness of the sense of duty,"[108]

Luther's concept was an excellent Biblically determined standard. Others, such as John Calvin, A. A. Hodge, William Davy, Francis J. Hall, Hans Larsen Martensen, and others have given definitions of conscience that may or may not include concepts such as education, judgment, wrong versus right, self, morality, etc. In general, the definitions have followed either a Biblical definition or definitions that have ignored the Scriptures, creating "hazy realms."[109]

Because the correct Biblical concept of conscience is not understood, men use their definition to support their philosophy. Because men do not understand, Dean John William Burgon said men are using

---

[106] Roger Douglass Congdon (misspelled in the journal as Congdong), "The Doctrine of the Conscience" (Bibliotheca Sacra, Vol. 102, Dallas Theological Seminary, 1945, Logos Software, 2002) 349.
[107] Ibid. 350 (Congdon).
[108] Ibid. (Congdon).
[109] Ibid. 357 (Congdon).

conscience as their primary guide in order to dethrone God's Words. He said:

> "The principle of private judgment,' (it is said,) 'puts Conscience between us and the Bible, making Conscience *the supreme interpreter.*' 'Hence,' it is said, 'we use the Bible,—some consciously, some unconsciously,—not to override, but to evoke the voice of Conscience....' 'The Book of this Law,' (as Hooker phrases it,) is dethroned; and Man usurps the vacant seat, and becomes a Law unto himself! God Himself is dethroned, in effect, and Man becomes his own god."[110]

Dean Burgon's comments reveal the **two** different viewpoints that line-up with modern and postmodern philosophies. The first part of the quote reflects modernism's philosophy:

> "The principle of private judgment," (it is said,) "puts Conscience between us and the Bible, making Conscience *the supreme interpreter.*" "Hence," it is said, "we use the Bible,—some consciously, some unconsciously,—not to override, but to evoke the voice of Conscience."

Modernists, as we shall see, believed that there was external truth, such as science, the Bible, etc., but the conscience overruled the Bible.

The next part of Dean Burgon's statement characterizes postmodern philosophy:

> "The Book of this Law,' (as Hooker phrases it,) is dethroned; and Man usurps the vacant seat, and becomes a Law unto himself! God Himself is dethroned, in effect, and Man becomes his own god."

---

[110] Dean John William Burgon, *Inspiration and Interpretation* (Dean Burgon Society Press, Collingswood, NJ, originally published in 1861, 1999) xxii.

The postmodernists reject external truth as existing at all—"Man becomes his own god."

Our Conscience is Our Witness

The Greek word for conscience used in Scripture, and used primarily in Paul's recording of Truth, is συνειδησις, which is transliterated suneidêsis.

> "The [Greek] word *suneidêsis* is literally "joint-knowledge" [to know with you and God] in Greek, Latin (*conscientia*) and English "conscience" from the Latin. It is a late word from *sunoida*, to know together, common in O.T., Apocrypha, Philo, Plutarch, New Testament, Stoics, ecclesiastical writers. In itself the word simply means consciousness of one's own thoughts (Heb 10:2), or of one's own self, then consciousness of the distinction between right and wrong (Ro 2:15) with approval or disapproval. But the conscience is not an infallible guide and acts according to the light that it has (1Co 8:7,10; 1Pe 2:19). The conscience can be contaminated (Heb. 10:22, evil *ponêrâs*)."[111] [HDW, my addition]

This definition is satisfactory, but most authors do *not* mention a major concept, the "one-word" definition for conscience. The "conscience" is your **witness** (Heb. 9:14, 1 Pe. 3:16), like **a witness** in a courtroom: **(1)** to the law of God written in our hearts (Rom. 2:15), and **(2)** to our thoughts, actions, and intents (see below). It is very helpful to the student of Scripture if he will substitute "witness" for "conscience" in the Scriptures, much like "Grace" can be substituted for "Christ" in the Scriptures or vice versa, to help *illuminate* what the Holy Spirit want us to understand in the Scriptures (Pro. 9:10). One caution, however, a witness

---

[111] Robertson's Word Pictures, Acts 23:1 (SwordSearcher, Ver. 5.1.1.1).

can be wrong, just like a witness in the courtroom. Read the following verses very carefully with the comments in brackets.

> *"For when the Gentiles, which have not the law, do by nature the things contained in the law, these, having not the law, are a law unto themselves: Which shew the work of the law written in their hearts, **their conscience**"* [Greek, συνειδησις, meaning "to know with" (e.g. with you and God), a witness **with** you of your actions and thoughts] *"also bearing **witness**"* (Greek, συμμαρτυρεω, testimony) *"and their **thoughts** the mean while accusing or else excusing one another" (Romans 2:14-15).* [HDW, my comments and emphasis].

> *"I say the truth in Christ, I lie not, my conscience"* (i.e. Greek, συνειδησις,"to know with" himself and God, e.g. a witness with you of your actions and thoughts) *"also bearing me witness"* (i.e. Greek, συμμαρτυρεω, testimony) *"in the Holy Ghost" (Romans 9:1).* (HDW, my comments).

In a saved, born again person, the Holy Spirit dwells **in** him and sheds light on Truth, which greatly influences the witness (conscience). Now, substitute "witness" for "conscience" in the following verse:

> *"For our rejoicing is this, the testimony of our conscience, that in simplicity and godly sincerity, not with fleshly wisdom, but by the grace of God, we have had our conversation in the world, and more abundantly to you-ward" (2 Corinthians 1:12).*

Man's spirit, the Lord Jesus Christ, the Holy Spirit, God, etc., are called witnesses in Scripture (Jn. 8:18, Rom. 1:9, 8:16, Heb. 10:15, Rev. 1:5, 3:14). Therefore, the KJB translators probably chose "conscience" for the Greek work, *suneidêsis,* in order to distinguish the faculty of conscience, which is our witness, from God, the Lord Jesus Christ, the Holy Spirit, etc., who are also called witnesses in Scripture.

John Bunyan in his book, *Holy War,* calls "conscience" a citizen of the city, Mansoul. Bunyan said Diabolus tried to kill Mr. Conscience when he captured the city, but he could not. Therefore, he placed him in a deep dungeon. Of course, in modern times, this would be called "tampering with a **witness**." When Emmanuel recaptured Mansoul, Mr. Conviction, opened a part of the city called "ear gate," and when he did, Mr. Conscience (Witness) could be heard screaming so loud from the dungeon that the entire city was aroused to remember their allegiance to Emmanuel.[112]

Our Conscience is an Inherited Faculty of The Mind

Keep these things in mind as you read the following concerning the "conscience." **Our** (each individual's) witness, the "conscience," is a faculty[113] of the mind given by God, which is aware of the *"law" "written in our hearts."* Many things in our environment can influence our "witness" (or conscience) as we mature. The conscience is not a development of our environment. We are born with a conscience; it is not

---

[112] J. Oswald Sanders, *A Spiritual Clinic* (Moody Press, Chicago, 5th printing and edition, 1961) 59.
[113] Webster's 1828 Dictionary, (only part of the definition for it is long) "FACULTY, n. L. facultas, from facio, to make.1. That power of the mind or intellect which enables it to receive, revive or modify perceptions; as the faculty of seeing, of hearing, of imagining, of remembering, &c.: or in general, the faculties may be called the powers or capacities of the mind. 2. The power of doing any thing; ability. There is no faculty or power in creatures, which can rightly perform its functions, without the perpetual aid of the Supreme Being. 3. The power of performing any action, natural, vital or animal. The vital faculty is that by which life is preserved." (The mind is classically associated with the soul of man, and not the spirit of man in the tripartite stricture of man (1Thess. 5:23).

acquired. For example, parental training or our experience does not place our conscience within us.

Our Conscience is Not Acquired

The origin of our conscience is *not* the result of parental discipline in childhood, or the lack of it. The environment influences our conscience, but that is not the origin of the conscience. Lewis Sperry Chafer said:

> "Some maintain that it is not an integral part of man, but is rather the voice of God speaking directly to the one who is exercised by conscience. On the other hand, and far removed indeed, is the notion that conscience is no more than a bent of mind received by the discipline of childhood. **Neither one of these extremes is sustained by Scripture.**"[114] (HDW, my emphasis)

It is a judgmental faculty or WITNESS attuned to God's law (Rom. 2:14-15) placed into **each** individual by **inheritance.** It is there from birth. The Scripture supports this view by the pronouns used and the context of passages. For example, the Scripture says: *"every man's conscience* (witness)" (2 Cor. 4:2), *"our," "your" "my" "man's"* conscience (witness) (1 Cor. 10:29, 2 Cor. 5:11, 1 Ti. 4:2).

God has done everything that He can to facilitate fallen man to believe on Him without seeing Him; that is, believe on Him by faith, the **key** to fellowship with Him and eternal life. Consider John 20:29b, *"blessed are they that have not seen, and yet have believed"* and Hebrews 11:6 *"But without faith it is impossible to please him: for he that cometh*

---

[114] Lewis Sperry Chafer, "Anthropology, Part V" (Bibliotheca Sacra, Volume 101, Dallas Theological Seminary, 1944; Logos, 2002) 145.

to God must believe that he is, and that he is a rewarder of them that diligently seek him." (cf. Heb. 11:1).

The Holy Spirit illuminates a born-again individual and member of the body of Christ by influencing the conscience *"with the washing of water by the word"* (Eph. 5:26). However, many have made the conscience *"shipwreck"* by abandoning faith in God's inscripturated Words and doctrines (1 Tim. 1:19).

> *"Holding faith, and a good conscience; which some having put away concerning faith have made shipwreck" (1 Timothy 1:19).*

In 1 Timothy 1:19:

> "**Faith** is used in two different ways in this verse. The first "faith" is subjective, referring to Timothy's own personal trust or faith in God; **holding faith** means that he is to maintain his confidence in God. The second "faith" is objective, referring to the body of revealed truth believed by the church, that is, "the faith which was once delivered unto the saints" [Jude 3]. The last half of verse 19 may be translated (interpreted): "which [a good conscience] some, having repudiated, have become shipwreck concerning the faith." Because some rejected their inner moral voice of conscience (their witness to the law of God written in their hearts), they have strayed far from the truth of God into theological heresy. Often religious error has its roots in moral rather than intellectual causes."[115] (HDW, not my emphasis, but my additions in parentheses).

Roy B. Zuck and others report their belief that the conscience (witness) is inherited. Zuck says:

---

[115] *The King James Study Bible* (Thomas Nelson Publishers, Nashville, TN, 1988) 1 Tim. 1:19.

> "The Scriptures seem to suggest that the conscience is inherent in all persons rather than an acquired trait. Second Corinthians 4:2 refers to "every man's conscience," and in 1 Corinthians 10:29 Paul, in speaking of his own conscience and the conscience of another, apparently is presuming that the conscience is universal and innate."[116]

The Holy Spirit is our God-witness. Man's conscience is our man-witness. It is apropos to remember that:

> "The conscience of a Christian himself may be evil (Heb 10:22), weak and ignorant (1 Cor 8:7, 10, 12), or strong (1 Cor 10:25–27) and pure (1 Tim 3:9). Similarly the conscience of the unsaved may be convicting (John 8:9) or seared (1 Tim 4:2), witnessing (Rom 2:15) or defiled (Titus 1:15). According to 2 Corinthians 4:2 all mankind has a conscience."[117]

Therefore, our conscience or man-witness cannot be *"the voice of the Lord,"* or the Holy Spirit, or the Lord Jesus Christ, or God because it can be evil, weak, ignorant, or defiled.

A Pure Conscience

This author recognizes a difficulty with the quote above concerning the word, "pure." The modern connotation of *"pure"* may be considered to mean without **any** defilement or impurities. This concept is different from the Greek original language word behind the word translated, "pure." The Greek word implies washed, cleaned or cleansed of

---

[116] Roy B. Zuck, "The Doctrine of the Conscience" (*Bibliotheca Sacra*, Vol. 126, Dallas Theological Seminary, 1969, Logos, 2002) 331.
[117] Roger Douglass Congdon, "The Doctrine of the Conscience" (*Bibliotheca Sacra*, Vol. 103, Dallas Theological Seminary, 1969, Logos, 2002) 408.

impurities (Mat. 23:26, Jn. 13:10, 15:3, 1 Jn. 1:7-10).[118] Nothing once defiled can ever be perfectly clean or pure again. It can only be washed or cleaned, but dirt will remain (e.g. the "old man").

The only "pure" conscience, which was never defiled, weak, seared, ignorant, or evil, and never in need of washing, is the conscience of the Lord Jesus Christ (the God-man). His conscience is not defiled in any way and is in no need of being cleaned or washed because of sin. Therefore, when Scripture says in 1 Timothy 3:9 that a deacon must be found, *"holding the mystery of the faith in a pure conscience,"* he does this in two ways: (1) by being *"in Christ,"* who only has a *"pure conscience."* Alternatively, another way to say this would be (2) by a conscience that is washed by the water of the Word through salvation. Gill says *"in a pure conscience"* means:

> "with a conscience sprinkled by the blood of Christ; with a conscience void of offence both towards God and man; with a suitable life and conversation; a conversation becoming the Gospel of Christ, and by which it is adorned: and this part of their character is necessary, that such may be able to instruct and establish those who are weak in the faith, and oppose and refute the erroneous, and also recommend the Gospel by their own example; otherwise should their principles or practices be bad, their influence on others might be very pernicious and fatal."

If a deacon is saved, he is *"in Christ;"* he has been washed by the blood of the Lamb and His Words; consequently, he is clean (Rev. 1:5, 7:14), but he is not pure like the Lord Jesus Christ. A virgin is pure in the sense of never having had sexual intercourse or never having been 'defiled;' but once 'defiled' is never a virgin again. Only Christ is *"pure"* in

---

[118] Strongs: καθαρος kath-ar-os' of uncertain affinity; clean (literally or figuratively):--clean, clear, pure.

the "virginal" sense of the word. He has never been defiled by any sin. He does not need to be purified.

In addition, the deacon and all men will continue to sin because the believer continues to fight the *"old man;"* therefore, a part of him will need washing or cleansing by confession, repentance, and forgiveness (1 Jn. 1:9, Jn. 13:10, Rom. 6 and 7). He is "pure" by virtue of the "covering" by the blood shed for those who trust and believe, but he is not pure like Christ—through and through *"for ever."* The context determines the meaning of pure in Scripture. It determines whether it is literal, that is pure like Christ; or whether it is figurative, that is pure by being washed.

A man's conscience is in need of DAILY washing by *"the words of the voice of the Lord"* and by confession of sin. Therefore, all should read God's Words daily, which provides the much-needed insight into and recognition of sin plus the instructions for cleansing designed for every man except One, the Lord Jesus Christ.

Our Conscience Is Affected by Original Sin

In addition, our conscience can never be completely pure because of original sin. Paul speaks of a *"pure conscience,"* but it must be understood in the light of all Scripture. Man can have a cleansed conscience, which could be called "pure" in a sense if it has been cleansed or purified by the blood of the Lord Jesus Christ. In addition, the Father, Son, and Holy Spirit dwell within a believer. Therefore, if we are born-again, we have the *"pure"* consciences of three persons within us, which are the perfect God-man's *"conscience,"* the Holy Spirit, and the Father. Some may question if the Holy Spirit and the Father have a conscience since they are spirit. However, we are made in the image of God, which implies similar faculties (Gen. 1:26).

When the Holy Spirit regenerates a man, he has much greater understanding; his conscience is cleaned, but the sin nature (original sin) limits complete perception and discernment by contaminating all things, including creation. Dr. L. S. Chafer quotes Dr. W. G. T. Shedd, saying:

> "Dr. W. G. T. Shedd has written at length on the injury to the original man by sin and the peculiar characteristics of the sin nature. He asserts:
> 'Viewed as natural corruption, original sin may be considered with respect to the *understanding*. (*a*) It is blindness. Isa. 42:7, a light to open blind eyes. Luke 4:18, "Recovering of sight to the blind." Rev. 3:17, "Knowest not that thou art blind." 2 Cor. 4:4, "The god of this world hath blinded their minds." All texts that speak of regeneration as "enlightening." 2 Cor. 4:6; Eph. 5:14; 1 Thess. 5:5; Ps. 97:11, etc. All texts that call sin "darkness." Prov. 4:19; Is. 60:2; Eph. 5:11; Col. 1:13; 1 John 2:11; 1 Thess. 5:4; Eph. 4:18, "Having the understanding darkened;" Rom. 1:28, "Reprobate mind." Sin blinds and darkens the understanding, by destroying the *consciousness* of divine things. For example, the soul destitute of love to God is no longer conscious of love; of reverence, is no longer conscious of reverence, etc. Its knowledge of such affections, therefore, is from hearsay, like that which a blind man has of colors, or a deaf man of sound. God, the object of these affections, is of course unknown for the same reason. The spiritual discernment, spoken of in 1 Cor. 2:6, is the immediate consciousness of a renewed man. It is experimental knowledge. Sin is described in Scripture as voluntary ignorance. "This they willingly are ignorant of, that by the word of God the heavens were of old," 2 Pet. 3:5. Christ says to the Jews: "If I had not come and spoken unto them they had not had sin:" the sin, namely, of "they know not him that sent me," John 15:21, 22. But the ignorance, in this case, was a willing ignorance. They desired to be ignorant.
> Another effect of original sin upon the understanding as including the **conscience** is: (*b*) Insensibility. It does not render **conscience** extinct, but it stupefies it. 1 Tim. 4:2, "having their conscience

> seared with a hot iron." (c) Pollution. Titus 1:15, "Even their reason and conscience are polluted," or stained. Rom. 1:21, They "became vain in their imaginations," or speculations. The pollution of reason is seen in the foolish speculations of mythology. The myths of polytheism are not pure reason. The pollution of conscience is seen in remorse. The testifying faculty is spotted with guilt. It is no longer a "good conscience:" spoken of in Heb. 13:18; 1 Pet. 3:16, 21; 1 Tim. 1:5, 19; Acts 23:1; nor a "pure conscience:" mentioned in 1 Tim. 3:9. It is an "evil conscience": a conscience needing cleansing by atoning blood "from dead works," Heb. 9:14. Dead works, being no fulfilment of the law, leave the **conscience** perturbed and unpacified.'"[119] [verse 'misquotes' were corrected to the KJB, HDW].

The conscience can be cleansed by divine things such as the Words of God and the atoning blood of our Saviour; so, in a sense it is pure, but it cannot be perfectly "pure" unless the pure conscience of the Lord Jesus Christ within us is referred to or until we are made pure and translated to heaven.

Conscience is Not the Voice of the Lord

Individuals should not "let your conscience be your guide." Our conscience is not the voice of the Lord speaking to us **in spite of** the proclamations of good authors and organizations who declare this precept. For example, The American Tract Society (1859) said:

> The existence of this faculty [the conscience] proves the soul accountable at the bar of its Creator, and its "*voice*"

---

[119] Chafer, Lewis Sperry, *Systematic Theology* (Kregel Publications, Grand Rapids, MI, 1993, Vol. 2) (285-286)

is in an important sense ***the voice of God**.*"[120] [HDW, my emphasis)

R. A. Torry (1856-1928) said:

> "**Conscience is the voice of God in the soul**, witnessing to our sinfulness, God's essential justice. The characteristic testimony of the human conscience has always been in accordance with the word of God, that, "after death comes the judgment."[121]

Isaak August Dorner (1888) makes conscience *"the voice of God."* He said:

> "An analogy to this certainty is seen in conscience in which also **the voice of God** becomes part of our personal knowledge; for good, which God wills and thinks, makes itself evident in the conscience by its own agency, as ethical truth, as the thought of God."[122]

The *"voice of God,"* the written Words in this dispensation, has an influence on the conscience, but the conscience is **not** *"the voice of God."* It recognizes the testimony of God written in our hearts.

Many Definitions Cause Confusion

We can also see the beginnings of postmodernism in some of the common definitions of conscience in the late 1800s. For example:

---

[120] American Tract Society Dictionary, "Conscience" (ATSD, A Dictionary of the Holy Bible, American Tract Society, 1859, SwordSearcher, Ver. 5.1, 2007).
[121] R. A. Torrey, The Master Christian Library, (Ages Software, Rio, WI) 38.
[122] Roger Douglass Congdon (misspelled in the journal as Congdong), "The Doctrine of the Conscience" (Bibliotheca Sacra, Vol. 102, Dallas Theological Seminary, 1945, Logos Software, 2002) 352.

> "Watson (1855) speaks of conscience as 'the right which man has to profess **his own opinions** on subjects of religion, and to worship God in the mode which he deems most acceptable to him.'"[123] (HDW, my emphasis and addition)

Also, Joseph Cook writing in 1879 said:

> "If, therefore, conscience be supposed to be, as the strict definition describes it, the souls sense of right and wrong in its own choices and intentions, and in those only, conscience is **infallible** within its own field."[124]

The conscience is **not** infallible or foolproof as proclaimed in the quote above at any time in the life of an individual as we have seen **from** Scripture. Man can never rely completely upon the conscience for guidance. It is a defective guide, but the Words of God can improve the conscience. Similarly, our feelings are often wrong, and cannot be a reliable guide in spite of the assertions of charismatics and postmodernists; the conscience in fallen man is defective, although it serves a very important function. The function is its significant duty to be aware of God's laws inherent in every man's heart (spirit). The problem is man's conscience is defiled by sin. The conscience can **cause** man to override the knowledge of God's law written in his heart.

Congdon sums up the problem of confusion about conscience by quoting Robert Vernell's *Systematic Theology*, saying:

> "Foster has well summarized the existing state of confusion when he says: "There has been a great diversity of opinion and also endless discussions, among philosophers and theologians, as to **what it is the word *conscience* should**

---

[123] Ibid. 354. (Congdon, Bibliotheca Sacra, Vol. 102) A quote from Richard Watson's, *Theological Institutes*, 1855.
[124] Ibid. 355 (Congdon, Vol. 102).

designate; the consequence of which is, that it really denotes **whatever** any given writer chooses to make it denote."[125] [HDW, 'Whatever' is a buzz word for the postmodern generations: "You believe what you want to believe, and I will believe what I want"—i.e. "whatever."[126]]

There are definitions that we can categorically say are incorrect definitions of conscience. These common "sayings" were obtained from an article by Roger Douglass Congdon, "The Doctrine of the Conscience" and J. Oswald Sanders' book, *A Spiritual Clinic*. For example:

1. "The conscience is the sense or consciousness of right and wrong."

This is a common definition among the unsaved of the world. It is wrong because it leaves out a "**standard**" by which to judge "right and wrong." The world likes this definition because it allows the modern and postmodern predilection for exalting "self" as the source of determining truth or "whatever."

2. "Conscience is regard for ordinary fairness or justice."

This is true for the unsaved man (the ordinary man), but it is wrong for the saved man (believer in the Lord Jesus Christ as His Saviour) because again no standard is held up by the ordinary man except customs (e.g. laws of a society) or the philosophy of man. His "defiled" conscience refuses to turn toward (face so that he can read it) the law of God. Therefore, the customs of the Buddhist, Muslim, Mormon, Seventh Day Adventist, New Ager, Shaman, and others become the "guide" as opposed to the work of the Holy Spirit who exalts the Word of God in the heart of the believer.

---

[125] Ibid. 356 (Congdon, Vol. 102).
[126] Williams, op. cit., 376-383 (The Lie).

3. "Conscience is the voice of God."

This is contrary to Scripture for several reasons. (a) In Scripture, the conscience is never the voice of God. (b) In Scripture, the voice of God is never the conscience (c) The conscience can be "evil," "defiled," and "seared."

The voice of God or the Lord is typically the Lord Jesus Christ, His voice through His prophets, His inscripturated Words or His Words revealed but not recorded (see Chapter 2). His voice **cannot** be "evil," "defiled," "seared," etc. Conscience is a faculty or property of the mind[127] of man according to Scripture (by the personal pronouns used attributing it to man), and the word "conscience" is never used as a faculty attributed to God, even though we are in His image. God does not want any confusion. God's mind, Spirit, heart, etc., cannot be equated with fallen man's body, soul, and spirit.

4. The conscience is "the verdict of our natural reason and judgment touching the moral quality of any act."

This definition is attributed to the French, nevertheless this author expects it is a result of the rule of *natural* reason. Natural reason is a rationalistic philosophy endorsing human reason above God's revelation that developed during the Reformation and was reinforced by the Enlightenment. The philosophy can be attributed to the Germans, to the English, and to others, also. Albeit, the grand staunch believer and author J. R. Graves (1820-1893) is credited with saying:

---

[127] T. Austin Sparks, *What Is Man?* (Premium Literature Company, Indianapolis, IN, unknown date, may be ordered from Testimony Book Ministry, Washington, D.C.) Many authors describe the conscience as a property of the Spirit as in T. Austin Sparks' *What Is Man?* and Watchman Nee's many books, Charles R. Solomon's books such as *The Ins And Out of Rejection).*

"The [French] apostles of this theory taught that every proposition, whether appertaining to religion, morals or politics, should be indorsed by human reason. Consequently, every system and policy, every relation of life and distinction in human society, every theory of government, and even the teachings of the Bible and the acts of the All-wise God are arrested and hailed before the tribunal of human Reason, and acquitted or condemned according to its, in their estimation, infallible decisions!...Following the dictates of their consciences, they murdered the king and subverted the throne, annulled the constitution and abolished the laws. They consigned the titled and the rich to the executioner and the block, and confiscated their property for no crime, except that they possessed titles and wealth by hereditary right, according to the law of the land. They sent to the guillotine or the dungeon all sexes who presumed to differ from them in opinion. Conscience, the voice of the understanding and reason, unguided by statute, human or divine, became the 'higher law' of France, and France became a hell."[128] [HDW, Does this sound like the present day course of America? Also, see Dean Burgon's comment under the heading, "A Neglected Doctrine"]

5. The conscience is the "practical intellect."

Alexander of Hales proposed this definition, and it was used by the Jesuits to explain away their atrocities. "As an outgrowth of the controversies which followed this definition, the Jesuits developed a warped moral system in which the end justified the means without regard to inherent right or wrong and conscience was 'a prejudice to be removed by probabilism'" (the choosing of favorable probability to oneself).[129]

6. Conscience is "a law to itself, the original law written on the heart."

---

[128] Congdon, op. cit., 408-409 "The Doctrine of the Conscience" (Bibliotheca Sacra, Vol. 103).
[129] Congdon, op. cit., 350 "The Doctrine of the Conscience" (Bibliotheca Sacra, Vol. 102).

This is A. H. Hodge's definition. The conscience is not "a law" or it would be fixed. The conscience may be aware of the law of God, but it may choose to disregard it, and the conscience may be overruled by man's will. "It is obvious that if this were true, conscience would be infallible as suggested by the popular saying: "Let your conscience be your guide" (i.e. equivalent to 'the voice of God," HDW)[130] The conscience is not "*the law written on their heart.*" Rather, as stated previously, it is a witness to that law.

The heart in the Scriptures has a broad array of meanings and can only be discerned by the context. For example, sometimes "heart" refers to one of the tripartite divisions of man called the spirit (1 Thess. 5:23, Heb. 4:12). At other times it may refer to the soul, or even the conscience located in the soul (cf. Jer. 17:1). However, the candle of the Lord is man's spirit (heart) where the law of God is written (Pro. 20:27) and from this central part of man, God searches the intent or will of man. In a lost man, his spirit is not quickened and therefore not as effectual as in a saved man whose heart (spirit) is turned toward God and His Words, which wash the conscience. The conscience is a separate faculty in man; it is like a separate room in a house, with doors leading to other rooms.

What Is Conscience—From the Scriptures?

So what is the conscience? We must turn to our authority, the Scriptures. Most works do not do an exegesis of the Scripture but give their "opinion."

> "Of all the doctrines which have their roots in the Bible the doctrine of conscience seems to be one of the few in which

---

[130] Congdon, op. cit. 351 "The Doctrine of the Conscience" (Bibliotheca Sacra, Vol. 102) and op. cit., 409. "The Doctrine of the Conscience" (Bibliotheca Sacra, Vol. 103).

special schools of thought [HDW, e.g. in systematic theology] are less prominent than the individual ideas on the subject."[131]

Congdon has done an excellent job outlining the Scriptural exegesis of this doctrine. Therefore, the conclusion of his paper on the conscience is presented. The only exceptions that this author would have from Congdon's comments, concern the conscience *and* the heart. The heart has many connotations in the Scripture as stated above. For example, by the use of "heart" in places such as Acts 2:37, Romans 14:22, 1 John 3:20, heart can be understood to be the conscience. Nevertheless, in general, the numerous references to the heart in Scripture seem to be associated with the spirit in the tripartite man (Deut. 4:9, 29, 10:12, Psa. 13:2, Jer. 4:19, Mat. 12:30; the tripartite man is found in 1 Thess. 5:23, Heb. 4:12), whereas the conscience is associated with the mind and its thoughts, a part of the soul. It is true that in Hebrew thought the heart was associated at times with the soul (mind) or with the spirit. The Apostle John describes the concept of conscience as the heart in 1 John 3:17-20. But, in this author's opinion, it helps to associate the conscience with the mind and thoughts of man located in the soul of man. Remember to substitute "witness" for conscience in Congdon's discussion.

Scope of the Doctrine of the Conscience

"In classifying our Biblical knowledge of conscience, we will find two divisions and two subdivisions for each major sections of the truth, the subdivisions being of like nature in each case. They are these: **(1)** the conscience of the saved, considered positively and negatively; **(2)** the conscience of the unsaved, considered positively and negatively. Using this outline we shall make a detailed classification of Scripture references. 2 Corinthians 4:2 may be used as a general

---

[131] Ibid. Vol. 102, p. 406.

introduction because it teaches that every man has a conscience whether he is saved or not. Many of the designations chosen to identify different types of conscience in the outline are taken directly from the Bible. Where such names were not found in the Word, terms were found which seemed to fit well.

a. *The Conscience of the Saved*

The conscience of the believer differs primarily from that of the unbeliever, in two ways: **(a)** it takes precedence over the sin nature, **(b)** its object is not to please self but to please God. From the positive side, then, eight details will be learned from Scripture about this kind of conscience: **(1)** It is a *Godward* type (1 Pet 2:19)—a conscience in which self is not considered, for God's will wholly controls. This is the victorious conscience of those who take no thought for their lives, how they appear to men; rather, they suffer and even die willingly, "wrongfully," because they have chosen to please God. Compare 1 Chronicles 28:9. **(2)** It is a *good* conscience (Acts 23:1; 1 Tim 1:5, 19; 1 Pet 3:16, 21). This means an intrinsically good conscience and not one concerned simply with an outward appearance of goodness, hence an inward satisfaction in having nothing between God and self. **(3)** It is a *pure* conscience (1 Tim 3:9; 2 Tim 1:3), one without guile before God as well as blameless in the sight of man. **(4)** It is a *good* conscience (Heb 13:18), which speaks of that which is outwardly good and useful. This is the manifestly practical aspect of a pure conscience. The practical element may arise out of the fact that this sort of conscience can expect an answer to prayer without doubting. **(5)** It is an *uncondemning* conscience, one void of offence (Acts 24:16, 1 John 3:21). This goal seems to have been the minimum desired by Paul and John. It is not a praising conscience, yet at least it does not condemn. Like the good (kalos) conscience it gives confidence before God in prayer. See Job 27:6 also. **(6)** It is a *witnessing* conscience (Rom 9:1; 2 Cor 1:12; 5:11). In this, another aspect of the work of conscience, Paul calls upon this faculty as a witness to the validity of his statements and actions, to indicate that they were done in the power and wisdom of the Holy Spirit. He also appeals to the conscience of his listeners as further witness to his sincerity. That which is perfectly open and manifest to God needs to be vindicated before man through conscience. See Joshua 14:7 on this. **(7)** It is a *civil* conscience (Rom 13:5) or one directed toward government in so far as it does not run counter to God, that which calls the Christian citizen to a blameless life. In this side to conscience the old Greek goal is fulfilled. (8) It is a *strong* conscience or the informed, developed conscience (1 Cor 10:25, 27) over against the weak faculty described in 1 Corinthians 8. This signifies the conscience free from the law, the desires of the flesh, superstition and unbiblical tradition. It is the disposition of the man who lives freely and fully in the benefits of grace to the glory of God.

From the **negative** angle the Scripture details several more points about a believer's conscience. **(1)** It may be a *weak* thing (1 Cor 8:7, 10, 12) or the ignorant conscience as over against the strong type. Such a one is still bound in the graveclothes of legality, its owner having "fallen from grace." Of course, he is saved and safe, though living in bondage instead of grace. **(2)** It may be an *unperfected* thing (Heb 9:9; 10:2)—the conscience of Jewish worshippers before Christ came. Their conscience was not perfectly cleansed from the sense of sins, proof lying in the necessity they felt to keep bringing sacrifices. **(3)** It may be an *uncleansed* thing (Heb 9:14). The blood of bulls and goats had power to sanctify for the cleansing of the flesh, while the blood of Jesus Christ has the "much more" power needed for a purging of defiled consciences, hurt by sin. **(4)** It may be an *evil* thing (Heb 10:22). It seems that one of the conditions for entering into the holy place with boldness "with a true heart and in fullness of faith" is to have one's heart "sprinkled from an evil conscience." *Heart* and *conscience* may be used synonymously here, to be sure, heart perhaps a more general term, *conscience* the more specific. **(5)** It may be a *condemning* thing. Although there is no occurrence of the word suneidēsis to which this terminology could be applied easily, there are nevertheless many clear passages for which this is the best description (1 John 3:20; Rom 14:22). It is the opposite of the uncondemning conscience, resulting in loss of confidence before God, failure in the prayer life, and a sense of frustration. Compare 1 Samuel 25:31. **(6)** It may be a *repentant* thing (Matt 21:29; Luke 15:17). This seems to be the best way to describe what the believer does in order to restore his good conscience. Note Genesis 3 in this connection. **(7)** It may be a *smiting* or oppressive thing (Matt 26:75; 2 Cor 7:9–10), that which reacts with violence. See 1 Samuel 24:5; 2 Samuel 24:10; Psalm 32:3–5 here.

a. The Conscience of the Unsaved

What can be said for the **positive** viewpoint first? Just as in the case of believers, the conscience of unbelievers may be approving and complimentary. But, surprisingly enough, we fail to find any examples of it in Scripture. Possibly this fact will afford further insight into the mind of God. In His omniscience He knows that the glorying of the proud is vanity; still, though they may boast of goodness the Lord permits no recording of it in His Word. On the contrary, God will show that their approving conscience is actually only a defiled thing. The only examples of a good conscience with the unsaved, then, are those which act to bring men to a saving knowledge of Jesus Christ. In addition **(1)** there is the *pricked* conscience (Acts 2:37), the word *heart* being used for the conscience here no doubt. Whether all who heard the apostles that day were pricked in heart we do not know, nor do we know whether all whose hearts were touched became Christians. But the record does tell that three thousand souls were convicted by the Holy Spirit and saved. **(2)** There is the *witnessing* conscience (Rom 2:15). This type refers to a general condition with the lost, representing a conscience which is in the process of hardening or trusting. **(3)** There is the *uneasy* conscience (Luke 2:35), too, similar to the last-named. It does not indicate a specific type, of course. Though it may tend toward the good, it seems to speak more usually of the bad conscience and unrepentant heart.

On the **negative** side the unsaved may have **(1)** a *convicting* conscience (John 8:9). The result of it may well be shame as in the example cited, still without a turning to Christ in repentance or trust. **(2)** They may have a *weak* conscience (1 Cor 10:28–29). Whether the lost or saved are in view here, can be questioned. According to one expositor, Paul warns Christians against giving people occasion to say something like this of them: "We thought him very narrow, we thought he recognized only Christ as God, but you see he partakes with us in the recognition of all our gods. He has so much more liberty than we thought."[10] Thus we discover the same sort of conscience here as was predicated of the believer. **(3)** They may have a *defiled* conscience (Titus 1:15), i.e., one dyed, polluted, stained, comparable to the "blinded mind" of the unbeliever. **(4)** They may have a *seared* conscience (1 Tim 4:2)—perhaps the sort of conscience which is in those who are "energized by Satan" himself (Eph 2:2). **(5)** They may have a *cut* conscience (Acts 5:33) similar to the condemning kind that the Christian has and the pricked sort which leads to salvation. In this new kind, however, the direction is downward toward wrath and fury, the opposite direction from that followed by the others. **(6)** They may have a *remorseful* conscience (Matt 27:3) such as led Judas to seek escape from himself, although it did not bring him to Christ in saving faith. Kelly observes in this connection how the chief priests exercised a *dead* conscience: "Conscience would have told them that *theirs* was the guilt of bribing Judas to betray Jesus, but it had long been seared with a hot iron, and now was utterly dead toward God, as it shows itself heartlessly cruel toward Judas."[11] **(7)** They may have a *revengeful* conscience (Gen 4), a type often illustrated in the Bible. It is the worst form of conscience, presiding as it does over the actions of the most degenerate. It was the kind possessed by the rulers of Israel who, being condemned by the purity of Christ, became hot with wrath and an insane desire to crucify the Holy and Just One.

Summary of the Doctrine

We have examined carefully all the Scripture which seemed in any way to present a truth about conscience. But even after classifying the evidence in what appeared the simplest possible and most natural order, many of the questions raised by scholars, philosophers, and theologians remain unanswered. The primary reason that they remain so is because they are not answered by the Word of God. And if any presume to add his own opinion to that, it profits nothing. Nevertheless let it be said that on some of the questions

---

[10] H. A. Ironside, 1 Corinthians, p. 303.
[11] William Kelly, Gospel of Matthew, p. 498.

presented down through the centuries the Bible does cast light, though perhaps indirectly.

a. Ideas Excluded

Conscience is not the voice of God speaking to man. Nor is it the mere "bent of mind received by the discipline of childhood. Neither one of these extremes is sustained by Scripture."[12] Conscience is not "the verdict of our natural reason."[13] And conscience is not infallible, as Cook erroneously maintains.[14] The conscience should not be classed with the body, soul, and spirit as major elements in personality. Nor should it be classed with the senses—hearing, seeing, smelling, feeling, tasting—which are, in their own realm, in a very real sense infallible. Red is red to any normal eye, hot is hot to any touch, but what is right to a Turk may be taboo to a Chinaman. What Saul did in all good conscience was exactly opposite to what his conscience permitted after he became Paul. Even among fellow Christians, some may regard a day and others regard all days alike; some may gain a defiled conscience by eating certain foods and others find all food is good.

"A quiet conscience makes one so serene!
Christians have burnt each other, quite persuaded
That all the Apostles would have done as they did."[15]

So we conclude that conscience is not to be classified with the senses.

b. Ideas Included

What, then, do we know about the conscience? It may err; it may be trained; it may be dulled, defiled, seared. But it cannot be eradicated: all men have this faculty. It is evident from the function and failings of conscience, on the contrary,

---

[12] Lewis Sperry Chafer, *Bibliotheca Sacra*, April, 1944, p. 145.
[13] J. R. Graves, What Is Conscience?, p. 4.
[14] Joseph Cook, Boston Monday Lectures: Conscience, p. 15.
[15] Byron, Don Juan, I, 63.

that this is a singular and specialized activity of the mind, associating with itself the emotions, the will, and, in fact, the whole being. **It is the mind "knowing with" God's law; it is the human, fallible link to God's eternal, infallible standard of holiness. And its degree of purity or defilement is in direct ratio to the strength of this relationship. Christians are not to live and act according to their conscience, but rather according to the Scripture, i.e., by "the mind of the Holy Spirit" (Rom. 8:27, Eph 4:30).**[16]

The words of John Bascom form a fitting conclusion to this piece of doctrinal research: "Conscience is the power which enables us to apprehend the holiness of God; to hold any doctrine, to entertain any belief concerning his character, decrees, actions, that violates our sense of right, is as wrong as to suppose that we understand his methods and government when they present themselves to us as unwise and irrational. Human reason enables us to comprehend the rationality of divine action, conscience its righteousness. When His conduct seems to us unreasonable or His judgments unjust, we may be sure that the adjustments of the instruments of our vision are imperfect, that we have not brought the intellectual or the moral telescope to a perfect focus, and hence the obscurity and contradiction. To say this is God's way, while the traces of folly or of wrong remain in it, is to check inquiry and mar truth; is to exculpate God by the plea of omnipotence; is to suppose it among the immunities of Deity to be permitted to do less well than man; is to sanctify tyranny by its grandeur and power, or to atone for the laxity of justice by the generous prodigality of grace. Conscience is the only glass in which God's moral character and government can be mirrored; and in proportion as this is brought to a perfect surface and complete reflection will all his ways be found fit and proportionate. Divine wisdom and law will reveal themselves in the soul according as it holds to the heavens a pure and unsullied conscience."[132] [HDW, my emphasis]

---

[16] Lewis Sperry Chafer, Unpublished Manuscript (*Theology III, Doctrine 34*).

[132] Congdon, op. cit., 75-81 (Bibliotheca Sacra, Vol. 103. Dallas Theological Seminary, 1946; Logos, 2002) Congdon used an article from: "Conscience, Its Relations and Office," Bibliotheca Sacra, January, 1867, pp. 165-66.

A Regenerated Conscience

If you have been taught or heard someone say, "I live by my conscience," it is wrong. Sin has crippled our conscience. However, when the Holy Spirit regenerates a believer and creates the *"new man,"* the conscience can once again be better tuned to the written "law" of God, but the conscience is not **His** "voice."

By extension, the term law is used for referring to all of the commandments in the Bible. "All the Old Testament was sometimes called the law"[133] and by extension, all of the New Testament (Mat. 5:18, Lk. 2:23, Jn 15:25, 1 Tim. 3:15, 2 Tim. 3:16). All the Words of God strengthen a weak conscience and help correct a defiled conscience.

We must remember that our witness (conscience) does **not** have executive privilege. Sanders said:

> "It must be noted that conscience is not an executive faculty. It has no power to make a man do right or cease to do wrong. It delivers its judgment, produces the appropriate emotion, but leaves it to the will of man to act in the light of its verdict. It has no further power of responsibility."[134]

Conscience is a Goad, Not a Guide

John Phillips said:

> "So conscience is **not a guide but a goad**. It must be educated and monitored by the Word of God. In the work of conviction, the Holy Spirit seizes upon conscience and brings God's Word to bear upon it with mighty power. Apart

---

[133] Albert Barnes, Notes on the Old Testament, Explanatory and Practical, (SwordSearcher, Ver. 5.1.1.1, originally published 1832-1872, 2007) comments on John 15:25.
[134] Sanders, op. cit., 59.

from God's word, conscience is a very uncertain faculty of the soul. While the ancient pagan would put his children into the red hot lap of Molech with the hearty endorsement of conscience, the strict Buddhist would have agonies of remorse over killing a fly. The one extreme is as wrong as the other."[135] (HDW, See Dr. Waite's comment concerning the study of Scripture and the conscience,[136] on page 56 of this work)

Our conscience is not the voice of the Holy Spirit. The Holy Spirit is **God's witness** with **our** spirit (Acts 15:8, Rom. 8:16, 2 Cor. 1:22, Heb. 10:15, etc.) and *"the eyes of the LORD run to and fro throughout the whole earth, to shew himself strong in the behalf of them whose heart is perfect toward him"* (2 Ch. 16:9, cf. Zech. 4:10, Rev. 5:6). The heart in this verse is that central part of man, the spirit, where God dwells in a saved man. The Holy Spirit illuminates God's Words using the faculties inherent in man that God created, such as our conscience, which is more reliable when the Words of God wash it.

Warnings

By extension of the above, it is wrong to let our conscience beat us to death. It is only a goad, which can be **VERY** wrong, just as any witness in a courtroom may be VERY wrong. This is why God demanded two or three witnesses. A believer must trust God's Words as His guide, over and above his feelings and conscience, and must remember and appropriate those Words calling often on 1 John 1:9. Do not let your conscience mislead you (1) by being overly condemning or (2) by justifying actions that are contrary to the Words of God.

---

[135] John Phillips, *Exploring Romans, An Expository Commentary* (Kregel Publications, Grand Rapids, MI, 2002) 44.
[136] Pastor D. A. Waite, *Romans: Preaching Verse by Verse* (Bible For Today Press, Collingswood, NJ, 2005) 63.

An individual's conscience may ***not*** condemn his actions or thoughts at any point in his life, but he will ***not*** necessarily be **justified**. Justification can only come through a right relationship to God. That "right relationship" can only be determined by the Words of God and by His Son, who is the Judge. If the relationship is "right," God imputes righteousness to man. Man is not righteous through any good work performed by him. Anyone can determine if he is in a right relationship to God by simply acknowledging, accepting, believing, and trusting Truth. Similarly, a person's conscience may be telling him he is wrong, while he may be perfectly justified in the eyes of God. For example, an overly condemning conscience that has resulted from an overly protective parent may make a person "feel" that he is wrong and that he needs to do penitence or good works; but in reality, he is in a perfect, justified relationship with God.

The judge is coming again (Jn. 12:47-48) when true judgment and justice will be adjudicated by "*the voice of the words of the Lord*" and by the Lord Jesus Christ (Jn. 5:22, Phil 1:9). The Holy Spirit acts as a guide also by proper illumination of God's Words, but He is not our goad. He guides us into **all** Truth given to God's prophets and Apostles (Jn. 16:13, 2 Pe. 1:18-21). God is the only true Guide. His guiding cannot be brought about unless a believer studies His Words. By extension, every believer should be involved in providing the Words of God in some way to people around the world.

Paul knew nothing that would be contrary to his conscience (1) either because his actions before his conversion were not condemning or (2) because his actions during his apostleship were right. Yet Paul knew his conscience was fallible, and so he said: "*For I know nothing by myself; yet am I **not hereby justified**: but he that judgeth me is the Lord*" (1 Corinthians 4:4). The Lord will judge us by His preserved Words

(Jn. 12:47-48). He has assured man that they will be available for us to know His will (Mat. 24:35, Mk. 13:31, Lk. 21:33, Psa. 12:6-7, Psa. 117, etc.).

Albert Barnes, paraphrasing and interpreting 1 Corinthians 4:4, indicates Paul was saying:

> "I am not conscious of *evil*, or *unfaithfulness* to myself; that is, in my ministerial life." It is well remarked by Calvin, that Paul does not here refer to the whole of his life, but only to his apostleship. And the sense is, "I am conscious of integrity in this office. My own mind does not condemn me of ambition or unfaithfulness. Others may accuse me, but I am not conscious of that which should condemn me, or render me unworthy of this office." This appeal Paul elsewhere makes to the integrity and faithfulness of his ministry. So his speech before the elders of Ephesus at Miletus and other verses (carry the same thoughts), Ac 20:18-19,26-27; Compare 2Co 7:2; 12:17."[137] (HDW, my addition for clarity).

Paul knew that he must exercise his conscience because his "witness" was not infallible (Acts 23:1, 24:16). For this reason, Paul always studied God's Words even while in prison awaiting his departure to be with the Lord (2 Tim. 4:13). However, at one time in Saul's (Paul's name before his regeneration) career, he was so spiritually blind to *"the voice of God"* that he persecuted the church. If the great Paul was blind at one point, could anyone be blind to the true meaning of Scripture? Sanders said:

> "So blinded by prejudice and bigotry was Paul that he thought he was obeying the voice of God in persecuting the church. How bitterly he repented when he saw the true nature of the actions to which his conscience had assented!

---

[137] Albert Barnes, *Barnes Notes* (SwordSeacher, Broken Arrow, OK, 2007) Comments on 1 Cor. 4:4.

Often when we think we are standing for principle we are only falling for prejudice."[138] (my emphasis, HDW).

However, a conscience properly exercised by the preserved, inerrant, inspired Words of God is less likely to lead anyone astray.

"So then conscience when regulated by **the Word of God** is the monitor in the **soul** of man which insists on right doing, condemns wrong doing, produces remorse when flouted, and imparts peace when heeded."[139] [HDW, my emphasis]

A Weak Conscience and "Babes" in Christ

A "*weak*" conscience is like a flag on a pole swinging back and forth in the wind. It is vacillating. It is like a man who is often of two opinions (1 Kg. 18:21), especially if he is not grounded in the Words of God. A weak conscience is oversensitive and overly scrupulous because it is not grounded, washed, cleansed, and stabilized by God's Words (1 Cor. 8:7-12). Surely one notices the many modern denominations, which thrive on works and conformity to the group's "Mishnah,"[140] which is indicative of a "weak" uninformed conscience. This is similar to the serious errors of the scribes and Pharisaical Jews (Mat. 23:13ff).

Sanders reports that a weak conscience is like a weak compass that vacillates easily.

---

[138] Sanders, op. cit., 61.
[139] Ibid. 61 (Sanders).
[140] Alfred Edersheim, *The Life and Times Of Jesus The* Messiah (Hendrickson Publishers, Peabody, MA, originally published in 1883, republished in 1993) 8. The Jewish Mishnah was the oral law which reached exponential proportions for a Jew to follow to prevent a transgression of the written law. It became more important in Israel than the written law. The oral Mishnah was eventually written down in the ?third century.

> "Its professor is constantly tormented by doubt as to whether an action is right or wrong and constantly digs up in unbelief what has been sown in faith."[141]

The possessor of a *"weak"* conscience is someone who is without sufficient knowledge of God's Words. A weak conscience is also easily defiled (corrupted) (1 Cor. 8:7). This is the reason Paul was very concerned about *"babes in Christ"* [1 Cor. 3:1-2, Heb. 5:12-13) (This author believes Paul wrote Hebrews)]. "Dirt" can defile a conscience, as dirt can clog the gears of a watch. For this reason, parents need to be very concerned about keeping their babes from dirt. They need to protect their babes from many things such as some movies and magazines, the internet, many in their peer group, and the myriad of false teachers, ordained of old to test us (Jude 1:4). Similarly, a pastor needs to be concerned with the same issues.

Remember, even a baby is born in sin and is not "pure" and is not without contamination (Psa. 51:5, 58:3, Isa. 48:8). Pure, in a strict sense of the word, is NO impurities; whereas the scriptural meaning in many instances is cleansed, but not absolutely pure. This is not true in all instances; it depends on context. No human being except Jesus Christ could be considered without contamination of any sort; that is, without sin, pure, and perfect. A believer is washed in the blood of the Lamb and is clean or cleansed, but the old man of sin remains (Isa. 53:6, Rom. 3:23, 7:17ff, 1 Jn. 1:9, Rev. 1:5, 7:14). We must guard ourselves after we are cleansed by the *"washing of water by the word"* made possible by His blood to keep ourselves free from additional *"spot"* or *"blemish"* (Eph. 5:26-27) by utilizing 1 John 1:9, by study of the Scriptures and by not participating in presumptuous sin.

---

[141] Sanders, op. cit., 62.

If we can possibly keep our *"babes"* in Christ, whether children or adults, free from dirt, that is, keep them clean and protected, then:

> *"Unto the pure all things are pure: but unto them that are defiled and unbelieving is nothing pure; but even their mind and conscience is defiled" (Titus 1:15, cf. Rom. 8:1ff).*

The postmodernist does not believe anything is truth (but himself and his experiences). Therefore, there is *"nothing pure"* but himself, *"but even their mind and conscience is defiled"* because they do not believe the pure and perfect Truth of God.

Beware of False Claims, False Teachers, and False Prophets

Beware of phony pronouncements and claims by individuals and by false prophets and teachers concerning the conscience. Jesus said, *"Beware of false prophets"* (Mat. 7:15). Paul said, *"Desiring to be teachers of the law; understanding neither what they say, nor whereof they affirm"* (1 Timothy 1:7).

This pertains to the many modern and postmodern false prophets who write books with their false interpretations and call them a "bible." God calls their words *"lying words," "perverted words,"* and *"chaff."* (Psa. 59:12, Isa 32:7, 59:13, Jer. 7:8, 23:6, 28, etc.). It would be dangerous for a believer to use their false words as a guide for his conscience. This also applies to those claiming new revelations from the Lord, which they shout abroad, frequently adding to or changing the written inscripturated Words of the Lord. We must use only the *received* Words of God given by *revelation* to God's *Biblical* prophets and Apostles (Eph. 2:20, 2 Pe. 1:21) and preserved by the orthodox Jews and the sanctified churches throughout the centuries (Rom. 3:1-2, 1 Tim 3:15). The Words were not preserved by cults such as the Essenes and Gnostics, or by apostate churches. It is very risky to use any other Words than those affirmed by the Holy Spirit in the sixty-six books of the Bible. Who doesn't want **all** of the inspired Words given to man by revelation, but "not one word more or less"?

It is those precise *received* Words from God that we can be certain are perfectly preserved as God promised and assure us that we are a child of God. If they were not perfectly preserved, we could not be certain. It is this author's contention that:

(1) doubt and

(2) confusion, created by scholars dragging

    (a) old corrupted MSS out of garbage dumps in Egypt and

    (b) neglected corrupted MSS off of dusty shelves in the

    Vatican and monasteries

to allegedly "reconstruct" the Words of God, has contributed significantly:

(1) to the explosion of people claiming they hear the audible voice of God and

(2) to the false philosophy of the last days.

In light of these factors, many believers are seeking reassurance that they are children of God, and unbelievers are looking for a stable foundation in something. The unfortunate result seems to be that everyone is turning to "himself," i.e. his own conscience.

The preserved Words of God tell us how to know we are His children by grace through faith without the use of the five senses (Eph. 2:8-10). His preserved *received* Words which have not been tampered with, which are tempered, and which are *"pure words: as silver tried in a furnace of earth, purified seven times,"* tell us how to have assurance (Deut. 4:2-6, Pro. 30:5-6, Rev. 22:18-19, Eze. 22:28, Psa. 12:6-7, 1 Jn.).

Assurance That a Believer is the Child of God

Although this work is not about assurance, some comments about it are appropriate at this point. The Apostle John wrote Words from the Lord for us so that we would know when we are His children.

> *These things have I written unto you that believe on the name of the Son of God; **that ye may know** that ye have eternal life, and that ye may believe on the name of the Son of God. 1 John 5:13*

This work cannot cover all of the aspects, but we will list the most important along with a few verses. The following comments are not meant to be exhaustive. Please understand there are hundreds of verses that confirm the concepts presented here. We know that we are a child of God when:

(1) We love God and desire to obey, guard, preserve, and watch-over the commandments of God, *"the voice of the words of God."*

> *"If ye love me, keep my commandments" (John 14:15). "If ye keep my commandments, ye shall abide in my love; even as I have kept my Father's commandments, and abide in his love" (John 15:10). "And hereby we do know that we know him, if we keep his commandments." (1 John 2:3). "He that saith, I know him, and keepeth not his commandments, is a liar, and the truth is not in him." (1 John 2:4). "By this we know that we love the children of God, when we love God, and keep his commandments" (1 John 5:2).*

(2) By keeping His commandments, our love of God grows and is perfected.

> "But whoso keepeth his word, in him verily is the love of God perfected: hereby know we that we are in him" (1 John 2:5).

(3) We love fellow believers.

> "He that saith he is in the light, and hateth his brother, is in darkness even until now. He that loveth his brother abideth in the light, and there is none occasion of stumbling in him" (1 John 2:9-10). "We know that we have passed from death unto life, because we love the brethren. He that loveth not his brother abideth in death" (1 John 3:14).

(4) We do not love the world.

> "Love not the world, neither the things that are in the world. If any man love the world, the love of the Father is not in him" (1 John 2:15). "For whatsoever is born of God overcometh the world: and this is the victory that overcometh the world, even our faith. Who is he that overcometh the world, but he that believeth that Jesus is the Son of God?" (1 John 5:4-5, cf. Jam. 1:15, etc.).

(5) We are not liars.

> "I have not written unto you because ye know not the truth, but because ye know it, and that no lie is of the truth" (1 John 2:21).

(6) We believe that Jesus is the Christ; that is, He is the door, the light, the Saviour, the only way to heaven and eternal life, and the virgin-born Son of God. We believe that He died, was buried and resurrected in three days; His body is flesh, and many similar things. Here are several verses among many:

> "Who is a liar but he that denieth that Jesus is the Christ? He is antichrist, that denieth the Father and the Son" (1 John 2:22). "Whosoever shall confess that Jesus is the Son of God, God dwelleth in him, and he in God" (1 John 4:15).

The next verse also confirms the importance of God's inspired, preserved Words called *"the record"* in these verses:

> *"He that believeth on the Son of God hath the witness in himself: he that believeth not God hath made him a liar; because he believeth **not the record** that God gave of his Son. And this is **the record**, that God hath given to us eternal life, and this life is in his Son. He that hath the Son hath life; and he that hath not the Son of God hath not life"* [1 John 5:10-12, cf. Lk. 24:13ff where Jesus affirmed that the **record** (Scripture) is about Him].

(7) We cleanse (purify) our lives by the washing of the Words of God; that is, we desire and hunger to know God's Words, commandments, will, precepts, etc. in order to serve our God and not sin. We turn ourselves over to and come under the Lord Jesus Christ's Words. In other words, we are sanctified to Him.

> *"And every man that hath this hope in him purifieth himself, even as he is pure"* (1 John 3:3). *"Little children, let no man deceive you: he that doeth righteousness is righteous, even as he is righteous"* (1 John 3:7). Paul's words amplify this concept by saying: *"...Christ also loved the church, and gave himself for it; That he might sanctify and cleanse it with the washing of water by the word, That he might present it to himself a glorious church, not having spot, or wrinkle, or any such thing; but that it should be holy and without blemish."* (Ephesians 5:25-27). And Paul said: *"But God forbid that I should glory, save in the cross of our Lord Jesus Christ, by whom the world is crucified unto me, and I unto the world"* (Galatians 6:14).

(8) We do not sin habitually or willfully. We do not practice sin.

> *"Whosoever is born of God doth not commit sin; for his seed remaineth in him: and he cannot sin, because he is born of God"* (1 John 3:9).

This verse does not mean that we never sin or have not sin. It is frequently misunderstood (cf. Heb. 10:26, 1 Jn. 1:8-10). *"Commit"* in this verse means "continue in" or "practice."

(9) We love not by words, but by acts and deeds toward our brothers and sisters.

> *"My little children, let us not love in word, neither in tongue; but in deed and in truth" (1 John 3:18, cf. 1 Jn. 3:17 Jam. 1:22, 2:18).*

(10) We test the spirits of people by confirming if they believe Christ came in the flesh.

> *"Beloved, believe not every spirit, but try the spirits whether they are of God: because many false prophets are gone out into the world. Hereby know ye the Spirit of God: Every spirit that confesseth that Jesus Christ is come in the flesh is of God:" (1 John 4:1-2).*

(11) We know that God dwelleth in us if we manifest the fruit of the Spirit, which no natural man will have without the Spirit. If you do not manifest the following fruit, which only you will know, you are not a child of God.

> *"But the fruit of the Spirit is love, joy, peace, longsuffering, gentleness, goodness, faith, (23) Meekness, temperance: against such there is no law" (Galatians 5:22-23). "Hereby know we that we dwell in him, and he in us, because he hath given us of his Spirit" (1 John 4:13). Jesus Christ affirmed this same principle when he said: "Abide in me, and I in you. As the branch cannot bear fruit of itself, except it abide in the vine; no more can ye, except ye abide in me" (John 15:4).*

(12) We live by faith in God the Father, God the Son, and God the Holy Spirit and their Words. (Rom. 1:17, Rom. 3, 2 Cor. 5:7, and many many many more passages).

(13) We understand that *"faith cometh by hearing and hearing by the word of God."* That means **all** of His inscripturated Words (Rom. 10:17, 2 Tim. 3:16).

(14) We believe and trust His promises and look for His glorious appearing (Gal. 3:29, Tit. 2:13, Heb. 6:12).

The Holy Spirit will illuminate, enlighten, and confirm if the above tenets apply to a person. The meaning of the following verse is often used incorrectly. Many claim that God speaks audibly to believers based on this verse. In reality, it confirms the Spirit's testimony in you. His fruit exhibits the Spirit's presence in our lives. We believe and live our lives according to His Words by the power of the Spirit. An unbeliever cannot live by the power of the Spirit.

> *"The Spirit itself beareth witness with our spirit, that we are the children of God:" (Romans 8:16).*

He gives us His witness or testimony by confirming His Words in us. He does not audibly tell us because God wants us to live by faith, not by sight.

Finally, you know you are a child of God by the assurance given in His Words, "then heirs; heirs of God, and joint-heirs with Christ; if so be that we suffer with him, that we may be also glorified together" (Romans 8:17). God's revelation given to us through the Words recorded by the prophets and Apostles is the most amazing, complete, perfect Book ever written. Everything a person needs is in the "old black Book." This is a loud claim by many believers through the ages. However, sometimes we need help from teachers, pastors, missionaries, and evangelists to understand God's "revelation" better.

So, what is "revelation?"

CHAPTER 4

REVELATION

> *"The secret things belong unto the LORD our God: but those things which are **revealed** belong unto us and to our children for ever, that we may do all the words of this law."*
> *(Deuteronomy 29:29, cf. Dan. 2:22)*

Revelation is the process of revealing truth. God has *"revealed"* His Truth to us through His Biblical prophets and Apostles. Not all revelation to His Apostles and prophets was inscripturated. The Words of revelation that God wanted man to know and to have are recorded for us *"for ever."*

The inscripturated Words of God in the Bible were chosen in eternity past (Psa. 119:89, Isa. 65:6, Dan. 10:21) by the Trinity before they were given to the Apostles and prophets to record (Jn. 16:13, 17:8, Eph. 2:20, 1 Pe. 1:23-25, 2 Pe. 1:20-21, 2 Pe. 3:2). The Words of the Lord were chosen before the foundation of the world (Mat. 13:35, Eph. 1:4, Rev. 13:8). They are *"for ever.. settled."* They were *"written before"* and are *"before"* Him in heaven *"for ever"* (Psa. 117, 119:89, Isa. 65:6). The angel who explained Daniel's vision of *"things to come,"* noted that he would *"show [Daniel] that which is noted **in the scripture of truth**"* (Dan. 10:21). The Words *"for ever...settled"* in heaven were given to Daniel to record for us even though He did not understand all of them (Dan. 12:8-9). The Apostle John noted the visions recorded in the book of Revelation were *"until the words of God shall be fulfilled"* (Rev. 17: 17, Jn. 17:17). In other words, the Words of God previously recorded would be fulfilled. Please note that the message is given through **Words** which are from the lips of Him who is the *"Ancient of days."* They are recorded in *"books"* that are before Him (Dan. 7:9-10).

His Truth comes to us in the form of precise, pure, perfect Words, which are like 'a legal contract' that are contained in books or epistles. The books are recognized by God's institutions that were given the responsibility to preserve them. The Holy Spirit guides them. Athanasius (b. 296 A.D.), an early church elder, and *The Muratorian Fragment* (dated 170 A.D.) are just two of several sources that document many of the books (the Canon of Scripture) by listing all of the New Testament books. Other writings, such as those of Irenaeus (120-190 A.D.), mention most of the New Testament books, but they do not record a list.[142] The canon of the Old Testament was closed before the time of Christ. Josephus (A.D. 37-101) indicated the closure in his book, *Against Apion,* found in the following quote:

> "One of the most important pieces of evidence in favor of the forming and closing of the canon at a time prior to Christ may be found in the writings of Josephus, the Jewish historian. He writes (at about 100 AD) "It is true our history has been written since Artaxerxes very particularly but has not been esteemed of the like authority with the former by our forefathers, because there has not been an exact succession of the prophets since that time."[143]

We have all of God's written revelation as He promised. If you truly believe God and His Son, if it is not a false profession, if it is not a "head" or intellectual belief, if you trust God with the hope that is in you and confirmed by the Holy Spirit who dwells in you, then effectually, you

---

[142] "The Canon of Scripture," see: http://www.bible-researcher.com/canon.html and http://www.bible-researcher.com/canon3.html
[143] "The Old Testament Canon," See: http://www.columbia.edu/cu/augustine/arch/sbrandt/canon.htm

Chapter 4—Revelation

as believer have signed God's "legal" contract, the Bible. The Words of the "Contract" cannot be changed (Deut. 4:2, Pro. 30:5-6, Mat. 24:35, Rev. 22:18-19). In addition, you are sealed *"for ever"* by the Holy Spirit, which is made possible by the blood shed on the Cross. The promises in God's 'Contract,' which are given by revelation to special people chosen by God to record, are yours *"for ever."*

> *"For ever, O LORD, thy word is settled in heaven" (Psalms 119:89). "Heaven and earth shall pass away, but my words shall not pass away" (Matthew 24:35, and many other places).*

Many authors will bring confusion to these issues by falsely claiming that God did not tell us how he would preserve the Words in His revelation to us. Therefore, many claim His revelation is preserved, but scattered in "all" the manuscripts.

For example, Dr. James B. Williams and Dr. Randolph Shaylor claim:

> "We believe that the Bible teaches that God providentially preserved His written Word (note that they do not say Words). This preservation exists in the **totality** of the ancient language manuscripts of that revelation. We are therefore certain that we possess the very Word of God."[144] (my addition, HDW).

Their statement would include well-known corrupted MSS such as Aleph (Sinaiticus), B (Vaticanus), A (Alexandrinus), Beza, and others. Furthermore, they imply that Words could be hidden in MSS yet to be discovered in secret places and possibly not available to anyone. This is contrary to clear Scriptural proclamations (see below). Their claim that "We are therefore certain that we possess the very Word of God" is mute

---

[144] "Williams and Shaylor, op. cit., iii (*God's Word in Our Hands*).

and empty. How do they know we possess the very Word of God if they are in "the totality of the ancient language manuscripts," and we do not have the original autographs? The only way to know and *receive* them is to believe God's Words, which state that they are available to every generation (see above). God says:

> *"For the LORD is good; his mercy is everlasting; and his truth endureth to **all generations**" (Psalms 100:5).* *"**I have not spoken in secret**, in a dark place of the earth: I said not unto the seed of Jacob, Seek ye me in vain: I the LORD speak righteousness, I declare things that are right" (Isaiah 45:19).* *"Come ye near unto me, hear ye this;* ***I have not spoken in secret from the beginning****; from the time that it was, there am I: and now the Lord GOD, and his Spirit, hath sent me" (Isaiah 48:16). "For this commandment which I command thee this day,* ***it is not hidden from thee, neither is it far off****. It is not in heaven, that thou shouldest say, Who shall go up for us to heaven, and bring it unto us, that we may hear it, and do it? Neither is it beyond the sea, that thou shouldest say, Who shall go over the sea for us, and bring it unto us, that we may hear it, and do it?* ***But the word is very nigh unto thee****, in thy mouth, and in thy heart, that thou mayest do it" (Deuteronomy 30:11-14).*

Since *"all"* the MSS are not available or accessible, in effect this claim would make *"all"* the Words of the contract unavailable, uncertain, and possibly corrupted by man for *vain* reasons. If their claims are true, how could we be certain of His Contract (Pro. 22:21) or believe Jesus' statement: *"Heaven and earth shall pass away, but my words shall not pass away"* (Matthew 24:35)? Could this be one of the significant causes or contributions to the acceptance of postmodern philosophy, which touts *uncertainty about everything*, especially God's revelation?

Revelation Does Not Need Reconstructing

Those who make the claim that the Words are in "all" the manuscripts, are called "Majority Text"[145] men. They believe the Words are in "all" the Greek MSS and in "all" the Hebrew/Aramaic MSS, whether they are available or whether they are still hidden in MSS yet to be discovered.[146] Their claims portend the need to "reconstruct" the Words of God back to or equal with the originals. However, they never tell or remind you **(1)** that the originals are not available, **(2)** that "all" the MSS have never been collated or even possibly found, or **(3)** that they never will be collated because the task is overwhelming. It is overwhelming because of the poor quality of the MSS, the variation in handwriting in old MSS, the fragility of the MSS, and limited access to them make collating "all" the MSS impossible. These men are still searching for "all" the Words that God said He would preserve for every generation. Would God hide

---

[145] "Majority Text" is a term which has changed in meaning in the last century. Previously, it meant the Bible *received* and confirmed in the majority of Greek manuscripts **examined,** which are "virtually identical," but it included a few words found in the Latin manuscripts, church elder writings, and lectionaries. However, the term Majority Text was changed by those who subscribe to the proclamations of Hermann von Soden, who collated approximately 400 manuscripts, but whose work was poorly documented, and by those who follow the work of Hodges and Farstead, or Pierpont and Robinson Majority Texts. Their majority texts are based upon a "few" manuscripts of the Byzantine tradition and basically follow von Soden. See http://www.wayoflife.org/articles/majoritytext.htm for a good article concerning the "Majority Text." Dr. D. A. Waite reports the Majority Text alters the Textus Receptus in about 1,800 places.

[146] Philip Comfort, *Encountering the Manuscripts, An Introduction to New Testament Paleography and Textual Criticism* (Broadman and Holman Publishers, Nashville, TN, 2005) 57. Many fragments of manuscripts are in the graves and garbage dumps in Oxyrhynchus, Egypt. They continue to be found and applied to the texts by New Testament textual critics. The wisdom related to this paleontology is faulty. The number of 'new' Greek manuscripts has risen from approximately 5,240 in the 1960s to over 5,500 in 2005. p. 56

His Words of revelation in MSS that are still not collated or even possibly still hidden in garbage dumps, in monasteries, or on Vatican shelves? Would a Holy God cause any of His Words to be unavailable over the last fifteen hundred years? As history confirms, God has preserved His revelation in the vast majority of manuscript evidence readily available. Under the guidance of the Holy Spirit God's servants preserved the texts by watching, guarding, and protecting the Words. *"Doth he thank that servant because he did the things that were **commanded** him? I trow (think) not"* (Luke 17:9) (HDW, my emphasis and addition).

Yet, men still praise Westcott, Hort, and many others for applying the often repeated refrain, "the oldest is the best," even though the words found in MSS dug up from grave sites are not in the MSS readily available and recognized by the sanctified churches. For example, Dr. Comfort praises Westcott and Hort for using those newly discovered words, saying:

> "In many instances where I would disagree with the wording in the Nestle/UBS text in favor of a particular variant reading, I would later check with the Westcott and Hort text and realize that they had often come to the same decision. This revealed to me that I was working on the same methodological basis as they. Of course, the manuscript discoveries of the past one hundred years have **changed** things, but it is remarkable how often they have affirmed the decisions of Westcott and Hort."[147]

If the Words of God are changing month-by-month or year-by-year based on new discoveries, then God is a liar. Whom do you think is right?

---

[147] Ibid. 100 (Comfort, *Encountering the Manuscripts*).

Confusion is Not From God

In addition, there are also many pastors, professors, teachers, authors, and speakers, who, by television programs, movies, magazines, and other media, portray a very confusing picture in relation to revelation. They quote versions that are reliant upon a few corrupted old texts or the alleged "majority" or "totality" of texts. They use many different versions whose words are as varied as the stars because of dynamic equivalent interpretations of corrupted texts. Subsequently, they cloud the Scriptural meaning of revelation, preservation, inerrancy, inspiration, and infallibility.

This is not a new problem. Confusion is not from God, and it started in the Garden (Gen. 3: 1-2, 1 Cor. 14:33). Knowing that His Words to us containing His promises are *"settled,"* brings peace (Psa. 119:89). Men, who claim the Canon of Scripture is open, the Words of revelation continue to need "work," and the search for MSS to confirm His Words is still necessary, are **not** bringing Words of peace, but words of confusion. Their texts and logic are unsettling because they vary so greatly. All of this searching by "scholars" has produced doubt and has helped usher in the postmodern age—uncertainty, extreme selfism, and doubt about any proclamation of truth. There is no need for confusion. We have *"the voice of the words of the Lord."*

The minute someone declares extra-Biblical revelation, promotes the need for more research to determine the accuracy of God's Words, or claims to hear the audible Words of God, he should be looked upon with great sorrow in our hearts and gently reproved with love. If he persists in making "unsettled" claims or claims that bring confusion because they are not Scripturally sound doctrines, he should be avoided (Rom. 16:17, 2 Jn 1:10-11, 2 Thess. 3:6, 14).[148]

Early Gnostics Brought Confusion

The early Gnostics did great damage to the cause of Christ and His Words during the immediate post-apostolic years. They often claimed extra-Scriptural revelation by the Holy Spirit. Irenaeus (120-192 A.D.), the disciple of Polycarp (69-155 A.D.) who was discipled by the Apostle John (d., c. 92-97 A.D.), speaks about these things in his book, *Against Heresies*. We caution the reader to understand that Irenaeus frequently wrote sarcastically because he was greatly disturbed by the pronouncements of Gnostics such as Valentinus and his disciples, the Marcionites, and others.[149] Irenaeus said:

> "These men falsify the oracles of God, and prove themselves **evil interpreters** of the good word of **revelation**. They **also** overthrow the faith of many, by drawing them away, under **a pretence of [superior] knowledge, from Him** who rounded and adorned the universe; as if, forsooth, they had something more excellent and sublime **to reveal**, than that God who created the heaven and the earth, and all things that are therein. By means of specious and plausible words, they cunningly allure the simple-minded to inquire into their system; but they nevertheless clumsily destroy them, while they initiate them into their blasphemous and impious

---

[148] Way of Life Literature, "Biblical Separation" (http://www.wayoflife.org/fbns/biblicalseparation.html).

[149] Roberts, Alexander ; Donaldson, James ; Coxe, A. Cleveland: Irenaeus, *Against Heresies*, The Ante-Nicene Fathers Vol. I : Translations of the Writings of the Fathers Down to A.D. 325 (Oak Harbor: Logos Research Systems, 1997). See the translator's preface, p. 312. The translators said about Irenaeus: "Not unfrequently he indulges in a kind of sarcastic humour, while inveighing against the folly and impiety of the heretics.'"

opinions respecting the Demiurge;[150] and these simple ones are unable, even in such a matter, to distinguish falsehood **from truth**."[151] (HDW, my emphasis)

Irenaeus knew he had the Words of God. He was only one generation removed from the Apostles. There is a claim that Irenaeus and other church elders quoted from texts other than the *received text*, also called the Traditional or Byzantine Text. However, these early authors had manuscripts, scrolls, or codices of papyrus, or leather, which were much harder to use than modern printed texts. So, church elders frequently quoted from memory; and just like us when we try to quote from memory, errors are made. Furthermore, they were often quoting and writing against heretics who changed the Words of God. They used the heretics' incorrect words in their quotes. They were not necessarily using a personal corrupted Alexandrian-type text, which originated in Alexandria, Egypt, a place where dozens of cults made their home. In other words, we can have great assurance that most of the early authors were using the *Received Texts* that originated in heaven. The Apostles and prophets recorded the Words given to them. Furthermore, recent careful analyses of church elder writings demonstrate the majority of quotes are the *Received Texts*.

The Gnostics, who frequently corrupted the texts, were guilty of claiming that the Holy Spirit revealed their speculations to them. For example, Montanus claimed that the Holy Spirit audibly spoke to him; and he led two alleged prophetesses around with him wherever he traveled. Dr. Harold O. J. Brown said:

---

[150] This fancied being was, in the Valentinian system, the creator of the material universe, but far inferior to the supreme ruler Bythus.
[151] Roberts et al, op. cit., Vol. I, p. 315.

"Montanus believed that he had a special prophetic gift, which was shared by his two female disciples, Maximilla and Prisca. He quotes the Spirit, supposedly speaking through him, 'Behold, man is like a lyre and I fly over it like the plectrum.'"[152]

This is similar to present day charismatic individuals claiming that angels speak to them and that they hear the audible *"voice of the Lord."* Irenaeus sarcastically said that the Gnostics claim:

"the Holy Spirit **taught them** to give thanks on being all rendered equal [the Aeons] among themselves, and led them to a state of true repose. Thus, then, they tell us that the Aeons were constituted equal to each other in form and sentiment, so that all became as Nous, and Logos, and Anthropos, and Christus. The female Aeons, too, became all as Aletheia, and Zoe, and Spiritus, and Ecclesia. Everything, then, being thus established, and brought into a state of perfect rest, they next tell us that these beings sang praises with great joy to the Propator, who himself shared in the abounding exaltation. Then, out of gratitude for the great benefit which had been conferred on them, the whole Pleroma of the Aeons, with one design and desire, and **with the concurrence of Christ and the Holy Spirit**, their Father also setting the seal of His approval on their conduct, brought together whatever each one had in himself of the greatest beauty and preciousness; and uniting all these contributions so as skilfully to blend the whole, they produced, to the honour and glory of Bythus, a being of most perfect beauty, the very star of the Pleroma, and the perfect fruit [of it], namely Jesus. Him they also speak of under the name of Saviour, and Christ, and patronymically, Logos, and Everything, because He was formed from the contributions of all. And then we are told that, by way of honour, angels of the same nature as Himself were simultaneously produced, to act as His body-guard."[153] [HDW, my emphasis]

---

[152] Harold O. J. Brown, *Heresies, Heresy And Orthodoxy In The History Of The Church* (Hendrickson Publishers, Peabody, MA, 1988) 66.
[153] Alexander Roberts; Donaldson, James ; Coxe, A. Cleveland: The Ante-Nicene Fathers Vol.I : Translations of the Writings of the Fathers Down to

Charismatic claims are not new. Eusebius Pamphilus (c. 250-341), the church historian, and Irenaeus (120-190 A.D.) comment on charismatic issues. For example, the translator of the epistle, *Pastor of Hermas* comments:

> "As Eusebius informs us, the **charismata** were not extinct in the churches when the Phrygian imitations began to puzzle the faithful. Bunsen considers its first propagators specimens of the *clairvoyant* art, and pointedly cites the manipulations they were said to practice (like persons playing on the harp), in proof of this."[154] [HDW, my emphasis]

In addition, Irenaeus draws the same conclusions that many of us claim today concerning the specious claims of individuals over and against God's *revelation*. Individuals need to be *under* God's revealed words rather than being *over* and *against* their literal meaning. Irenaeus said:

> "Such, then, is the account which they all give of their Pleroma, and of the formation [of their opinion] of the universe, striving as they do, to adapt **the good words of revelation to their own wicked inventions.** And it is not only from the writings of the evangelists and the apostles that they endeavour to derive proofs for their opinions by means of **perverse interpretations and deceitful expositions**: they deal in the same way with the law and the prophets, which contain many parables and allegories that can frequently be drawn into various senses, according to the kind of exegesis to which they are subjected. And others of them, with **great craftiness**, adapted such parts of Scripture to their own figments, lead away captive from the truth those who do not retain a

---

A.D. 325. (Oak Harbor : Logos Research Systems, 1997) 318. (Irenaeus' Against Heresies).
[154] Ibid. Vol. II (Translations of the Writings of the Fathers Down to A.D. 325) 4. (Introductory Note to The Pastor of Hermas; Irenaeus is mentioned as dealing with charismatic problems in this passage.).

stedfast faith in one God, the Father Almighty, and in one Lord Jesus Christ, the Son of God."[155] (HDW, my emphasis)

The Doctrine Of Revelation

In general, revelation, the revealing of truth, is broken into two broad categories called *general* and *specific* revelation:

> "or that which is *natural* and that which is *supernatural*, or that which is *original* and that which is *soteriological*."[156]

Theologically, *revelation* is:

> "restricted to the divine act of communicating to man what otherwise man would not know."[157]

Revelation is a supernatural act that reveals **some** of the secret things of God, which God wants man to know. God has other secrets that are not necessary for man to know presently. We repeat:

> *"The secret things belong unto the LORD our God: but those things which are revealed belong unto us and to our children for ever, that we may do all the words of this law"* (Deuteronomy 29:29, cf. Job 15:8, Dan. 2:19, 22, 27, 47).

But, of those *"secret things which are revealed,"* (Deut. 29:29, Rom. 16:25) *"[t]he secret of the LORD is with them that fear him; and he*

---

[155] Alexander Roberts; Donaldson, James ; Coxe, A. Cleveland: The Ante-Nicene Fathers Vol.I : Translations of the Writings of the Fathers Down to A.D. 325 (Oak Harbor : Logos Research Systems, 1997) 320 (Irenaeus' Against Heresies). Section 6.
[156] Lewis Sperry Chafer "Revelation" (Bibliotheca Sacra, Vol. 94, Dallas Theological Seminary, 1937, Logos, 2002270.
[157] Ibid. 264.

will shew them his covenant" (Psalms 25:14). King Nebuchadnezzar recognized that God is the revealer of secrets. He said to the great prophet Daniel: *"Of a truth it is, that your God is a God of gods, and a Lord of kings, and a revealer of secrets, seeing thou couldest reveal this secret"* (Daniel 2:47).

His revealed Old and New Covenants are like a legal contract, which is made with Words that cannot be changed and that are given by *"the voice of the Lord,"* who walked in the Garden. The Lord Jesus Christ relates that He received the Words from the Father (Jn. 17:8). Whether this applies just to the Words during the first Parousia is not clear. However, we believe that all the Words were *"settled in heaven"* among the Trinity before they were given to the prophets and Apostles to record (Psa 119:89). So, by generalization, all the Words were given to the Son, who is called the Word of God, from the Father, and the Holy Spirit reveals only what He hears (Jn. 16:13). The Trinity is in absolute agreement with all of the Words given (Jn. 14:23-24, 26, 16:13, 28, 17:8, Psa. 119:89); and the Words given to the prophets and Apostles are the very ones which lead us to a saving knowledge in the Lord Jesus Christ (Jn. 17:20).

In a sense, revealed Words are secret Words. The unregenerate cannot understand them, even though they are "revealed" and before them. They were revealed by a person, who is the Word of the Lord. He dwelt between the cherubim in the Holy of Holies. He spoke with Moses out of heaven and face to face. He is *"the secret of his tabernacle"* in the Holy of Holies part of the structure. The entire tabernacle in the wilderness is typologically representative of the Lord Jesus Christ. He *"tabernacles"* or dwells with or in man (Psa. 27:5, Jn. 14:23, 15:4, 7). He is the *"shadow"* that offers protection from danger just as His Words do (Psa. 91:1); His *"secret is with the righteous"* (Pro. 3:32). His revelation is not a *"secret"* (Isa. 45:19, 48:16). It is revealed and available for man. But, it is not understood by unbelievers because they do not have the Holy Spirit (Jn. 14:16, 1 Cor. 1:18, 21, 2:11). However, the secret things of God are revealed to "all" who would believe **and** trust on the Lord Jesus Christ. Even the demons believe, but they do not trust in Him. So, they are not saved (Jas. 2:19). There is a divide between believe **and** trust that separates eternity in heaven from eternity in hell. If only they would believe **and** trust on *"the voice of the words of the Lord,"* our Redeemer (Lk. 1:6, Jn. 3:16, Gal. 3:13, Rev. 5:9), whose Words were written that all might believe on Him (Jn. 20:31, Col. 1:5-6, 1 Tim. 4:10). We must always hold any teaching accountable to **all** of the preserved, inerrant, inspired, infallible, revealed, written Words of our Lord, *"search[ing] the scriptures"* like the Bereans (Acts 17:11). They are His *"voice."* They are *"the scripture of truth"* and *"the holy covenant"* (Dan. 10:6, 21, 11:28, 30).

The category of revelation, called *general* revelation, is sometimes called practical or common revelation; the second category, *specific* or *supernatural* revelation, which includes *special* revelation.[158] General revelation will be examined first.

General (Common, Practical) Revelation

General revelation does not give us **special** *Words*, but it does speak to us spiritually and mentally like a metaphor through **one** of its aspects, creation. History and providence are the other aspects of general revelation (see below).

---

[158] Dr. Roy Wallace, *Studies in Systematic Theology* (LinWel, Shreveport, LA, 2001) 55-56. For "practical," see Lewis Sperry Chafer, "Revelation" (*Bibliotheca Sacra*, Vol. 94, Dallas Theological Seminary, 1937, Logos, 2002) 271. Also, see Lewis Sperry Chafer, "Revelation" (*Bibliotheca Sacra*, Vol. 94, Dallas Theological Seminary, 1937, Logos, 2002) 270.

Creation *typically* has a "voice" (Psa. 19:3) because it speaks to us by its grandeur, beauty, perfection, and complexity. By creation's representation as a metaphor, it declares that there is and has to be a creator who designed it (Psa. 19, Isa. 40:22, Rom. 1:20). That is, the "voice" of creation gives "testimony" to a creator, who also has a literal voice. Creation is a witness of and to the Grand Designer. The verses in Romans 10:17-18 demonstrate Paul's typological use of creation. He uses Psa. 19:4, about creation in verse 18 of Romans 10. Paul indicates the gospel is a testimony, which is powerful. This is similar to the fact that creation is a powerful testimony to a creative God. Creation alludes to and indicates God's creative ability by His powerful Words. For those who are redeemed, they understand their power. His Words saved them. Their power was experienced. By simply believing God's Words, which testify about His Son, a man can become *"a new creature."* (2 Cor. 5:17), designed by God.

A similar correlation to the need for a designer can be made using a clock as an analogy. A time-keeping clock made from pieces of metal must have a creator. The clock has a "voice" that testifies to its creator.

We often appeal to the "voice of reason." Of course, reason does not literally have a voice, but we may use this metaphor to appeal to someone for a reasonable approach to a problem.

Similarly, creation has a voice, which speaks to a "reasoning" man because of its design. A complex inhabitable creation must have a creator and by virtue of the creation, it has a "voice" (Isa 45:18). In Psalm 19:2-3, "speech," "language," and "voice" are metaphors. A metaphor is a figure of speech that applies a word or phrase to somebody or something that is not meant literally. It is designed to make a symbol or form a comparison that does not represent *real* things. In other words, creation is not God; it is not "real" to speak of creation as God. Rather, creation represents the knowledge and power of God. In Psalm 19, the metaphors combined with the descriptive language declare the power of *"the voice of the **words**"* of the Creator.

The creation is an aspect of *general* revelation of an Almighty God and Creator. The use of the word, general, does not mean that creation is not complex. For example, we might say, "In general,.....", meaning approximately. However, there is nothing approximate about creation. It is a complex, awesome, precise design, which has a voice or message about our Creator.

> *"The heavens declare the glory of God; and the firmament sheweth his handywork. Day unto day uttereth speech, and night unto night sheweth knowledge. There is no speech nor language, where their voice is not heard" (Psalms 19:1-3).*

A Blind Watchmaker?

The contention that creation has a "blind watchmaker" is ludicrous![159] Some scientists tenaciously hold to the theory of "non-

---

[159] Richard Dawkins, The Blind Watchmaker (W. W. Norton & Company, NY, NY, reissue edition (September 1996). An advertizing flyer for the book gives some insight into the fallacious thinking in the book:
"One of the most famous arguments of the creationist theory of the universe is the eighteenth-century theologian Willam Paley's: Just as a watch is too complicated and too functional to have sprung into existence by accident, so too must all living things, with their far greater complexity, be purposefully designed. But as Richard Dawkins, professor of zoology at Oxford University, demonstrates in this brilliant and eloquent riposte to the Argument from Design, the analogy is false. Natural selection, the unconscious, automatic, blind yet essentially non-random process that Darwin discovered, has no purpose in mind. If it can be said to play the role of watchmaker in nature, it is the blind watchmaker."

random evolution," also called "selective evolution," allegedly discovered by Charles Darwin. The process is fallaciously said to be a "blind watchmaker." Obviously, creation is awesomely complete, as well as complex; but its imperfection because of the fall drives some men to deny that it was designed by a Creator (Gen. 3:17-19, Rom. 8:22). "Selective evolution" is not evolution at all. It is "adaptation of species" to the environment. Man continually seeks to understand His environment, but without God's wisdom, it is foolishness. The Preacher said:

> *"Then I beheld all the work of God, that a man cannot find out the work that is done under the sun: because though a man labour to seek it out, yet he shall not find it; yea further; though a wise man think to know it, yet shall he not be able to find it."(Ecclesiastes 8:17).*

What are these foolish theories of astrophysics such as a "Big Bang," or of evolutionists such as long days, long gaps, etc., that are contrary to the Words of God? The Bible makes it clear that the cause and creator of all things is God. Man does not have an excuse for not *"understanding"* and having *"knowledge of the Holy"* (Pro. 9:10). His Words, which have never been shown to have an error or to be fallible, declare that He is the creator. Can anyone deny that very special Words (*jots and tittles*) were used to create this magnificent Creation?[160] What a mess the universe would be if a nonspecific "message" were used.

Anyone who has studied the complexity and completeness of creation by observing the amazing micro-computers and intracellular factories that exist within a living cell can not help but declare the glory of

---

Well, this whole concept by Dawkins is ridiculous. The first and second laws of thermodynamics have proven that randomness does not organize into something more complex! Period!
http://www.simonyi.ox.ac.uk/dawkins/writings/blindwatchmaker.shtml
[160] Bill Sheffield, *The Beginnings Under Attack* (21st Century Press, Springfield, MO, 2003) 11-14.

God's creative ability. Otherwise, he is unregenerate or a reprobate; and in addition, he must deny the first and second laws of thermodynamics.[161] Science has never demonstrated an increase in complexity. The first and second physical laws of thermodynamics have NEVER been refuted. For

---

[161] Dr. Henry Morris said: "As far as the laws or processes of the physical universe are concerned, these all devolve upon two extremely broad and powerful principles, the so-called first and second Laws of thermodynamics. Let it be emphasized that, if there is really such a thing as a law of science, these two principles meet that definition. There is no other scientific law supported more fully and certainly by more numerous and meaningful lines of evidence than are these two laws. All physical processes (and all biologic processes, for that matter) involve the interplay of two basic entities called energy and entropy. One could say that any event occurring in space and time is a manifestation of some form of exchange of energy. The particular event or process basically is just this transformation of one or more forms of energy (kinetic or motion energy, electrical, chemical, light, heat, sound, electromagnetic, nuclear, or other forms of energy) into one or more other forms. In this process, the total energy remains unchanged; no energy is either created or destroyed, although its form may and does change. This is the first law of thermodynamics, the law of conservation of energy. This law has been validated on both the cosmic and sub-nuclear scales and is a truly universal law, if there is such a thing. And, since energy really includes everything, even matter, in the physical universe, it is as certain as anything can possibly be, scientifically, that no creation of anything is now taking place in the universe, under the normal conditions which science is able to study. But in the process, some of the energy is always transformed into non-usable heat energy, and thus becomes unavailable for future energy exchanges. The concept of entropy has been developed to describe this phenomenon, entropy being a measure of the unavailability of the energy of the system or process. The second law of thermodynamics describes this by stating that there is always a tendency for the entropy of any closed system to increase. Or, in more general terms, the second law states that there is always a tendency for any system to become less organized. Its disorder or randomness tends to increase. If isolated from external sources of order or energy or "information," any system will eventually run down and "die." (Institute of Creation Science, http://www.icr.org/home/resources/resources_tracts_tbiatos/) Accessed 10/25/07.

someone to believe a complex living cell could evolve from a "primordial soup" to the amazing complexity of living organisms is ludicrous. It is blasphemy of the worst kind against God's revelation.

About two millennia before science unraveled the secrets of DNA, *complex* cell interaction, intra-cellular "factories," atomic structure, and so much more, Irenaeus (120-190 A.D.) recognized the need for a Creator, because creation has a voice. He recognized that creation could not have occurred without a Designer and he exalts God's life-giving Words (Jn. 6:68). He said the following:

> "For if the manifestation of God which is made by means of the creation, affords life to all living in the earth, much more does that **revelation** of the Father which comes through the Word, give life to those who see God."[162]

Physicists, mathematicians, biologists, astronomers, and other scientists are **not** even close to unraveling the complexity of the universe or of life, and this author believes they never will. The pride and arrogance of the unbelievers in the various scientific disciplines is appalling.

The Unifying Principle

The search for a "unifying universal principle" by scientists, particularly by quantum physicists, is causing the God in heaven to laugh (Psa. 2). They try to escape *"the voice of the words"* in Scripture that declares the unifying principle, which is a person, the Almighty Creator, who is the Lord Jesus Christ. He is *"upholding all things by the **word** of*

---

[162] Alexander Roberts; Donaldson, James ; Coxe, A. Cleveland: The Ante-Nicene Fathers Vol.I : Translations of the Writings of the Fathers Down to A.D. 325 (Oak Harbor : Logos Research Systems, 1997) 490. (Irenaeus' Against Heresies).

his power" (Heb. 1:3) because He created *"all things,"* which includes *"heaven"* and *"earth,"* and things *"visible and invisible"* by the voice of His Almighty Words (Col. 1:16).

> *"God, who at sundry times and in divers manners spake in time past unto the fathers by the prophets, Hath in these last days spoken unto us by his Son, whom he hath appointed heir of all things, by whom also he made the worlds; Who being the brightness of his glory, and the express image of his person, and upholding all things by the word of his power, when he had by himself purged our sins, sat down on the right hand of the Majesty on high" (Hebrews 1:1-3). "For by him were all things created, that are in heaven, and that are in earth, visible and invisible, whether they be thrones, or dominions, or principalities, or powers: all things were created by him, and for him:" (Colossians 1:16)*

Many scientists, atheists, and agnostics are surrendering to the obvious "integrated complexity" or organization of life and the universe. Many evolutionists are concluding there must be an intelligent designer of the universe. However, they continue to resist the personal involvement of the Designer. They are deists. Even Antony Flew, the man who influenced the atheist Richard Dawkins the most, gave up to the obvious evidence:

> "Former Darwinian atheist philosopher Antony Flew has published a new book, 'There Is a God: How the World's Most Notorious Atheist Changed His Mind,' to explain his move from being one of the world's leading exponents of the pure materialist Darwinian philosophy to belief in the existence of a personal deity who created the universe. Flew, an Oxford educated philosopher described by some as 'legendary,' first announced his discovery of 'a god' in 2004. Flew had been one of the 20th century's leading proponents of the pure atheistic Darwinian doctrines that categorically reject any possibility of a creative divine being. His ideas paved the way for thinkers such as Richard Dawkins, the UK's most virulent opponent of

religious belief. ... 'It was empirical evidence,' he told an interviewer, 'the evidence uncovered by the sciences. But it was a philosophical inference drawn from the evidence.' Flew told Dr. Benjamin Wiker that two factors in particular 'were decisive.' 'One was my growing empathy with the insight of Einstein and other noted scientists that there had to be an Intelligence behind the integrated complexity of the physical Universe. The second was my own insight that the integrated complexity of life itself--which is far more complex than the physical Universe--can only be explained in terms of an Intelligent Source.'... He told Wiker, 'I believe that the origin of life and reproduction simply cannot be explained from a biological standpoint despite numerous efforts to do so. With every passing year, the more that was discovered about the richness and inherent intelligence of life, the less it seemed likely that a chemical soup could magically generate the genetic code.'... Emphasizing that he remains a Deist, not a Christian, he told W ker that he does not 'accept any claim of divine revelation' but is continuing to study them, particularly those of Christianity "[163]

History, Providence, and General Revelation

History and providence are included under general revelation because of **(1)** the providential prophetic fulfillment of *written* prophecy. For example, consider that over 300 prophecies concerning Jesus Christ were perfectly fulfilled. In addition, consider prophecies such as: (a) Isaiah's prediction that a king of Babylon by the name of Cyrus would issue a proclamation to rebuild the foundation of the temple in Jerusalem (Isa. 44:28, Ezra 1:2), and (b) the many prophecies declaring the Jewish dispersion (Lev. 26:33, Deut. 4:27) and the regathering (Isa. 56:7, Jer. 31:8). **(2)** The providential preservation of the jots and tittles of inspired

---

[163] David Cloud, FAMOUS ATHEIST PUBLISHES BOOK DESCRIBING "CONVERSION" (Friday Church News Notes, November 9, 2007, www.wayoflife.org fbns@wayoflife.org)

Scripture through the nation Israel and the sanctified churches (Psa. 12:6-7, Mat. 24:35, Rom. 3:1-2). **(3)** The progressive march of mankind (nations and individuals) to the decreed will of God through seven dispensations as described in His Words, and **(4)** the clear lack of archaeological evidence to support the evolution of created species (i.e. there are no evolutionary links). Adaptation within species occurs, but there is no evolution from one species to another.

Lewis Sperry Chafer calls these aspects of **general** revelation:

> "(a) God revealed through Nature,
> (b) God revealed through Providence,
> (c) God revealed through Preservation."[164]

Specific Revelation, Including **Special** Revelation

Dr. Chafer lists the categories of **specific** (supernatural) revelation as:

> "(d) God Revealed through Miracles,
> (e) God Revealed through Direct Communication (HDW, "the words of the voice of God," which may or may not have been recorded)
> (f) God Revealed through the Incarnation,
> (g) God Revealed through the Scriptures."
> (HDW, **specific** revelation through **special** revelation of His Words recorded by the prophets and Apostles)."[165]

It must be quickly added that none of the **general** revelations or **specific** revelations could be completely understood without **all** the **Words** of **special** revelation: "God Revealed through the Scriptures." For example, man has claimed that creation is a result of many gods as

---

[164] Chafer, op. cit, 270-274 ("Revelation").
[165] Ibid. 274-280.

found in Hinduism, that the universe is the result of a big bang, or that species of animals and plants are a result of evolution. All of these theories or humanistic philosophies are false. The second person of the Trinity demonstrated the creative ability of God during His first Parousia. Eyewitnesses reported God's creative power when they recorded the miracles of our Lord Jesus Christ in Scripture. Those instantaneous miracles of creation and control over nature assure us that He is the creator. For example, remember the instantaneous and completely mature restoration of the withered arm of a man. It was **not** restored like a baby's arm, but fully matched his other arm.

> *"Then saith he to the man, Stretch forth thine hand. And he stretched it forth; and it was restored whole, like as the other" (Matthew 12:13).*

Only God, who is the Creator, could do such wonderful things.

Special (written) revelation makes it clear that God created the universe (Gen. 1:1ff, Jn. 1:3, 1 Cor. 8:6, Eph. 3:9, Heb. 1:1-2). In addition, without special revelation man would not understand, for example, that miracles were **(1)** authentication of **(a)** the *received* Word(s) of God (Jn. 17:8), **(b)** His messengers (Lk. 11:49, Eph. 2:20, 3:5, 2 Pe. 3:2), **(c)** the person and work of the perfect God-man, Jesus Christ (Heb. 4:15), and **(d)** a change in dispensations (Lk. 16:16, Eph. 1:10, 3:2). **(2)** Also, written revelation discloses that the maintaining and upholding of the universe by the Creator is a miracle, and we would not know how it is sustained without **special** revelation (e.g. Heb. 1:3). **(3)** Special revelation reveals the "voice" of our conscience; our thoughts are not "*the voice of the Lord*" because our conscience can be defiled, seared, and evil and our thoughts and ways are not God's. (Gen. 6:5,6, 8:21, Isa. 55:8-9, Jer. 17:9, also see chapter 3).

Furthermore, without His pure, perfect written Words, man would be dependent on his own reason, which is corrupted by the fall and by personal sin. The dependence on man's reason without **specific** revelation in **all** of its aspects (see above) results in heathenism (Isa. 55:7-9). Chafer said:

> "Man's true estate under reason and when isolated from revelation is partially demonstrated by the lowest forms of heathenism;"[166]

Man left to ***his own*** "*conscience*," reason, will, intellect, emotions, thoughts, mind, spirit, soul, and body inevitably leads to anarchy and debauchery. Because of the fall of man, the individual's carnal mind left to "self" would become the dominant "law" in a society (2 Tim. 3:1-5); and the carnal mind *"is enmity against God"* (Rom. 8:7, 1 Tim. 5:6). But, the Scripture reveals that the Restrainer, the Holy Spirit, is presently keeping the world in check (2 Thess. 2:7). However, the United States has drawn further and further away from Biblical revelation. Therefore, anarchy and debauchery are on the streets of America, and for that matter, around the world.

The crime stats secondary to juvenile gangs are soaring (cf. Hos. 4:6, Mal. 4:5-6). Consider New Orleans after hurricane Katrina! Carnality in our homes against **Biblical** morals is at an all time high. For example, note the increase in unisex marriages, abandonment, and dissolution of marriages. The dishonesty in government, business, and personal relationships is obvious. Consider the greed of Enron's executives, the well-publicized acceptance of bribes by government officials, and the fornication of officials at the highest level of government. The deceit in the pulpit is accelerating. Remember the Ted Haggard debacle, Jim and

---

[166] Ibid. 264.

Tammy Baker of the PTL Club, and the Jimmy Swaggart disaster. Think about the 'pastors,' deacons, and teachers who say one thing in church, but do not live their lives according to *"the voice of the words of the Lord."*

These are all evidences of failure in the church age, the dispensation of grace. Praise God for the work of the Restrainer, restraining the prince of this world, evil man, and *"the iniquity [that] doth already work"* (2 Thess. 2:7). But, surely the Restrainer will be removed soon. Without the Restrainer present in the world, man's conscience will justify any evil. The justification will be assisted by the tenets of the philosophy of man called postmodernism (see chapter 6). Evil men already believe their thoughts and their conscience are *"the voice of the Lord."* Therefore, when all restraint is removed, sin will abound, and man will commit every imaginable sin.

It is surprising that one of the greatest corrupters of Scripture, Origen,[167] understood the influence of the written Words of God, **special** revelation, on the conscience, saying:

> "And John, too, when he speaks of his eating the one roll (Rev. 10:9-10) in which both front and back were written on, means the whole of Scripture, one book which is, at first, most sweet when one begins, as it were, to chew it, but bitter in the revelation of himself which it makes to the conscience of each one who knows it."[168]

---

[167] Dean John William Burgon, *The Traditional Text of the Holy Gospels* (The Dean Burgon Society Press, Collingswood, NJ, originally published 1898, republished 1998) 10-11.
[168] Alexander Roberts; Donaldson, James ; Coxe, A. Cleveland: Origen, Commentary on the Gospel of John, The Ante-Nicene Fathers Vol. X : Translations of the Writings of the Fathers Down to A.D. 325. (Oak Harbor : Logos Research Systems, 1997) 348.

Special revelation (written Words) began with Moses. He was the first to write the inspired Words of God. All of the personal communications through face-to-face meetings, dreams, visions, or *"voice of the words of God"* to individuals **prior to** Moses is included in **specific** revelation, but the inspired Words of **special** revelation were not recorded until Moses wrote the Pentateuch. **Specific** revelation of the truth began with Adam in the Garden, and included Eve, Cain, Enoch, Noah, Abraham, Isaac, Jacob, and many others. Many get this wrong. For example, one author said:

> "Up to the time of Abraham we have what is often called "common revelation" i.e., the knowledge of God available to all men everywhere and always. But with Abraham God began a "**special** revelation" and from then on he was known as Yahweh." [169] (HDW, my emphasis)

Cessation of Revelation

Many of us believe **special** revelation has ceased. There are several reasons. **(1)** The last few verses in Revelation combined with 1 Corinthians 13:10 indicate the closure of Scripture, saying:

> *"For I testify unto every man that heareth the words of the prophecy of this book, If any man shall add unto these things, God shall add unto him the plagues that are written in this book: And if any man shall take away from the words of the book of this prophecy, God shall take away his part out of the book of life, and out of the holy city, and from the things which are written in this book" (Revelation 22:18-19). "But when that which is perfect is come, then that which is in part shall be done away" (1 Corinthians 13:10).*

---

[169] James L. Kelso, "Abraham As Archaeology Knows Him Part II — Abraham the Spiritual Genius" (Bible and Spade, Vol. 2, Associates for Biblical Research, 1973, 2005) 38.

The passage in 1 Corinthians 13:10 is misinterpreted very often because the original language text is not consulted. Many exegetes consider the word *"perfect"* to refer to the Lord Jesus Christ based upon the context, especially verse twelve. However, the Greek word, τέλειον, translated *"perfect"* is neuter and refers to the Bible (βιβλιον), or Book, which is neuter. The Greek word, scripture, in the Bible is feminine, and of course, the Lord Jesus Christ is a masculine construction.

In the context of this passage, Paul was indicating that when the Bible was completed: (a) certain gifts would cease and (b) they knew only *"in part"* at that time, and so, certain gifts were necessary (v. 12) until the Bible was complete. (c) Paul gave the example or simile of knowing **"as"** a child until maturity came, when "childish needs" (such as the special, temporary gifts) could be put aside.

(2) In addition, the Holy Spirit and the Lord Jesus Christ speaking through Paul use the Greek word, τελεος, translated perfect in many passages, to indicate *"revealed."* For example, consider 2 Corinthians 12:9. In this verse, God's strength, which is perfect, is not weak. Therefore, we must understand that God's strength is *revealed* through someone else's weakness, not God's weakness or feebleness [cf. Phil. 3:12, Heb. 2:10, Heb. 9:9 (make = τελεον = reveal), etc.].

(3) If we were uncertain as to completed special revelation and we were constantly looking for more Words of special revelation as we enter the last of the last days, then we would take our eyes off of the Lord Jesus Christ and be looking "for another prophet like unto [Moses]" (Deut. 18:15, Acts 3:22, 7:37). The Scriptures are finished and are *"for ever settled."* The best translation in English of the completed, revealed Words is the King James Bible.

Ruckmanites

Some people such as Dr. Peter Ruckman believe that the King James Bible is "advanced revelation" and may be used to correct the *received* Hebrew and Greek Texts. Dr. David Cloud, with whom this author agrees concerning Ruckman, reports:

> Peter Ruckman, on the other hand, SAYS he believes the KJV is advanced revelation. Consider:
> "The A.V. 1611 reading, here, is **superior to any Greek text**" (Peter Ruckman, *The Christian's Handbook of Manuscript Evidence*, Pensacola Bible Press, 1970, p. 118).
>
> "Mistakes in the A.V. 1611 **are advanced revelation!**" (Ruckman, *Manuscript Evidence*, p. 126).
>
> "A short handbook, such as this, will not permit an exhaustive account of the marvelous undesigned 'coincidences' which have slipped through the A.V. 1611 committees, unawares to them, and **which give advanced light, and advanced revelation** beyond the investigation of the greatest Bible students 300 years later" (Ruckman, *Manuscript Evidence*, p. 127).
>
> "A little English will **clear up the obscurities in any Greek text**" (Ruckman, *Manuscript Evidence*, p. 147).
>
> "**If all you have is the 'original Greek,' you lose light**" (Ruckman, *Manuscript Evidence*, p. 336).
>
> "If you are able to obtain a copy [of Ruckman's proposed new book] you will have, in your hands, a minimum of **200 advanced revelations that came from the inerrant English text**, that were completely overlooked (or ignored) by every major Christian scholar since 90 A.D." (*Bible Believers' Bulletin*, Jan. 1994, pp. 2,4).
>
> "We shall deal with the English Text of the Protestant Reformation, and our references to Greek or Hebrew will only be made to enforce the authority of that text or **to**

demonstrate the superiority of that text to Greek and Hebrew." (Peter Ruckman, *Problem Texts*, Preface, Pensacola Bible Institute Press, 1980, p. vii).

"We candidly and publicly confess that the King James text of the Old Testament (Authorized Version) is far superior to Kittel's Hebrew text, Derossi's Hebrew text, Kennicott's Hebrew text or any Hebrew text that any of you are reading. We do not hesitate to state bluntly and openly that **the King James text for the New Testament (Authorized Version) is superior to Erasmus' Greek text**, Aland's Greek text, Metzger's Greek text and **any other that you are reading** (or will read in the future)" (Ruckman, *Problem Texts*, page xii). [Brother Cloud: You see that Ruckman treats the Greek Received Text with the same lightness as he does the modern critical text.]

"If you had the original manuscripts, you couldn't find what a soul was, no matter how educated you were, because **the key for 'finding out' had nothing to do with the Hebrew or Greek**" (Ruckman, *Problem Texts*, p. 145).

"Observe how accurately and beautifully **the infallible English text** straightens out Erasmus, Griesbach, Beza, Nestle, Aland, Metzger, Trench, Vincent, Davis, Wuest, Zodhiates, Elzevr, and Stephanus with the poise and grace of a swan as it smoothly and effectively breaks your arm with one flap of its wings. Beautiful, isn't it? **If the mood or tense isn't right in any Greek text, the King James Bible will straighten it out in a hurry"** (Ruckman, *Problem Texts*, pp. 348, 349). [*Editor*: Why does Ruckman put critical, modernistic textual editors Nestle, Aland, and Metzger on the same level with Beza, Elzevir, and Stephanus who honored the Word of God and handed down to us the Text Received from the Apostles?]

"The original Hebrew had nothing to do with Genesis 1:1-3 at all [referring to Ruckman's unique idea that the flood of 2 Peter 3:5-6 speaks of a flood that took place in Genesis 1:2]. It only muddied the issue. **Hebrew is of** no help at all in understanding the passage" (Peter Ruckman, *The Unknown Bible*, Bible Baptist Bookstore, 1984, p. 67).

"**The King James text is the last and final statement that God has given to the world**, and He has given it in the universal language of the 20th century ... The truth is that **GOD SLAMMED THE DOOR OF REVELATION SHUT IN 389 BC AND SLAMMED IT SHUT AGAIN IN 1611**" (Peter Ruckman, *The Monarch of Books*, Pensacola, 1973, p. 9). [Brother Cloud: In fact, God slammed the door of revelation shut in about 90 A.D. with the completion of the New Testament.]

While I believe the Authorized Version is an accurate translation of the preserved Word of God, I reject Ruckman's contention that the Authorized Version is superior to the Hebrew and Greek from which it was translated, or that God only slammed shut the door of revelation in 1611, or that the English straightens out the Greek, or that the Authorized Version contains advanced revelation.

If Ruckman is right, where was the inspired Word of God prior to 1611? What did the churches do from the time of the apostles until the 17th century? And what did they do before Ruckman came upon the scene to create this doctrine, because it is certain that no one taught it at an earlier date?"[170]

Other Examples of Confusion and Modern Gnostics

Another example of misunderstanding revelation and illumination is found in the writings of T. Austin-Sparks (1888-1973), a magazine editor and pastor in England, who wrote:

---

[170] Dr. David Cloud, "What About Ruckman?" (Way Of Life Literature, Port Huron, MI, FBIS, April 19, 2004, http://www.wayoflife.org/articles/ruckman.htm).

> "The only knowledge of God which is of spiritual value for ourselves, or for others by our ministry, is that which we have by revelation of the Holy Spirit within our own spirits."[171]

If Austin-Sparks had used *illumination* for "revelation" in the sentence above, it would be correct. However, illumination and revelation are frequently misunderstood. Many people blatantly reject the difference, such as the charismatics, which leads to rejection of the cessation of revelation. Many are non-cessationists, who believe revelation is continuing. They are in clear opposition to the Scriptures (1 Cor. 12-14). In this instance and many other places in the Bible, the original language texts need to be consulted for accurate interpretation and determination of the passage.

We are dependent upon **special** revelation in the *received* Hebrew, Aramaic, and Greek texts. Although a text may be a faithful and accurate translation, the bottom-line stops with the received original-language texts. Translations into the languages of the world may be excellent, but the original-language texts are the texts of final authority. However, because divine authority is transferred to accurate and faithful translations, those Words are illuminated by the Holy Spirit to give us enlightenment (Psa. 19:8, Eph. 1:18, Heb. 6:4). If a believer grieves or quenches the Holy Spirit, then he will not be able to understand the Scriptures properly. Furthermore, He will not bring individuals across your path that will edify you. You must turn your face toward a Holy God and do His commandments, and then illumination will come as *"the sun of righteousness"* sheds light in your heart and heals you (Mal. 4:2).

"Modern" Gnostics, who make outlandish claims of additional revelation or claims concerning the need for additions to the canon of

---

[171] T. Austin-Sparks, *What Is Man?* (Premium Literature Company, Indianapolis, IN, unknown date, may be ordered from Testimony Book Ministry, Washington, D.C.) 71.

Scripture, are a dime a dozen in these last days.[172] As we shall see, many postmodernists are modern Gnostics who have revived a sense of mysticism and transcendentalism in everything, including the Words of revelation from God. They elevate secret knowledge known only to "self." Their vocabulary often consists of new words thought up by academics; words that are only double-speak, which add to the confusion for sick and lost souls seeking peace in all the wrong places. What they truly need is the indwelling Holy Spirit who illuminates the Words of Scripture. The prophets and Apostles recorded them for anyone seeking God. Jesus said to the Father concerning the Apostles and prophets:

> *Neither pray I for these alone, but for them also which shall believe on me through their word; (John 17:2),*

"Their Word" was the Words given to them by God.

So, what is inspiration and illumination?

---

[172] Jeffery Khoo, "Canon, Texts, and Words: Lost and Found or Preserved and Identified?" (*The Burning Bush,* Vol. 13, Nu. 2, July, 2007) 74-75. Dr. Khoo, Dean, Far Eastern Bible College in Singapore discusses the Gnostics associated with modern Gnostics and "pop-culture." It is also available at www.febc.edu.sg/VPP63.htm.

CHAPTER 5

INSPIRATION AND ILLUMINATION

Inspiration

"All scripture is given by inspiration of God, and is profitable for doctrine, for reproof, for correction, for instruction in righteousness:" (2 Timothy 3:16).

Theopneustos Means "is Given by Inspiration of God"

2 Timothy 3:16 is a very technical verse. It was placed in Scripture to refute those who would claim only "parts" of the canon of Scripture are inspired. A careful analysis of the passage where this verse occurs counters that false claim. First, the phrase translated *"is given by inspiration of God"* comes from one Greek word, θεοπνευστος, theopneustos, an adjective in this verse. A part of the problem associated with translation of this verse concerns some technical grammatical features. If the verse is translated as an attributive adjective, then the verb, "is" would be placed **after** God and would read, "All given by inspiration of God is scripture." This would concur with those who believe only parts of Scripture are inspired. However, the Greek is a predicate adjective construction, which requires the verb "is" **before** θεοπνευστος.

Furthermore, a translation that reads like the NASB, NIV, or NLT such as "All scripture is God-breathed" leaves the open-ended question of deciding what is Scripture and what parts of Scripture in the canon are inspired. In other words, a person could again claim only a part of Scripture is God-breathed. Only the KJB allows the proper understanding that all the God-breathed Words of the Bible *"is given"* by inspiration. Theologians call this "plenary inspiration," which refers to all the Words and none of the Words are limited or restricted in any sense. The inspiration of the Words is complete and full. The other Words in the verse influence this conclusion when compared to each other and to the context, particularly verse 15.

Pasa Means "All," Not "Every"

The Greek πᾶσα (pasa) translated *"all,"* is used with an anarthrous (without an article such as "the") Greek noun, γραφή (graphé), which is translated *"scripture."*[173] It is well documented that this construction is translated "all" and not "every" (see Mat. 3:15, Acts 2:36, 7:22, Col. 4:12).[174] *Young's Literal Translation, Amplified Bible,* and *Darby's Translation* inappropriately translate pasa as "every." The translations using "every" leave the door open for selecting what is considered Scripture.

Graphe Means Scripture

Graphe is a technical word which is used to refer to Scripture either in whole or in part (cf. Jn. 5:39, Acts 17:2 Rom. 1:2 with Mat. 21:42, Jn. 13:18, Gal. 4:30). In 2 Timothy **2:15**, the Holy Spirit speaking through

---

[173] H. E. Dana and Julius R. Mantey, *A Manual Grammar of the Greek New Testament* (The Macmillan Co., New York, NY, 1927, © 1955) 149ff.
[174] Dr. Thomas Strouse, Dean, Emmanuel Baptist Theological Seminary EBTS), "The Translation Model Predicted by Scripture" (*EBTS Online Resources*, http://www.emmanuel-newington.org/seminary/resources/) p. 2.

Paul uses the Greek word, γραμματα (grammata) in a phrase: *"he hagia grammata,"* which means *"the holy scriptures."* Grammata refers to the temple's **copies** or apographs of the Old Testament Scriptures. The Greek word, *graphe,* in 2 Tim. **3:16** refers to the autographs.[175]

Dean John William Burgon succinctly points out that in verse sixteen there is no Greek eta, (**H**) between pasa and graphe. The significance is 'that' the word "that" would be placed in the verse to read: "All Scripture that is given..." Burgon says:

> "St. Paul does not say that *the whole* of Scripture, collectively, is inspired. More than *that:* what he says is, that *every writing,—every several book* of those ἱερά γράμματα, or Holy Scriptures, in which Timothy had been instructed from his childhood,—is inspired by God...St. Paul is careful to remind us that every Book in the Bible is an inspired Book.[176]

These very purposeful verses, 2 Timothy 3:15-16, were given to Paul to record. They are carefully constructed verses by the Holy Spirit to defend the verbal (Words), plenary (all the Words), inspiration of Scripture.

The Process of Inspiration

The "process" of *Inspiration,* the receiving of the Words, is poorly understood by any of us because we have never received the inspired Words of God to be recorded as Scripture (2 Tim. 3:16, 2 Pe. 1:19-21, 3:2, Eph. 2:20). We must accept by faith the proclamations of Scripture concerning the reception and recording of **special** revelation by God's

---

[175] Strouse, op. cit., ("The Translation Model Predicted by Scripture")
[176] Dean John William Burgon, *Inspiration and Interpretation* (Dean Burgon Society Press, Collingswood, NJ, originally published 1861, republished 1999) 53.

prophets and Apostles. Theories must be cast aside! Other verses refer to inspiration without using the word, inspiration, but teach that men were *"moved by the Holy Spirit"* to record the Words in the autographia, the original manuscripts. The Words were copied and preserved. For example, the following verses confirm how the Scriptures are received.

> *"For the prophecy came not in old time by the will of man: but holy men of God spake as they were moved by the Holy Ghost" (2 Peter 1:21).*

Paul records his knowledge that the Words he recorded were Scripture:

> *"Which things also we speak, not in the words which man's wisdom teacheth, but which the Holy Ghost teacheth; comparing spiritual things with spiritual" (1 Corinthians 2:13).*

Peter calls the Words given to Paul by the Holy Spirit to recorded Scripture:

> *"As also in all his epistles, speaking in them of these things; in which are some things hard to be understood, which they that are unlearned and unstable wrest, as they do also the other scriptures, unto their own destruction" (2 Peter 3:16).*

We find the OT prophets were repeatedly commanded to record the inspired Words, vision, commands, etc. (Ex. 17:14, 34:1, 27, Deut. 10:2, Jer. 30:2, Hab. 2:2).

The Model For Making Copies

The model for preservation of inspired Words is also included in the Bible. **God made the first copy of His inspired Words** as the model. He copied the exact same Words that were on the first tablet containing the Ten Commandments (Ex. 34:1). He commanded Jeremiah to make a copy of the **exact** Words He gave him to record in the scroll that King Jehoiakim cut-up and destroyed with a penknife and by burning the manuscript (Jer. 36ff).

Many good theologians do not express inspiration, the process of inspiration, and the recording of the Words very well. It leaves the door open for people to declare God has preserved His message, but not His Words. For example, in the quote to follow, a better way to state the definition is bolded. Dr. Wallace said:

> "The theological use of the term "inspiration" is a reference to that controlling influence which God exerted over the human authors (**recorders, not authors, HDW**) by whom the Old and New Testaments were written (**recorded, HDW**). It has to do with the reception of the divine message (**NO! the divine Words, HDW**) and the accuracy (**perfection, HDW**) with which it is transcribed (**recorded, HDW**). Inspiration therefore superintends the communication of the (**Words of, HDW**) truth that revelation produces."[177] [HDW, my additions in bold for clarification].

Dr. Thomas Strouse, Dean of Emmanuel Baptist Theological Seminary, offers a concise correct definition: He said:

> "Inspiration is the process whereby the Holy Spirit led the writers of scripture to record accurately His very words; the product of this process was the inspired original."[178]

This author probably would not have used "accurately" in the quote from Dr. Strouse, although it is not wrong. The word "perfectly"

---

[177] Wallace, op. cit., 57.
[178] Strouse, op. cit., 2 ("The Translation Model Predicted by Scripture").

would seem better because it reflects the Word used in Scripture (Psa. 19:7, Rom. 12:2, 1 Cor. 13:10).

Paul clearly proclaims the Words that he gave were *received* from God. He said:

> *"For this cause also thank we God without ceasing, because,* **when ye received the word of God which ye heard of us,** *ye* **received** *it not as the word of men, but as* **it is in truth, the word of God,** *which effectually worketh also in you that believe"* (1 Thessalonians 2:13). (HDW, my emphasis)

Spurgeon comments on inspiration, saying:

> "Let those give up the inspiration of the Bible who can afford to do so, but you and I cannot. Let those cast away the sure promise of God who have got something else to comfort them, who can go to their philosophy or turn to their self-conceit. But as for you and for me, it is a desperate matter for us if this book be not true. And therefore let us be ready to defend it at all hazards, and if need be to die for it. Oh, brethren, it were better to die, that book being true, than to live, that book being false.
>
> If we are left in doubt as to which part is inspired and which is not, we are as badly off as if we had no Bible at all. I hold no theory of inspiration; I accept the inspiration of the Scriptures as a fact.
>
> If I did not believe in the infallibility of this book, I would rather be without it. If I am to judge the book, it is no judge of me. If I am to sift it, and lay this aside and only accept that, according to my own judgment, then I have no guidance whatever, unless I have conceit enough to trust my own heart. The new theory denies infallibility to the words of God, but practically imputes it to the judgments of men. At least, this is all the infallibility they can get at. I protest that I will rather risk my soul with a guide inspired from heaven, than with the differing leaders who arise from the earth at the call of "modern thought."
>
> The Bible must have been written by our Creator, for nobody but the Lord who created men could know so much

Chapter 5–Inspiration & Illumination

about them. This volume reveals the secrets of all hearts. It unveils our private thoughts.

Everything in the railway service depends upon the accuracy of the signals. When these are wrong, life will be sacrificed. On the road to heaven we need unerring signals, or the catastrophes will be far more terrible. It is difficult enough to set myself right and carefully drive the train of conduct. But if, in addition to this, I am to set the Bible right, and thus manage the signals along the permanent way, I am in an evil plight indeed.

We will not have it that God, in his holy book, makes mistakes about matters of history or of science, any more than he does upon the great truths of salvation. If the Lord be God, he must be infallible. And if he can be described as in error in the little respects of human history and science, he cannot be trusted in the greater matters.

Men talk of "the mistakes of Scripture." I thank God that I have never met with any. Mistakes of translation there may be, for translators are men. But mistakes of the original word there can never be, for the God who spoke it is infallible, and so is every word he speaks, and in that confidence we find delightful rest.

I am prepared to believe whatever it says, and to take it believing it to be the Word of God. For if it is not all true, it is not worth one solitary penny to me.

We believe in plenary, verbal inspiration, with all its difficulties, for there are not half as many difficulties in that doctrine as there are in any other kind that men may imagine.

There are many who refuse to believe in the verbal inspiration of the Scriptures. But I fail to see how the sense of Scripture can be inspired if the words in which that sense is expressed are not also inspired. **I believe that the very words, in the original Hebrew and Greek, were revealed from heaven,** and notwithstanding every objection that can be brought from any quarter, I have never been able to get away from the firm belief that, if I give up my Master's words, I give up his thoughts also."[179]

David Cloud said:

---

[179] Tom Carter, *Spurgeon at His Best* (Baker Book House, Grand Rapids, MI, 1988) 23-25.

"The [KJB] translators believed that the Bible is the infallible Word of God. To my knowledge, a loftier testimony of the Bible's divine inspiration has never been written than that which is contained in the Preface to the 1611 King James Bible."[180]

The following is from the King James Bible translator's "Preface to the Readers:"

"THE PRAISE OF THE HOLY SCRIPTURES"

"But now what piety without truth? what truth (what saving truth) without the word of God? What word of God (whereof we may be sure) without the Scripture? The Scriptures we are commanded to search. John 5:39. Isa 8:20. They are commended that searched and studied them. Acts 8:28-29, 17:11. They are reproved that were unskilful in them, or slow to believe them. Matt 22:29. Luke 24:25. They can make us wise unto salvation. 2 Tim 3:15. If we be ignorant, they will instruct us; if out of the way, they will bring us home; if out of order, they will reform us; if in heaviness, comfort us; if dull, quicken us; if cold, inflame us. Tolle, lege; Tolle, lege, Take up and read, take up and read the Scriptures [S. August. confess. lib 8 cap 12], (for unto them was the direction).

It was said unto S. Augustine…"Whatsoever is in the Scriptures, believe me," saith the same S. Augustine, "is high and divine; there is verily truth, and a doctrine most fit for the refreshing of men's minds, and truly so tempered, that everyone may draw from thence that which is sufficient for him, if he come to draw with a devout and pious mind, as true Religion requireth" [S. August. de utilit. credendi cap. 6]. Thus S. Augustine and S. Jerome: "Ama scripturas, et amabit te sapientia etc." [S. Jerome. ad Demetriad]. Love the Scriptures, and wisdom will love thee.

And S. Cyril against Julian; "Even boys that are bred up in the Scriptures, become most religious, etc." [S. Cyril. 7

---

[180] David Cloud, "THE KJV TRANSLATORS ON BIBLICAL INSPIRATION" (Fundamental Baptist Information Service, email, 10/04/07, FBIS News Service [fbns@wayoflife.org].

contra Iulianum] But what mention we three or four uses of the Scripture, whereas whatsoever is to be believed or practiced, or hoped for, is contained in them? or three or four sentences of the Fathers, since whosoever is worthy the name of a Father, from Christ's time downward, hath likewise written not only of the riches, but also of the perfection of the Scripture?

"I adore the fulness of the Scripture," saith Tertullian against Hermogenes [Tertul. advers. Hermo.]. And again, to Apelles an heretic of the like stamp, he saith; "I do not admit that which thou bringest in (or concludest) of thine own (head or store, de tuo) without Scripture" [Tertul. de carne Christi.]. So Saint Justin Martyr before him; "We must know by all means," saith he, "that it is not lawful (or possible) to learn (anything) of God or of right piety, save only out of the Prophets, who teach us by divine inspiration."

So Saint Basil after Tertullian, "It is a manifest falling way from the Faith, and a fault of presumption, either to reject any of those things that are written, or to bring in (upon the head of them) any of those things that are not written.

We omit to cite to the same effect, S. Cyril B. of Jerusalem in his 4::Cataches., Saint Jerome against Helvidius, Saint Augustine in his 3::book against the letters of Petilian, and in very many other places of his works. Also we forebear to descend to later Fathers, because we will not weary the reader.

The Scriptures then being acknowledged to be so full and so perfect, how can we excuse ourselves of negligence, if we do not study them, of curiosity, if we be not content with them? Men talk much of [an olive bow wrapped about with wood, whereupon did hang figs, and bread, honey in a pot, and oil], how many sweet and goodly things it had hanging on it; of the Philosopher's stone, that it turned copper into gold; of Cornucopia, that it had all things necessary for food in it, of Panaces the herb, that it was good for diseases, of Catholicon the drug, that it is instead of all purges; of Vulcan's armor, that it was an armor of proof against all thrusts, and all blows, etc. Well, that which they falsely or vainly attributed to these things for bodily god, we may justly and with full measure ascribe unto the Scripture, for spiritual.

It is not only an armor, but also a whole armory of weapons, both offensive and defensive; whereby we may save ourselves and put the enemy to flight. It is not an herb, but a tree, or rather a whole paradise of trees of life, which bring forth fruit every month, and the fruit thereof is for meat, and the leaves for medicine. It is not a pot of Manna, or a cruse of oil, which were for memory only, or for a meal's meat or two, but as it were a shower of heavenly bread sufficient for a whole host, be it never so great; and as it were a whole cellar full of oil vessels; whereby all our necessities may be provided for, and our debts discharged.

In a word, it is a Panary [Pantry] of wholesome food, against fenowed [mouldy] traditions; a Physician's shop (Saint Basil called it) [S. Basil in Psal. primum.] of preservatives against poisoned heresies; a Pandect [a treatise which contains the whole of any science] of profitable laws, against rebellious spirits; a treasury of most costly jewels, against beggarly rudiments; finally a fountain of most pure water springing up unto everlasting life.

And what marvel? The original thereof being from heaven, not from earth; the author being God, not man; the inditer [composer], the holy spirit, not the wit of the Apostles or Prophets; the Penmen such as were sanctified from the womb, and endued with a principal portion of God's spirit; the matter, verity, piety, purity, uprightness; the form, God's word, God's testimony, God's oracles, the word of truth, the word of salvation, etc.; the effects, light of understanding, stableness of persuasion, repentance from dead works, newness of life, holiness, peace, joy in the holy Ghost; lastly, the end and reward of the study thereof, fellowship with the Saints, participation of the heavenly nature, fruition of an inheritance immortal, undefiled, and that never shall fade away: Happy is the man that delighted in the Scripture, and thrice happy that meditateth in it day and night."[181]

Alleged Inspiration Problems

Any book, which considers the question of inspiration in-depth, always gives multiple views for inspiration. Most of the views are humanistic because:

---

[181] Edgar J. Goodspeed's translation of a portion of the "Preface: 'To The Reader'" in the 1611 King James Bible with paragraph additions and definitions inserted for clarity by this author.

Chapter 5–Inspiration & Illumination

(1) They eliminate *"receiving"* all the inscripturated Words as inspired, and begin the journey down the road of picking and choosing which Words, verses, chapters, books, etc. may or may not be inspired within the sixty-six books. The choices of inspired passages vary from author to author. This is dangerous and contrary to Scripture. There is no indication anywhere in the Scripture that the Holy Spirit would **NOT** guide God's people to all Truth; that is, recognizing all of the inspired Words. As a matter of fact, it is just the opposite (Jn. 16:13, 1 Jn. 2:20-21). Therefore, recognizing the Words recorded by the Apostles and prophets comes about by the *illumination* or *enlightenment* by the Spirit. They are the Words found recorded in the sixty-six books of the *received* Bible.

Numerous books and corrupted books were proposed as inspired along the way, such as the Shepherd of Hermas, but were rejected by the sanctified churches. The Words *received* in an inspired book were ALL accepted as the very Word of God and preserved from generation to generation as commanded by God.

(2) Another humanistic trap that is often uncovered in books on inspiration is the attempt to deal with the human recorders and the various linguistic qualities of the books in the Bible. The tendency of most expositors is to immediately propose that the human (quote) "writers" (unquote) of Scripture chose the Words as they were "guided" by the Holy Spirit. This is pure fiction. This is contrary to Scripture. Peter clearly informs us that Scripture was of **no** private interpretation (2 Pe. 1:21). In other words, the Words are not an interpretation of the Words that God was speaking, but they were the actual Words *received* (Jn. 17:8). Paul makes it clear that the Words are from the Holy Spirit (1 Thes. 2:13).

The correct way of viewing this 'sticky wicket' of different linguistic qualities of the books is to understand that God knew the vocabulary within the minds of the Apostles and prophets and He chose the Words from their vocabulary to record, which were infallible, inerrant, and inspired, since they were from Him. Because God is omniscient, he knew the Apostles and prophets in eternity past. He knew what their experiences, vocabulary, way of life, and many other things would be.

Any views other than verbal, plenary inspiration and preservation immediately entice speculators to second-guess the origin of Scripture. In short order, the verbal, plenary translation of the Words is also dropped in favor of dynamic equivalent translating.

Furthermore, any other views than those outlined above concerning inspiration, start a journey down the road of mysticism and unscriptural experiences, such as hearing an audible voice of God, seeing visions that provide 'new' revelations, speaking in tongues, giant angels, etc. Mysticism, which is subjectivism, eventually results in pantheism, a view that asserts God is present in everything material and immaterial. Dr. Browne said,

> "Again, it is well known how mysticism tended to Pantheism. Striving after absorption in god, men learned to identify their own minds, more or less, with Deity. The Divine Spirit was believed to dwell in **all** human souls, and needed only to be stirred within them. The inclination to look wholly within, neglect of the objective, cultivation only of the subjective—all this too readily takes a pantheistic direction."[182]

All ages of the church have experienced the phenomenon of mysticism. It is no less today, and probably much more so. The inspiration of Scripture is destroyed by mysticism and extreme spiritualism. No one under the tenets, claims, and conditions of mysticism can determine where inspiration begins and ends. The

---

[182] Browne, op. cit., 15-16 (*The Inspiration of Scripture*).

sufficiency of written Scripture for all that pertains to life has been well attested to and confirmed by godly men through the ages. Why seek guidance from sources that are uncertain, such as recently discovered discarded MSS, or rely upon some man's thoughts such as dynamic equivalent translations (2 Pe. 1:18-21)?

Illumination

*"But call to remembrance the former days, in which, after ye were **illuminated**, ye endured a great fight of afflictions;" (Hebrews 10:32) "The eyes of your understanding being **enlightened**; that ye may know what is the hope of his calling, and what the riches of the glory of his inheritance in the saints," (Ephesians 1:18).*

Dr. John Walvoord, writing about illumination of God's Words in Scripture without an audible voice, said:

> "God is able, however, to speak to the heart of man with such reality that the effect is produced **without** the need of actual words. Such is the experience of the Christian who is frequently taught by the Holy Spirit **the truths of God**, and yet the Christian would have difficulty finding words to express all that the Spirit had made known."[183] [HDW, my emphasis]

The *"truths of God"* are the Words of Scripture (Jn. 17:17). This quote by Walvoord is not mysticism, which is a subjective overriding of objective and authoritative Truth. It is "light" shed on the literal, non-allegorical understanding of the Scriptures that is sometimes enhanced by the figures of speech in Scripture. Lewis Sperry Chafer said *illumination* is:

> "the influence or ministry of the Holy Spirit which enables all who are in right relation with God to understand the Scriptures."[184]

Chafer continued his discussion saying:

---

[183] John F. Walvoord, "The Work of the Holy Spirit in the Old Testament," (Bibliotheca Sacra, Vol. 97, Dallas Theological Seminary, 1940, Logos, 2002) 315.
[184] Chafer, op. cit., 267 ("Revelation").

"It is significant that in one passage, namely, 1 Corinthians 2:9-13, there is reference to **Revelation** in verse 10, to **Illumination** in verse 12, and to **Inspiration** in verse 13. Finally, both Revelation and Inspiration may be distinguished from Illumination in that the last named is promised to all believers; that it admits of degrees, since it increases or decreases; that it depends not on sovereign choice but rather on personal adjustment to the Spirit of God; and without it none is ever able to come to personal salvation (1 Cor. 2:14), or knowledge of God's revealed truth" [special revelation].[185] [HDW, not my emphasis, but my addition]

The Cause of Poor Illumination

Apparently, *illumination* or *"enlightenment"* of *"the voice of the words of the Lord"* has reached a low point because the Holy Spirit is so grieved and quenched by sin in this present rebellious world (Eph. 4:30, 1 Thess. 5:19). If so many people, who are claiming to be God's children cannot understand Christ's declaration: *"Heaven and earth shall pass away, but my words shall not pass away"* (Matthew 24:35, and dozens of similar passages), then illumination of God's people is at a low point in history. God's Words are not illuminated in the lives of "believers" so that they can "hear" God's voice in His written words. They are listening to their *own* thoughts, imaginations, conscience, dreams, and exegetical manipulations, which would lead any of us astray, bar none. The only *"sure word of prophecy"* and authoritative guidance are God's inspired Words recorded for believers in the canon of Scripture and illuminated by the Holy Spirit. However, they must be *"illuminated"* along with a clear conscience (1 Jn. 1:9), sanctified lives, and attendance to the reading of God's **special** revelation as simply literal Words with literal meaning in the ordinary sense of the meaning. The Words must be studied in relation

---

[185] Ibid. 268.

to Biblical culture and ALWAYS with daily meditation, prayer, and a sanctified life.

Illumination of God's Words is not to be confused **(1)** with the mechanism and method of *inspiration* of God's Words given to the prophets and Apostles to be recorded, **(2)** with the *"conscience,"* **(3)** with the audible *"voice of the Lord"* or (4) with *revelation*.

Illumination and Conscience

The Holy Spirit through illumination of God's inspired Words may influence our conscience (or witness). The conscience is a judge of our thoughts and actions. But the conscience can be defiled, seared, and weak (see the chapter on conscience). Peter explains that the **written** *"voice of the words of the Lord"* are far more valuable than the "voice which came from heaven," because the *"perfect,"* which is the Scriptures, *"has come"* and is complete (1 Cor. 13:10, 2 Pe. 1:18). We no longer know *"in part"* (1 Cor. 13:9). The book of Revelation completed God's *revelation* to us (see the section "Cessation of Revelation" in chapter four). We can hold all sixty-six (66) books in our hands to God's glory.

Our desire should be to do nothing that would *"quench"* or *"grieve"* the Holy Spirit who sheds light on a believer's understanding of the written *"voice of the words of the Lord,"* not with an audible voice, but by illumination of His Words. Intuition (hunches) of the carnal mind is light years apart from God's Words illuminated. The postmodernists depend on intuition or feelings, not enlightenment, as we shall see. Another big reason their hunches are so far off is that they are using 'new' versions, which contain primarily the interpretations of man. They are not accurate and faithful translations of God's preserved, *received* Words (see below).

The ability to recognize the true Word of God has been with sanctified churches since the beginning of the age. Harold Browne, D.D., states:

> "...that the illuminating grace of God has ever been with His Church."[186]

The secret of how God illuminates His Words for the sanctified believer is a mystery, but for those who have experienced it, they hunger for its persistence. It is like coming out of the darkness into the light (Jn. 12:46, 1 Pe. 2:9). Do not trust any other source, including your "self;" and trust only the believer's light, the Holy Spirit, who illuminates the Words so that the believer can see and hear them. Illumination will be seriously affected by unconfessed sin, habitual sin, and presumptuous sin (see 1 Jn. 1:8-2:4 for unconfessed sin; 1 Jn 3:9 for willful or habitual sin; Nu. 15:30-31, Deut. 17:9-13, 2 Pe. 2:10 for presumptuous sin).

The factitious claim that the ordinary believer *"hears"* the audible voice of the Lord is ludicrous. Even Saul, God's first anointed King over Israel, had to go to the prophet Samuel to know the Words of the Lord; and when Saul did not precisely obey the **specific** revelation of God's Words conveyed to him by the prophet, the Kingdom was "rent" from him (1 Sam. 15:27-28). Part of the **specific** revelation for Saul from the prophet is in God's **special** revelation to us.

Another example relates to King David. King David received visits from the prophets, Nathan and Gad, who delivered messages to him from God (2 Sam. 12:1ff, 1 Ch. 21:11ff). God did not speak directly to David on every occasion. As a matter of fact, it was rare.

---

[186] Rt. Rev. Edward Harold Browne, D.D., *The Inspiration of Holy Scripture* (T. Whittaker, New York, NY, 1878) 112.

Another example is the episode involving King Zedekiah when he secretly sought out the prophet Jeremiah for a Word from God (Jer. 37:17). God did not speak directly to the king of His nation. Also, the great Apostle Paul was taught by the Lord for a significant period of time in Arabia; probably at Mount Sinai or Horeb, the same place where Moses received the Law and where Elijah was ordered to go by the Lord (Ex. 19:11, 1 Kg. 19:7-8, Gal. 1:11-12, 15-18). We do not know all the precise Words shared with Paul by specific revelation as the Lord taught him in Arabia. However, the special written Words God wanted us to have were later recorded by Paul. Paul was an Apostle who had the rare privilege of hearing God's audible voice, but ordinarily he operated based on the Words already revealed.

Because the apostolic age is over, and the Scriptures are complete, God expects us to conduct our lives and the administration and organization of His church according to His inscripturated Words by faith and not by hearing His audible voice. In other words, not by "sight" or the senses, which would include all of the physical senses such as hearing? This author cannot find any reference by *respected* orthodox ante-Nicene church elders (before 325 A.D.) that they heard God audibly speaking. Rather, invariably, they claimed reliance on God's written Words.

A believer does not need to claim "God spoke to me" or "God told me" to try and impress others that one is sanctified and special in the sight of God. God is no respecter of persons (Acts 10:34). You are special in God's sight if you understand God's written **special** Words to you found in the canon of Scripture.

A believer should not trust his thought patterns (Gen. 6:5, 8:21, Isa. 53:6, etc.), particularly if he is involved in *presumptuous* sin(s) (**Nu. 15:30-31,** Psa. 19:13, 2 Pe. 2:10).

Chapter 5–Inspiration & Illumination

*"But chiefly them that walk after the flesh in the lust of uncleanness, and despise government. **Presumptuous** are they, **selfwilled**, they are not afraid to speak evil of **dignities**." (2 Peter 2:10)*

In addition, this author would add for this day and time especially, *"dignities"* applies not only to rulers, but also to the dignity of the Words of God. Is presumptuous sin the reason why so many believers do not understand the frequent occurrence of Scriptural verses attesting to preservation of God's Words? Is this why they speak against their perfect preservation?

A Major Cause For Rejection of God's Preserved *Received* Words

In this postmodern age, this author believes that the misunderstanding, and misuse, and misinterpretation, and misreading, and misconception of the terms presented in this work are contributing to the rejection of the precise Words given by a Holy God and preserved to *"the jot and tittle."* These factors are a major cause for the lack of recognition and support of the *received* Hebrew, Aramaic, and Greek Words found in the Textus Receptus/Traditional Text from God. Individuals are offhandedly rejecting any plea for understanding. They are refusing insight from Scripture, proof from history, and testimony from thousands of MSS attesting to the Words. They are following either the tenets of modernism or postmodernism. This may be a conscious or unconscious process or decision. The tenets of postmodernism are so ingrained in our culture that the reason is frequently not recognized.

The postmodernists prefer to listen to their own conscience. It often leads them to their favorite teacher, scholar, or "community" who favors their position on issues because the postmodernist considers his thoughts are truth. They deny the need for external guidance from Scripture or from counselors who are wise in the ways of the Lord. This problem can only continue to grow in a postmodern world deluded by a false philosophy. Thousands upon thousands of our students are influenced every day in the institutions of learning in this nation, and many other nations around the world, by the false tenets of postmodernism.

Here is an example. When talking with a young student or young adult about preservation of God's Words, usually the young person will quickly inform you, "That is your opinion!" This happens even while showing them several passages in Scripture that confirm God's promise of preservation. They relate that they are "uncertain" about the interpretation of the verses. Their teachers foster their doubt about the preserved text of Scripture and its literal interpretation. This kind of conversation with young people has happened to this author on several occasions around the world.

The acceptance of the tenets of postmodernism is leading to an acceleration of rejecting:

(1) the significant history of the *received words* (Jn. 17:8) in the handwritten manuscripts in Hebrew, Aramaic, and Greek, which are called uncials and minuscules,[187]

(2) the significant support for the Received Texts (the Hebrew Masoretic text and the Received Greek text) from church father writings,[188]

(3) the significant history and evidence that demonstrates the heretical men involved with pushing the constructed, eclectic *critical text*,[189]

---

[187] Dr. Jack Moorman, *Forever Settled* (Bible For Today Press, Collingswood, NJ, 1999) The entire book should be read.

[188] Dr. Jack Moorman, *Early Manuscripts, Church Fathers, and the Authorized Version* (Bible For Today Press, Collingswood, NJ, 2005) The entire book should be reviewed carefully. It will also demonstrate the doctrinal problems in the critical text.

(4) the significant doctrinal problems in the *critical text* and the 'new' bible versions based on texts such as Nestle/Aland and the UBS Greek text,[190] and

(5) the significant support for the *received* Words in Hebrew, Aramaic and Greek in other translations such as the Peshitta (Aramaic), Gothic, Latin, etc., and the early lectionaries.

(6) Lastly, postmodernism is helping to excuse the significant demonstrations and proof of the corruptions of a small group of manuscripts that are used to usurp the *Received Texts*,[191]

So what is postmodernism?

---

[189] Pastor D. A. Waite, *The Heresies of Westcott and Hort, As Seen In Their Own Writings* (Bible For Today Press, Collingswood, NJ, 2004). The entire book should be studied.

[190] Pastor D. A. Waite, *Defending the King James Bible* (Bible For Today Press, Collingswood, NJ, 9th printing, 2006). This book is now a classic. It should be in the library of any serious student of Scripture and history. Also see Dr. Jack Moorman, *Early Manuscripts, Church Fathers, and the Authorized Version* (Bible For Today Press, Collingswood, NJ, 2005). Dr. Moorman's book documents 356 doctrinal passages and problems in the 'new' texts.

[191] Dean John William Burgon, *The Revised Version* (Dean Burgon Society Press, Collingswood, NJ., 2nd printing, 2000) The entire book should be studied.

CHAPTER 6

POSTMODERNISM

> *"This know also, that in **the last days** perilous times shall come. For men shall be lovers **of their own selves**, covetous, boasters, proud, blasphemers, disobedient to parents, unthankful, unholy, Without natural affection, trucebreakers, false accusers, incontinent, fierce, despisers of those that are good, Traitors, heady, highminded, lovers of pleasures more than lovers of God; Having a form of godliness, but denying the power thereof: from such turn away" (2 Timothy 3:1-5).*

A Concept For Academia Or A New Era

As philosophers, and thinkers, and researchers, and scholars, and believers began to consider the recent changes that are noted in the actions, speech, and writings of individuals, the question arose: "Is postmodernism a real change from modernism and therefore, a major shift in society called a paradigm shift?" For example, in 1996 Zane C. Hodges wrote the following:

> "In the cloistered halls of academia one of the newest buzz words is *postmodernism*. Postmodernism expresses the widely held view that modernity has somehow come to an end and that we have entered the postmodern age. Obviously there is a kind of pretentiousness to this perspective, but perhaps after all this entire concept is true."[192]

Thomas C. Oden has concluded that modernism is dead. He said:

---

[192] Zane C. Hodges, "Post-Evangelicalism Confronts The Postmodern Age, A Review of The Challenge of Postmodernism" (*Journal of the Grace Evangelical Society,* Vol. 9, Grace Evangelical Society, 1996, Logos, 2002) 3.

> "There is no need for believers in grace to despair over the losses of modernity. There is no reason to fight something already dead."[193]

We can conclude from Dr. Oden's comments and the statements of many others that scholars believe either the modern age has ended or the residual philosophy of the modern age will soon depart. The overwhelming conclusion of twenty-three contributors to a book, *The Challenge of Postmodernism: An Evangelical Engagement*,[194] (hereafter called TCOP) is that postmodernism is a phenomenon that must be considered and dealt with from a pastor's pulpit and the teacher's podium. The person in the pew must be aware that a new and godless philosophy is sweeping the world.

The tenets of modernism have ceased as a viable construction or attempt at construction of truth, as a way to relate to others, as a 'new' epistemology, and as an anchor to sustain the manner in which an individual thinks, reads, and considers truth. Perhaps the demise of modernism is good for others because of its arrogance in favor of science and relativity. No believer is sad to see the haughtiness of modernism, the reliance on humanism, and the enthroning of science by modernism pass away. Many writers assert that:

> "[t]he Enlightenment assumed that human thinking can solve everything."[195]

---

[193] Thomas C. Oden, "The Death of Modernity and Postmodern Evangelical Spirituality" (Essay by Dr. Oden in *The Challenge of Postmodernism: An Evangelical Engagement,* Victor Books, Bridgepoint, Wheaton, IL, 1995) 21.
[194] David S. Dockery, Editor, *The Challenge of Postmodernism: An Evangelical Engagement* (Victor Books, Bridgepoint, Wheaton, IL, 1995) 23 essays in 400 pages.
[195] Kimball, op. cit., 49 (The Emerging Church).

However, modernism's replacement, postmodernism, alleges "no" absolute truth(s), "no" universal solutions, "no" one-way to God, etc. The Postmodernists exhibit many contradictory views. For example, they declare there is no absolute Truth, but at the same time, they claim the tenets of postmodernism are "true."

Postmodernism contains features, as we shall see, which indicate that it is like a ship being tossed to and fro on the high seas without any anchor whatsoever except to "self." In addition, although the postmodernists are ready to assail the arrogance of modernism, the overconfidence of postmodernism's complete reliance on "self" far exceeds the haughtiness of modernism's reliance on rationalism, relativism, science, and philosophical theories. At least many modernists acknowledged external truth, and some even recognized the Bible as an authority. However, there were not many people who recognized or put into practice the final absolute authority, the Bible.

The Definition of Postmodernism

Although the precise definition varies slightly from author to author, there seems to be a consensus that is best expressed by David S. Dockery in TCOP:

> "As we move into the twenty-first century, a new way of viewing the world has emerged. The "modern" way of thinking, that dominated the nineteenth and twentieth centuries, has become obsolete. The modern ideas are no longer relevant."[196]

---

[196] Ibid. 13 (TCOP).

John MacArthur (whom this author disagrees with concerning many doctrines and beliefs) gives a concise definition in a well-written book, *The Truth War*. Dr. MacArthur defines postmodernism as:

"the rejection of every expression of certainty."[197]

The author of this work prefers to call postmodernism: **extreme selfism** and **the rejection of truth from any external source**. It is *uncertainty* about everything. According to the postmodernists, truth can only be determined or discerned by the individual, because he is dependent on his bubble of reality secondary to his experiences. Truth is embodied in a mystical or transcendental concept, only knowable and experienced by each individual without regard to precise written Truth. The postmodernist fails to recognize that his claims of uncertainty about truth as "truth" negate his propositions. In addition, revelation, as defined in this work (see chapter 4), identifies the significance of providence and history in relation to Scriptural Truth. It appears that the postmodernist operates from limited knowledge of facts about the Bible. For example, scholars have claimed inaccuracy in the Scriptures, but year after year archaeological discoveries have demonstrated the extreme accuracy of the Bible when pitted against recorded secular history.[198]

---

[197] John MacArtur, *The Truth War, Fighting for Certainty in an Age of Deception* (Thomas Nelson, Nashville, TN, 2007) 12.

[198] For example, the recent discovery of a "tiny tablet" confirms a relatively unimportant officer in King Nebuchadnezzar's Babylonian government mentioned in Jeremiah 39. "The full translation of the tablet reads: (Regarding) 1.5 minas (0.75 kg) of gold, the property of Nabu-sharrussu-ukin, the chief eunuch, which he sent via Arad-Banitu the eunuch to [the temple] Esangila: Arad-Banitu has delivered [it] to Esangila. In the presence of Bel-usat, son of Alpaya, the royal bodyguard, [and of] Nadin, son of Marduk-zer-ibni. Month XI, day 18, year 10 [of] Nebuchadnezzar, king of Babylon." Although the name is spelled slightly differently in Jeremiah, the experts believe it is the same

Dan Kimball, a postmodernist, does not give a failing grade to modernism or postmodernism; and he defines them for us, saying:

> "But modernism actually produced wonderful things, great advances in sciences, in medicine, and in technology [and] did line up well with many aspects of our faith,... [but] when modernism then assumed we could figure out God and systematize our faith, we went astray...[T]he emerging church is to rethink what aspects or values of modernism became more or less accepted standards, rather than Scripture, for how we go about ministry... Pure modernism held to a single, universal worldview and moral standard, a belief that all knowledge is good and certain, truth is absolute, individualism is valued, and thinking, learning, and beliefs should be determined systematically and logically. Postmodernism, then, holds there is no single universal worldview. **All truth is not absolute**, community is valued over individuals, and thinking, learning, and beliefs can be determined nonlinearly. Stanley Grenz explains that postmodernism "is an intellectual mood and an array of cultural expression that call into question the ideals principles and values that lay at the heart of the modern mind-set."[199]

Kimball goes on to say: "But today, contradiction is accepted."[200] Therefore, even though Jesus said, "I am the way, the truth, and the life: no man cometh unto the Father, but by me" (John 14:6) and told the Father, "thy word is truth" (Jn. 17:17), there is no problem with the obvious contradiction and belief by many postmodernists that no truth is absolute. He explains, for example, that this is the reason celebrities wear crosses around their necks, but amalgamate Buddhism, Hinduism, and other religions into their personally constructed belief system; and their

---

person. See http://www.telegraph.co.uk/news/main.jhtml?xml=/news/2007/07/11/ntablet111.xml
[199] Dan Kimball, *The Emerging Church, Vintage Christianity For New Generations* (Zondervan, Grand Rapids, MI, 2003) 57-58.
[200] Ibid. 52 (Kimball).

behavior is certainly less than compatible with Christianity. In fact, it is despicable. The current generation's thinking and behavior, which can be obviously contradictory, is called "both/and" logic.[201] It is called the "mosaic generation," because of 'picking and choosing' incompatible beliefs from various belief-systems.[202]

We can no longer call upon the terms liberalism or modernism or neo-evangelicalism to conjure up a picture of the present generation. J. Gresham Machen used these words to describe liberalism and modernism during the modern age. He said:

> "In the sphere of religion, in particular, the present time is a time of conflict; the great redemptive religion which has always been known as Christianity is battling against a totally diverse type of religious belief, which is only the more destructive of the Christian faith because it makes use of traditional Christian terminology. This **modern** non-redemptive religion is call "**modernism**" or "**liberalism**."…the many varieties of modern liberal religion are rooted in naturalism—that is, in the denial of any entrance of the creative power of God (as distinguished from the ordinary course of nature) in connection with the origin of Christianity."[203]

Machen's comments were written in 1923. During the modern age, a significant concern of the born-again believer related to the possible destruction of Christianity by scientific and archaeological studies and findings (e.g. as from Darwin's *Origin of Species*). For example, they feared some archaeological finding would be uncovered that would "prove" the Bible was wrong, destroying inerrancy, infallibility,

---

[201] Consider modernism = either/or" or either "science versus self.' Postmodernism = both/and = "self" only, although the both/and concept has gradually overtaken the world over the last several centuries.
[202] Williams, op. cit., 375-378 (*The Lie*).
[203] J. Gresham Machen, *Christianity and Liberalism* (Wm. B. Eerdmans Publishing Company, Grand Rapids, MI, 1923) 2.

and inspiration. Of course, it has not happened, and it never will. The attempt to amalgamate and accommodate liberalism with Christianity failed! Millard J. Erickson said:

> "J. Gresham Machen ...essentially argued that liberalism might be true, but that it was not Christianity and did not deserve to be known by that name."[204]

Why did the liberalism that began with the modern age and that spawned neo-evangelicalism fail? It did not revere *"every word"* in the Bible as truth. All of the inerrant Words of the Bible are God's Words, which were given to certain men by revelation to be recorded for man in all ages. The Words will be available *"to all generations"* and *"for ever"* to anyone who seeks God *"with all the heart"* (Psa. 100:5, 117, Mat. 4:4, 24:35, Mk. 12:33, etc.). They are Truth (Jn. 17:17). The message in the Scriptures is fixed (Mat. 24:25, Gal. 1). The Words that form the message will always be available, in spite of the men who fall victim to God's enemy, change them, and declare the revised words are God's Words. Man has always attempted to change the message by mixing it with human philosophy in every age, just as they are doing in the postmodern age. The New Testament writers warned repeatedly about this pitfall. They quite often gave specific rebuttals to human philosophies such as Docetism, Apollinarianism, Eutychianism, and Arianism in their writings (e.g. John, 1 John, Galatians). Paul's warnings should be heeded by all theologians who try to hide behind the influence and excuse of cultural philosophical changes as a reason to adapt the message to the age and to the church (Gal. 1:6-12, Col. 2:8).

---

[204] Millard J. Erickson, *The Postmodern World, Discerning the Times and the Spirit of Our Age* (Crossway Books, Wheaton, IL, 2002) 77. This book is well written and is a worthwhile addition to a library.

As we shall see, postmodernism does "not deserve to be known by [the] name," of Christianity either, because it changes the message *received* in the precise, preserved Words. In addition, the excuse trumpeted by modernists and postmodernists for adapting the message by claiming the "interpretation" is not fixed is hogwash. It is another excuse to vary the fixed gospel message to meet humanistic goals of greed, large church numbers (i.e. for members, collections, space, etc.) and fame under the guise of love, care, compassion, tolerance, need, and reaching the lost. Let me repeat, the lost cannot be reached by "*any other gospel*" than the precise gospel *received* in Scripture. If anyone changes the Words, the message changes; and we add that if permission is granted to man to change one Word, over time man will change more and more until the message is not recognizable at all. Who hasn't played the game of passing a message around a circle of a dozen or so people? The discovery is the last person to receive the message receives an entirely different message—it becomes "*any other*" message than the original.

Machen's comments above were written about 300 years after the subtle beginning of modernism. Modernism has failed and postmodernism will completely fail if time lasts for creating *uncertainty* in God's message, God's truth, and God's Son. The *uncertainty* that has arisen is due primarily to the differing messages in many so many 'so-called' bibles and texts, and secondarily, because of the extreme subjectivism that has arisen as a result.

Dates

Some are giving a solid date for the beginning of modernism such as Bastille (1789) and the end of modernism for example as the fall of the Berlin wall (1989). Dr. Hodges quotes Dr. Dockery who said:

> By *postmodern,* we mean the course of actual history following the death of modernity. By *modernity* we mean the period, the ideology, and the malaise of the time from 1789 to 1989, from the Bastille to the Berlin Wall.[205]

For this author, these dates are too restrictive because, as with most trends, or fads, or paradigm shifts, or *herd* change in thinking,[206] the onset is gradual and the end is nebulous. Therefore, it is better to consider that modernism:

> "had its beginning in the Reformation and reached its pinnacle with the publication of Charles Darwin's fallacious book, the *Origin of Species,* in 1859. It was spurred on by the intense and dramatic results of science in the twentieth century. However, man began to realize that science does not bring about a utopia or demonstrate man's goodness; rather just the opposite. For example, the rationality for the development of the atomic bomb, and its subsequent use in World War II, cast a cloud over the tenets of "reason" (and rationality in modernism).[207] (HDW, my addition).

Since the tenets of modernism have failed, the proponents of the philosophical tenets of postmodernism are now a thundering 'herd.' The tenets are entrenched in the halls of our educational institutions. The purveyors of the tenets of postmodernism are loudly denying revealed truth and an omnipotent, omniscient, omnipresent God. The tenets have affected all professions and all levels of society from the poor to the rich.

> "As artists, philosophers, and architects reject modern values and embrace postmodern ideas, this change was reflected in university classes, which in turn began

---

[205] Hodges, op. cit., 4 (as quoted from Oden, op. cit., 20).
[206] As fads, changes in thinking, etc. begin in a society, and more and more jump on board until it is like a *herd* stampeding across a western plain.
[207] H. D. Williams, "Postmodernism Versus Scripture" (*Dean Burgon Society News,* Number 80, April-July, Dean Burgon Society, 2007) 3.

> influencing new literature, art, architecture, and even educational methods. Little by little as students studied this new form of creativity and philosophy, we began seeing actual changes slowly surfacing in experimental forms of music, movies, and the arts. We saw some of this rejection of modern values begin surfacing on university campuses in the 1960s."[208]

The 1960s date is accurate. As the shock of the atomic bomb, its significance, and its threat, soaked into the consciences of philosophers, their postmodern thoughts were recorded. Their ideas were disseminated by the rapid distribution of information through new technology into classrooms in a short time period of about 15-20 years. In other words, the shock of the events of World War II accelerated the rejection of modernism. At least, modernism had clung to a modicum of *external* truth, although it was misunderstood and misappropriated. The seed of the 'perceived' right of a person to weigh in the balance **any** fact, proposition, precept, writing (narrative), or systematic evaluation of truth AND to reject it, was birthed in modernism. 'Scholars' began to publish *critical* evaluations of the Bible at the beginning of modern period. The German critics were especially harsh toward the historical events, miracles, and facts recorded in the Bible. They denied prophecy and the customary early dates attributed for the written revelation. Unfortunately, they were simply carrying on the severe attack on the Scriptures in the first few generations after the Apostles (Acts 20:29).

> "Malcus Porphyry (234?–305? A.D.), that learned and spiteful Syrian whom Jerome calls "Rabidum adversus Christum canem" (a rabid dog against Christ), wrote fifteen books against Christianity."[209]

---

[208] Kimball, op. cit., 58 (*The Emerging Church*).
[209] J. Aall Ottesen Stub, *Verbal Inspiration* (Lutheran Publishing House, Decorah, Iowa, 1915) 67.

The Bible has survived all of the attacks against it. A careful analysis of the assults against it reveals that the opponents were proposing theories. The theories are eventually espoused as truth. Unfortunately, many believe a lie that is often repeated. Nevertheless, every suggested contradiction or failure of the Bible concerning its accuracy, science, and history has been soundly countered. Every claim will continue to be defeated. It is God's Truth. It cannot be defeated.

The Search For Truth Without God

Man had always believed that truth exists, at least until postmodernism began. Although man has tried to explain or identify truth without God's help, he has been totally unsuccessful. John MacArthur (although this author disagrees with many of his beliefs and doctrines) gives an excellent "thumbnail sketch" about the change in thinking over the centuries.

> "Ancient Greek philosophers simply assumed the validity of truth and human knowledge without attempting to account for how we know what we know. But about five hundred years before the time of Christ, Socrates, Plato, and Aristotle, began to consider the problems of how to define knowledge, how to discover whether a belief is true, and how to determine whether we're actually justified in believing anything. For some two thousand years, nearly all [unregenerate or believing] philosophers more or less presupposed that knowledge is conveyed somehow through nature…Then in the middle of the seventeenth century, at the dawn of the so-called Enlightenment, philosophers such as Rene DesCartes and John Locke began to grapple very seriously with the question of how we gain knowledge. That branch of philosophy became known as epistemology—the study of knowledge and how human minds apprehend truth. Descartes was a rationalist, believing that truth is known by reason, starting with a few foundational, self-evident truths and using logical deductions to build more sophisticated

structures of knowledge on that foundation. Locke argued, instead, that the human mind begins as a blank slate and acquires knowledge purely through the senses. (Locke's view is known as empiricism.) Immanuel Kant demonstrated that neither logic alone nor experience alone (hence neither rationalism nor empiricism) could account for all human knowledge, and he devised a view that combined elements of rationalism and empiricism. G. W. R. Hegel argued in turn that even Kant's view was inadequate, and he proposed a more fluid view of truth, denying reality is a constant. Instead, he said, what is true evolves and changes with the advancement of time. Hegel's view opened the door to various kinds of irrationalism represented by "modern" systems of thought ranging form the philosophies of Kierkegaard, Nietzche, and Marx to the pragmatism of Henry James....After thousands of years, the very best human philosophers have all utterly failed to account for truth and the origin of human knowledge apart from God [revelation].

In fact, the one most valuable lesson humanity ought to have learned from philosophy is that it is impossible to make sense of truth without acknowledging God as the necessary starting point."[210] [HDW, my additions and emphasis]

Postmodernism Is Here To Stay Until Christ Returns

As the twentieth century closed, many observers began to notice that there was a significant change in thinking from modernism and from the previous millennia of man's history. In fact, a scan of recent literature in theological journals and writings revealed almost 4,000 references to postmodernism. A "Google" search turned up 5,370,000. David S. Dockery, President of Union University in Jackson, Tennessee, writes a statement worth repeating:

---

[210] John MacArthur, *The Truth War, Fighting for Certainty in an Age of Deception* (Thomas Nelson, Nashville, TN, 2007) 5-7.

"As we move into the twenty-first century, a new way of viewing the world has emerged. The "modern" way of thinking, that dominated the nineteenth and twentieth centuries, has become obsolete. The modern ideas are no longer relevant."[211]

Kimball said:

"Those who think that postmodernism is a figment of the academic imagination, a passing fad, could not be more wrong. Postmodernism has flowed right out of the musty corridors of academia into the world of popular culture; it is on the pages of youth magazines, on CD boxes and the fashion pages of Vogue."[212]

Kimball goes on to say:

"In the modern era, a person would grow by taking in the nutrients of modern soil, including monotheism (belief in one God) and a rational, logical system of learning. Religion was a good thing in modern soil. A modern person learned propositionally… In the post-Christian era (beginning c A.D. 2000), the values and beliefs of a person raised in America are shaped by a global, pluralistic atmosphere. This person has instant exposure to global news, global fashion, global music, and global religions. There are many gods, many faiths, many forms of spiritual expression from which to choose. In a postmodern atmosphere, a person grows up learning that all faiths are equal but that Christianity is primarily a negative religion, known for finger-pointing and condemning the behaviour of others. In this atmosphere, the Ten Commandments aren't taught and the Bible is simply one of many religious writings. Ethics and morals are based on personal choice, as families encourage their children to make their own decisions about religion [as if they were capable] and to be tolerant of all beliefs. A major influence on

---

[211] Dockery, op. cit., 11 (TCOP). Also, a discussion of postmodernism from a literary standpoint by Mary Klages may be found at http://www.colorado.edu/English/courses/ENGL2012Klages/pomo.html.
[212] Kimball, op. cit., 55.

a postmodern person's ethics and morals is what they learn from the media and what is accepted by their peers. Although relativism is more of a norm in a postmodern world, most agree on some absolutes such as wrongness of excessive violence, murder, or evil like the September 11th tragedy."[213] [HDW, my addition]

This author could not have said it better. However, if someone has understood what has just been outlined, it should almost scare him or her to death for the young people growing up in this milieu because it will lead many to the gates of hell.

Deepok Chopra is one of the leading spiritual "gurus" of the postmodern age who is helping to promote and spread postmodernism by an amalgamation of Hinduism, Buddhism, and Christianity. He was a student of:

"Maharishi Mahesh Yogi (born January 12, 1917), the founder of the Transcendental Meditation program, [who] has inspired numerous schools, colleges, universities, health-care facilities, Peace Palaces, and Invincibility centers that bear his name." [Wikipedia, the free encyclopedia]

The books by Chopra are about Buddha, the "third" Jesus, and spirituality. He has a spirituality center in California with international appeal called "The Chopra Center For Wellbeing." He is making appearances around the world on television and radio such as Glenn Beck's TV program on CNN's Headline News where he affirms the information presented here. Dr. Chopra is

"an Indian medical doctor and writer. He has written extensively on spirituality and diverse topics in mind-body medicine. He claims to be influenced by the teachings of Vedanta and the Bhagavad Gita from his native India, and

---

[213] Ibid. 58-60 (Kimball).

quantum physics. He also said that he has been profoundly influenced by the teachings of J Krishnamurti." [Wikipedia, the free encyclopedia]

Chopra uses key words for many postmodernists such as "cosmos," "collective consciousness," and "universal mind." The eastern religions have penetrated deeply within our society.

> "The Buddhist is now your neighbor, the Muslim your child's schoolteacher...[and] this is the religious anthem of those growing up in a post-Christian world: 'All paths lead to God.'"[214]

This belief is peddled every day on national and international television by the modern gurus like Oprah and the late Mother Teresa.

Fritjof Capra, a physicist and the author of *The Tao of Physics, The Web of Life,* and *The Hidden Connections, Integrating the Biological, Cognitive, and Social Dimensions of Life Into A Science of Sustainability,* has also contributed to the social revolution and paradigm shift instigated in the halls of academia. Capra said:

> "One of the most important philosophical implications of the new understanding of life is a novel conception of the nature of mind and consciousness, which finally overcomes the Cartesian division between mind and matter... In other words, cognition is the very process of life. The organizing activity of living systems, at all levels of life, is mental activity. The interactions of a living organism—plant, animal or human—with its environment are cognitive interactions. Thus life and cognition are inseparably connected. Mind—or, more accurately, mental activity—is immanent in matter at all levels of life... the behavior of the living organism is

---

[214] Kimball, op. cit., 71, 73 (The Emerging Church).

determined, but rather than being determined by outside forces, it is determined by the organism's own structure "[215]

In other words, there is a "universal consciousness," a "collective consciousness," a "cosmos." However, the ultimate determiner is "self," one of the mantras of postmodernism. Nonetheless, the confusion within postmodernism is exemplified by the claim that "community" is over "self." For example, Dan Kimball relates:

> "Postmodernism, then, holds there is no single universal worldview. All truth is not absolute, **community is valued over individualism**, and thinking, learning, and beliefs can be determined nonlinearly."[216]

A Warning to Postmodern Organizations

What is not realized by postmodernist leaders, and particularly the young people who exalt an "individual's right" to decide what is truth, is the ultimate challenge to any "community" to hold a group together that thrives on diverse ideas, experiences, and culture such as the postmodern emerging church. There is only a superficial unity, a nonconformist-type unity, which will eventually fly apart with disastrous results. Often, any psychologically disabled or compromised member, in a community based on diversity of authority, interpretations, and culture, who is given "freedom to decide truth," will quite often seek retribution against others in the community when shamed, embarrassed, or thought to be harassed. We have seen this phenomenon in shootings at schools, workplaces, and other institutions in America.

---

[215] Fritjof Capra, *The Hidden Connections, Integrating the Biological, Cognitive, and Social Dimensions of Life Into A Science of Sustainability* (Random House, Doubleday, NY, 2002) 31-36.
[216] Kimball, op. cit., 49 (The Emerging Church).

Although the postmodernist organizations consider that their thinking is ideal, it is idealism at the height of impracticality and danger. Because postmodern "communities" do not consider these realities, this author predicts dire consequences in due course for this shortsightedness on the part of organizers of a "community of faith" based on "whatever." It is contrary to the clear teaching of Scripture. The *"voice of the words of the Lord"* charges the church to unite around the person of Jesus Christ through doctrine, strict organization, and spiritual gifts and *"not as other Gentiles walk, in the vanity of their minds"* for very good reasons (Eph. 4:17, cf. Eph. 4:11-17, 1 and 2 Timothy, Titus). The mystical, imaginary, non-judgmental Jesus Christ proposed by the postmodernist is an entity that cannot be reproduced, defies unity around His person, and instigates more arguments "than Carter has little liver pills." The mysticism of postmodernism is not a firm foundation. It is like a troubled sea with large undulating waves and cross currents.

MODERNISM VERSUS POSTMODERNISM

Some of the Postulates of Modernism

Some of the significant tenets of modernism pulled from several recent sources are (see the attachments for additional comparison charts):

(1) Dependence on human reason called *enlightenment rationalism*.
(2) Rejection of supernatural phenomena.
(3) The belief that there is truth, but it is relative (spurred on by the
(4) theory of relativity).
(5) Scientific discoveries will lead to a better society and world.
(6) Scientific discoveries will usher in an era of peace on earth.
(7) Man is basically good.
(8) Almost all religions have truth in their basic tenets, which should
(9) serve to unite man.
(10) The 'new' religion of Humanism will serve gradually to unite

(11) different societies around the world (collectivism).
(12) Humanism will improve education worldwide and remove
(13) prejudices evoked by religions, particularly fundamentalism.
(14) Humanism will be elevated to an acceptable level for man by the
(15) future discoveries of science (e.g. the reason for the intense search for life on other planets, and evolutionary links to prove
(16) the Bible wrong).
(17) Skepticism is legitimate for any fact.
(18) Tolerance is accepting any social behavior and belief, and never
(19) pointing out that it may be wrong or that it deviates from acceptable norms. This began in the modern age and reached its pinnacle in the postmodern age. In pre-modern times, intolerance meant being able to express a different opinion peacefully; not violently objecting to someone's opinion or behavior. In today's culture, a person who is expressing intolerance in an appropriate, peaceful way will be verbally or physically abused or attacked. Which way is truly intolerance?
(20) Knowledge should be for practical use; spiritual knowledge is not
(21) practical (pragmatism).
(22) There is only the universal fatherhood of man.

Also, please take note of the charts at the end of this work comparing modernism, Christianity, and postmodernism in the attachment section.

The result of the various features of modernism is paganism. Machen relates:

> "Paganism is that view of life which finds the highest goal of human existence in the healthy and harmonious and joyous development of existing human faculties... Paganism is optimistic with regard to unaided human nature, whereas Christianity is the religion of the broken heart."[217]

---

[217] Machen, op. cit., 65 (*Christianity and Liberalism*).

Postmodernism is The Worst Humanistic Philosophy in Man's History

The features of postmodernism are even worse, which will lead to open heathenism as we are beginning to see in disgusting events on the streets of America and around the world. Gay Pride parades, the prevalence of pornography everywhere, exploding pedophilia, and overt celebrity whoredoms and fornication are examples.

The thinking of the postmodernists is much worse in relation to Scripture when compared with previous philosophies. Openly aggressive homosexuals such as the Frenchman, Michael Foucault, have promoted it.[218] It is completely antagonistic to clear Scriptural statements, which are called propositional statements by postmodernists,[219] and to rationality as presented in Scripture, particularly Paul's writings. God calls upon us to come reason with him (Isa. 1:18). Undoubtedly, the philosophical catastrophe of postmodernism is contributing to the clear rejection of the pure Words of God, of the clear "propositional" statements of Scripture, of the clear pronouncements of church creeds and statements of faith, and of the testimony of God-fearing, outstanding church elders in the past and present.

The Scriptures clearly state that truth exists in a Person and a Book and that it cannot be broken.

> *"Jesus saith unto him, I am the way, the truth, and the life: no man cometh unto the Father, but by me." (John 14:6) "Sanctify them through thy truth: thy word is truth." (John 17:17) "If he called them gods, unto whom the word of God came, and the scripture cannot be broken;" (John 10:35).*

---

[218] Dockery, op. cit., 58-59 (TCOP).
[219] John MacArtur, *The Truth War, Fighting for Certainty in an Age of Deception* (Thomas Nelson, Nashville, TN, 2007) 15.

Man's continuing failure to recognize the source and place of truth, to arrogantly declare man's thinking superior to God's thoughts, and to place their *"ways"* and *"thoughts"* above His *"ways"* and *"thoughts"* will truly hasten the end of the church age (Isa. 55:6-11, Rev. 22: 20-21). It is obvious that the turning from Scripture is causing tremendous spiritual failures at all levels in spite of the successes of technology.

There is much debate by scholars over postmodernism, such as the extent of "relativism," "reason," and "deconstructionism," and in the character of those holding to postmodernism,[220] but, as usual, it depends on the author. Some authors are radical, others are moderate; some are secular, others are 'religious.' For example, some authors will declare relativism and/or reason is bankrupt in postmodernism while others will defend them as an integral part of postmodernism. This author will take the worst features of postmodernism in all the groups as identified in various author's writings and the reader can apply the variable and variety concept to each tenet. The tenets can be identified in the writings of early authors such as Jacques Derrida (1930-2004), Richard Rorty,[221] Michael Foucault;[222] later writers such as Dick Jellema and John Cobb,[223] and

---

[220] Dockery, op. cit., see the essays by ten contributors to TCOP.

[221] Richard Rorty, "Pragmatism is a Philosophical Therapy. It Helps You Stop Asking the Unhelpful Questions"
(http://www.believermag.com/issues/200306/?read=interview_rorty) "Richard Rorty may be America's most influential living philosopher; he is certainly both the most controversial and the most widely read. The son of Trotskyite journalists, he grew up in New York and New Jersey, where his family farm occasionally hid Trotskyites fleeing Stalinist assassins. After studying philosophy at the University of Chicago and Yale, he took a post teaching at Wellesley in the early Sixties. He soon moved to Princeton, where he taught for twenty years."

[222] Michael Foucault, home page, http://www.csun.edu/~hfspc002/foucault.home.html

more recent authors such as Stanley Grenz,[224] John Franke,[225] and John Armstrong.[226]

Some of the Postulates of Postmodernism

The postmodernist (some-times!) indicates some or all of the following as tenets (talk about confusion!):

(1) The rejection of any 'so-called' truth (a crisis in epistemology), or at least a tendency to discharge any fact generally considered truth by a significant body of individuals.
(2) The rejection of reason and rationality, which is replaced by absolute relativism (i.e. centered in the person).
(3) The rejection of strong convictions about any truth based on postulates or foundationalism. Foundationalism is: "the belief that knowledge consists of sets of beliefs that rest assuredly on

---

[223] John Cobb, (http://en.wikipedia.org/wiki/John_B._Cobb) "John B. Cobb, Jr. (born February 9, 1925) is an American United Methodist theologian who played a crucial role in the development of process theology. He integrated Alfred North Whitehead's metaphysics into Christianity, and applied it to issues of social justice." [HDW, process theology is bankrupt because it declares God is learning over time.]
[224] Stanley J. Grenz, home page, http://www.stanleyjgrenz.com/index2.shtml
[225] John Franke, from his university's home page, "Dr. Franke is particularly interested in engaging postmodern thought and culture from the perspective of Christian faith in order to explore the opportunities and challenges they present for the witness and ministry of the gospel. In addition to teaching Bible, he has lectured and taught on the relationships between theology, ministry, and postmodernity in the United States, Canada, England, and New Zealand and is actively involved in research and writing. In addition to publishing numerous articles and reviews, he is the coauthor of *Beyond Foundationalism: Shaping Theology in a Postmodern Context* and the author of *The Character of Theology* and *Barth for Armchair Theologians*." (http://www.biblical.edu/pages/discover/faculty-directory.htm)
[226] John Armstrong, home page, http://www.johnharmstrong.typepad.com/

	still other sets of beliefs and that the whole is supported by irreversible foundational beliefs."[227]
(4)	The rejection of considering anything "evil" except the very worst crimes or the very worst sins.
(5)	The rejection of relativism by some, its use by others, but subjectivism for sure with a little objectivity thrown in occasionally to establish their position and "whatever" "fits" the moment becomes truth.
(6)	The rejection of any generalized, religious, or civic morality.
(7)	The rejection of every dogma.
(8)	The argument against, and the annihilation of, every definition.
(9)	The belief that there is no such thing as truth outside of "self."
(10)	The belief that language written or spoken by anyone is biased.
(11)	The belief that language written or spoken must be deconstructed to understand the attempt at personal benefit and bias for the author (deconstructionism, see footnote 44).
(12)	The questioning of every axiom and the corollary of elevating mysteries and paradox, and dwelling on ambiguities.
(13)	The belief as a result of the above that nothing is *certain*. Certainty becomes arrogance in their philosophical stance. (e.g. the postmodern pastor, Joel Osteen, who responds to most questions concerning serious Biblical doctrine with "I don't know." For example, when asked: "Will Muslims or Hindus go to heaven?" The answer: "I don't know." Most postmodernists believe that there is danger in seeking to be right.
(14)	Skepticism absolutely rules.
(15)	Approves pluralism ("philosophy: the philosophical theory that reality is made up of many kinds of being or substance; social: the existence of groups with different ethnic, religious, or political backgrounds within one society" from Encarta) i.e. ecumenism and universalism.
(16)	Pragmatism replaces foundationalism.
(17)	"**Meaning resides not in external reality or texts but in the interpreter.**"[228]

---

[227] Carl F. H. Henry, "Postmodernism, The New Spectra?" (Essay in TCOP) op. cit., 42.
[228] Ibid. 41 (Henry, TCOP).

A Warning to Church Elders

One significant character trait of postmodernists, which is not mentioned in the articles and books reviewed by this author, but observed in postmodern acquaintances, is their ability to "**live in boxes**." What is meant by this term is their chameleon-like characteristic. They are able to change their behavior depending on their environment and the people near-by without a twinge of a guilty conscience. In other words, if they are at church, they act one way; if they are at work, they act another way; and if they are at home, they act still another way. Each place is a "box" that requires different thoughts and actions for them. Obviously, this is a result of accepting any behavior, even outrageous behavior by individuals. This is a product of their definition of tolerance, which results in no confrontation because it might interfere with acceptance, or "step" on someone's belief, or hinder "my" status in the "box." No one can truly know postmodernists unless a person is exposed to their behavior in each of the boxes in which they live for a significant amount of time. This is a warning to church elders to:

> "*Lay hands suddenly on no man*, neither be partaker of other men's sins: keep thyself pure" (1 Timothy 5:22). (HDW, my emphasis).

Some Quotes

The change in philosophies over the last few centuries from pre-modern, to modern, to postmodern is well illustrated by Walter Truett Anderson in TCOP. He explained the differences in their methods using an extended baseball umpire metaphor or parable. Starting with the pre-modern philosopher, he said:

"There's balls and there's strikes, and I call 'em the way they are." The second, a modernist, asserts "I call 'em the way I see 'em," The third umpire, a postmodernist, claims "they ain't nothin' until I call 'em."[229]

For the 'religious' postmodernists, "I" comes first. A "believer" is asked to focus on four aspects of his life that is characterized by an anagram, EPIC. EPIC is (1) experiential (2) participatory (3) the image-driven (4) the connected. Surely anyone can discern that the "objective," called the Lord Jesus Christ and the Scripture, is missing in this 'formula.' D. A. Carson comments on this anagram and its explanation by Leonard Sweet, saying:

> "Some of this is very helpful. But it is disquieting that he fails to say why we are not to embrace postmodernism. Is it not, at least in part, because strong postmodernism sacrifices the category of **objective truth**, a category (as we shall see) that both historic Christianity and the Bible itself have always insisted on?"[230] (HDW, my emphasis)

Sadly, Dr. Carson rejects THE objective truth himself by embracing corrupt texts and versions, which is explained below.

Why Are Young People Leaving The Church? A Primary Reason

The major reason we are losing our young people in the church is because God's people have been so vacillating, or of two minds, concerning the assurance of "objective truth" found in the Words of

---

[229] R. Albert Mohler, Jr., "The Integrity of the Evangelical Tradition and the Challenge of the Postmodern Paradigm" (TCOP) 55-56.
[230] Carson, op. cit., 126.

God.[231] Most professors, teachers, or scholars cannot tell a student seeking objective, absolute truth where *"every word"* of God (Mat. 4:4) can be found, i.e., in a book that the student can hold in his hands and say that he has *"every word."* The reason is because many teachers claim: (1) that the Words are scattered in every manuscript (the majority text view), or (2) that they were only in the originals called autographs, which are no longer available, or (3) that we have only the message, idea, or concept of God's Words, which is adequate. Any student, who seriously considers these "pronouncements" by teachers, will be able quickly to discern:

(1) the futility of such statements,
(2) the *uncertainty* of such statements,
(3) the subsequent ease of corrupting the "message" from God by man, if many of the precise, contractual, legal Words or *"voice" of God"* are lost, and
(4) the conflict with the clear statements of Scripture (Mat. 24:35, Mk. 13:31, Lk. 21:33, etc.).

An example is the well-known teacher, D. A. Carson, who uses and defends the NIV Bible as the best translation,[232]

(1) which was *interpreted* from a *critical-text* 'made' from corrupted manuscripts (primarily the B and Aleph manuscripts), and
(2) which cannot be collated because of the thousands of differences.

---

[231] Chuck Missler, "Saving Our Youth" (*K-House eNews,* Coeur d'Alene, ID, Aug., 14, 2007) "A large number of young people are leaving the Church after high school, according to a survey of 1,023 Protestants age 18 to 30. While 35 percent of those who leave generally resume regular church attendance by age 30, and another 30 percent attend sporadically, significant numbers of Christian youth are leaving and never coming back." This is a very common report by others also, such as *Barna Research.*

[232] D. A. Carson, *The King James Version Debate, A Plea For Realism* (Baker Book House, Grand Rapids, MI, 1979) 97. Although Dr. Carson's book was written in 1979, no change in his thinking has been demonstrated in his writings since that date, which this author has read.

He prefers the NIV over the texts *received*:
(1) which have few differences, and
(2) which were accurately and faithfully *translated* by the KJB translators.

If D. A. Carson's position does not undermine absolute "objective truth," then what does? If believers (and particularly our alleged 'scholars') cannot agree on where God's Words can be found, and they present several "texts" AS THE WORDS OF GOD, then obviously this gives 'thinking' young people the permission to be **_uncertain_** about many things. The *Received Text* is the text used by the Reformers because it was the text used by the previous generations of sanctified churches and the priesthood of believers. It conforms to God's promise:

> *For the LORD is good; his mercy is everlasting; and **_his truth endureth to all generations_**. (Psalms 100:5).*

In light of His promise in Psalm 100:5, why would God's Words not be available from generation to generation? Why would any 'thinking' adult accept translations of the *critical text* **constructed:**
(1) from corrupted manuscripts unavailable for approximately fifteen hundred years,
(2) that were:
  (a) pulled out of garbage dumps,
  (b) found in graves, and
  (c) discovered on shelves in storage rooms.
(3) that were discarded by the early church, since they were obviously constructed by cults and Gnostics secondary to their heresies?[233]

---

[233] Philip Comfort, *Encountering the Manuscripts* (Broadman & Holman, Nashville, TN, 2005). Throughout Dr. Comfort's book, he exalts the manuscripts found in Egypt at the garbage dump at Oxyrinchus, or in the grave sites of Gnostics. Dr. Comfort is a knowledgeable man, but his starting place is not the precise, preserved promises of God handed down through the generations, without which no man has hope. Also, see http://petragrail.tripod.com/nicea.html for exposure of Gnostic books.

Surely, everyone knows that Brooke Foss Westcott (1825-1903) and Fenton John Anthony Hort (1828-1892) set out to dethrone the *Received* Greek Text by their constructed Greek text and to "cast upon the world" their 'new' text, the ultimate unclear "voice.".[234] Surely, everyone knows by now that the United Bible Society and Nestle/Aland texts base their work on Westcott and Hort's labor.

Although many 'scholars' will declare this primary reason as overly simplistic (i.e. *uncertainty* about where "*every word of God*" is found) for the progress and success of postmodernism and its effects, such as young people leaving the church and rejecting absolute truth, so be it. It is the truth. It has hastened the insidious infection by postmodern tenets spreading through our society and culture. Satan has used this primary reason (doubt and uncertainty about God's Words) greatly, undermining God's Words to benefit his rebellion against "The Living Word" and "His Living Words."

A second primary reason postmodern young people are leaving the church is because the *uncertainty* generated throughout Christendom:

(1) by the confusion generated in churches through the use of multiple conflicting "bible" versions in assemblies, and

(2) by the volatile growth of sin by professing Christians. The subject of this work will not allow an exposition of these factors, but all of these issues have resulted in the explosive acceptance and infusion of postmodern tenets into societies around the world.

Many 'thinkers,' such as Dr. C. Matthew McMahon, are rightfully proclaiming the dangers of postmodernism. He declared:

> "Liberal Protestantism is one of the most destructive movements within modern Christian thought because it 1)

---

[234] Williams, op. cit., 57-61 (*The Lie*).

redefines and reinterprets orthodox idea to fit new categories of thought, and 2) removes objective truth and **absolute standards**. In other words, though postmodernists would not claim this in every area (though some would) *truth* changes.

If this is not blatantly stated, it is practically accomplished. This movement gave way to atheistic theories such as Darwin's evolutionary theory. If the pseudo-intellectual theory of evolution can take root in Postmodern thought, and reside there with any degree of comfort, then its existence in relativity to Christian teaching and the God of the Bible, is at complete odds with it, or at least should be at odds with it. **For the postmodern theologian, almost all Christian beliefs will come to be regarded as "seriously" out of line within modern cultural norms.** Most of the time, Christian beliefs are "completely" redefined, or orthodox beliefs abandoned, as liberal theologians reinterpreted them. This can be seen in the writings of men like Albrecht Ritschl who saw the Kingdom of God as "ethical values" for culture, or men like Karl Barth and Reinhold Neibhur who regarded liberal Protestantism as based upon an optimistic view of human nature and having faith in faith. Others, such as Paul Tillich wanted to see a correlation between theology and culture, culture obviously giving the foundation and structure of what is to be believed. They believe the Gospel must speak to culture, thus, as culture changes, so does the Gospel. Postmodern Liberalism places an immense weight on the notion of universal human religious experience, and denies absolute truth, as well as the objectivity of truth. It emphasizes transient cultural relationships, and surrenders Christian theology at the expense of changing times or the need for a new and fresh redefining of terms. **Postmodernism has come to be known as a "cultural sensibility" without absolutes, fixed certainties, or foundations. It delights in pluralism, and divergence, and thinks in terms of situational ethics.** Postmodern philosophers are as diverse in their theological outlook as they are many. They are primarily concerned with the developments of liberal theology, and how theology affects and interpolates with culture... **Evangelical Postmodern Diversification within the contemporary church, then, is one of the most dangerous antagonists to the Bible, and the historical Christian faith**. It allows a sinful pragmatism to enter the church, and novelty in creating new ways to redefine, thus destroy, orthodox doctrine[235] (HDW, my emphasis).

Four Postmodern Streams

Postmodern 'theologians' identify four streams within their movement. Diogenes Allen relates that they are:

> "(1) the confessional stream represented by Karl Barth, (2) the existentialist-hermeneutical stream, (3) theological deconstruction, and (4) process theology. Allen sees the emergence of the postmodern movement as a new opportunity for theology, and a new openness for faith. The situation of the Christian church "is not far better than it has been in modern times because our intellectual culture is at a turning point." He continues:
>
>> A massive intellectual revolution is taking place that is perhaps as great as that which marked off the modern world from the Middle Ages. The foundations of the modern world are collapsing, and we are entering a postmodern world. The principles forged during the Enlightenment… are crumbling."[236]

However, under the guise of postmodernism, these streams in many instances are an attempt to return to the sacramentalism of some denominations. For example, Karl Barth's return to the "confessions" of his church (the creedal statements of the Reformed Faith) is heralded as a return to orthodoxy; when in fact, he advocates a return to "tradition,"

---

[235] Dr. C. Matthew McMahon, "Evangelical Postmodern Diversification," found at this website, http://www.apuritansmind.com/HistoricalTheology/McMahonEvangelicalPostmodernDiversification.htm. However, this author is sad that Dr. McMahon uses the modern versions based upon a 'constructed' text, a text not *received*.
[236] Mohler, op. cit., 63 (Mohler, TCOP).

which subtly overrides the Words of God by placing tradition on an equal par with God's Words. Karl Barth (1886-1968), a Swiss Reformed theologian, advocated "freedom" from the gospel; that is, from the literal Words of God.

> "The source of theology (which can also be called the gospel) is also its subject-matter, to which it is tied just as all other branches of knowledge pursued at the university are tied to their subject-matter. Without it theology would and could dissolve into amateurish excursions into history, philosophy, psychology, and so on... Bound to its subject matter though it is in this way, **it enjoys complete freedom of inquiry and doctrine**...and it accepts no instructions or regulations from anyone; **it even serves the Church in its independence of its own responsibility**. And since God from whom it takes its name is no dictator, it cannot behave dictatorially. Bound only to its subject matter, but also liberated by it, the teacher of theology can have and desires to have only pupils who are free in the same sense." [237]

This type of thinking and subtlety helped spur the onset and subsequent progress of postmodernism, which developed as man realized that scientific advancement could result in humanitarian failure; for example, the development of germ warfare. Contrary to Karl Barth's thinking, we are NEVER free from the Words and "voice" of God as a theologian, student, or man in the pew (Rom. 7:7-13). The Words are absolute truth, which should always be the standard, foundation, or starting point. Logically, freedom from absolute truth would drive an individual exposed to *uncertainty about* and *freedom from* all things, particularly God's Words, to arrive at "self" as the determiner of truth. "I" would become central in thinking and the foundation used for decision-making. Our society is beginning to experience the negative results of this

---

[237] John Webster, "The Cambridge Companion to Karl Barth" (http://assets.cambridge.org/052158/4760/sample/0521584760WS.pdf).

type of philosophy in every aspect of its functioning (e.g. crime, educational breakdown, corporate disasters, political debacles, home failures, etc.).

Postmodernists Object to Being Challenged To Define Their Beliefs

The attitude of the proponents of the postmodern movement about those being affected by it is significant. Their outlook as it affects various cultural phenomena, such as the arts, literature, architecture, or the emerging church, reflects their *uncertainty* related to defining anything. In other words, the postmodernists that this author knows are uncertain about which tenets of postmodernism affect their proclamations. This reason relates to their exaltation of individual thoughts and actions, even though they may be conflicting. They are particularly ambivalent about accepting God's Words as a contract with man (Heb. 9:16), about where the Words are found (Rom. 3:1-2, 1 Tim. 3:14-15), and about how the Words are interpreted (2 Pe. 1:19-21). Certainly, if they accepted a signed, secular, legal contract, they would know the wording precisely and they would know where the contact is kept. The practical aspect they fail to see any longer is the personal characteristic of the Scriptures. It is addressed to all men, but it is a personal "letter" to each believer. God expects each of us to study *"every word"* (2 Tim. 2:15, Mat. 4:4).

Why did the most important document for man become less important than a personal contract between men? The reason lies in the denial by postmodernists of the **effects** of the tenets of postmodernism on them personally. Postmodernists are *uncertain* about what they believe and where truth is found and, therefore, uncertain that their neglect of precise Words from God is significant. They seem unable to discern the duplicity and contradictions in their lifestyles and actions, and the lack of doctrine determined from a fixed foundation.

John S. Hammett, Professor of Theology, Southeastern Baptist Theological Seminary, writes:

> **"Moreover, the movement is so diverse as to open anyone who speaks of it as a whole to the charge of misrepresentation**. In fact, the most substantive response to D. A. Carson's book charges him with just that. David Mills says: "while Carson himself noted the complexity and diversity of the ECM [emerging church movement], he failed to keep these factors in view as he critiqued the movement." 7. The leaders of the movement acknowledge that there is neither unanimity nor even a consensus of opinion among them as to what emergent is, and they deny that any single theologian or spokesperson represents the movement as a whole."[238]

But in spite of their uncertainty about their beliefs, one significant aspect they all subscribe to either subtly or overtly is their disdain for the authority of Scripture and its primacy for the believer. This is a result of the following influences:

(1)   higher and lower criticism of the Bible,

(2)   deconstructionism, and

(3)   postmodern literary criticism, which reduces the Bible to "narratives" or "stories" that have some relevance, but no absolute authority.

Stanley Grenz, professor of theology and ethics at Carey Hall/Regent College in Vancouver, British Columbia, believes that

---

[238] John S. Hammett, "AN ECCLESIOLOGICAL ASSESSMENT OF THE EMERGING CHURCH MOVEMENT" (http://ateam.blogware.com/AnEcclesiologicalAssessment.Hammett.pdf).

Scripture in the 'new' world is "ultimately unnecessary." His intent is to join with other postmodernists who claim that the "faith community" contains individuals who interpret 'narratives' differently. Therefore, the Bible becomes "the book of the community," but it is subservient to the community's interpretation. Subsequently, he states:

> "Consequently, the divine nature of Scripture or its status vis-à-vis revelation need not be demonstrated in the prolegomenon to theology."[239]

The Bible becomes simply like any other book, which the individual may or may not elevate as the prime book in his home, but perhaps will accept as **a** "book of the community." Does anyone see the seed—"like any other book"—of Hugo Grotius/John Fell/Richard Bently/J. A. Bengal/Johann Semler/J. J. Griesbach/Westcott/Hort and others in this heresy?

In the postmodern world, is it any wonder that **(1)** the Bible is not read, **(2)** experience is elevated to truth, **(3)** reason is dethroned, **(4)** the divine is ridiculed, and so, Jesus is called 'just' a great prophet, **(5)** doctrine is irrelevant, and so, His virgin birth is denied, **(6)** miracles are debunked, **(7)** Biblical morality is shunned, etc..........?

Two Major Divisions of Postmodernism

The two major divisions of postmodernism, called Destructive and Constructive Postmodernism by some authors, have tenets that overlap in theory, but have shades of differences; tenets that are wholly separate, and tenets that are compatible in both groups. It is beyond the scope of this work to outline all the points. But, most articles have missed the point that there is a secular and a religious division in

---

[239] Mohler, op. cit., 65-66 (Mohler, TCOP).

postmodernism. Some have called it hard and soft postmodernism without recognizing this division.[240] Similarly, postmodernism has retained some of the aspects of modernism, particularly the branch called "soft" or "Constructive Postmodernism."[241] The constructive postmodernist is often the religious person who is capable of a charismatic-like persuasion that is aloof from God's Revelation. This is the "soft" postmodernist who picks and chooses what he believes and what he casts in or out of his construction of a religious system.

The Reason For Rejection of Modernism

The rejection of modern philosophy by postmodernists centers primarily on the frightening development of technologies and the desire to be free from any authority. Along with the progress of technology came World War I, World War II, Auschwitz, the Korean War, the Vietnamese War, the wars in Africa, Russian satellite wars, environmental disasters, and many more tragedies. It became obvious that man could not and would not control his environment, that man under modernistic philosophy had missed the mark, and that visible Christianity had failed. Therefore, other "truths" (but they dare not call them truths) were sought. They dare not turn to a Holy God's absolute revelation of truth, *"the voice of the words of God."*

The Postmodern Church

Postmodernism has spawned the *emerging church movement*, which includes the early *seeker-sensitive* churches (some authors place

---

[240] D. A. Carson, *Becoming Conversant with the Emerging Church, Understanding a Movement and Its Implications* (Zondervan, Grand Rapids, MI, 2005) 105-106.
[241] Henry, op. cit., 38-39, 48, (Henry, TCOP).

the *seeker-sensitive* church toward the end of modernism). The *seeker-sensitive* churches are already evolving into another type with more features of postmodernism emerging. The *emerging church movement* is defined by Mark Driscoll as:

> "a growing, loosely connected movement of primarily young pastors who are glad to see the end of modernity and are seeking to function as missionaries who bring the gospel of Jesus Christ to emerging and postmodern cultures."[242]

Dan Kimball, a postmodernist, reacting, and relating to the postmodern phenomenon in his church writes:

> "I didn't know it yet, but we were feeling the effects of emerging generations being born into a post-Christian (and what I will define here as a post-seeker-sensitive) world."[243]

Rick Warren's church is an example of the *seeker-sensitive* church. The rapid changes in the organization and administration of postmodern churches to reflect cultural phenomena in technology and philosophy are astounding. For example, the *seeker-sensitive* postmodern church pastor is being replaced by churches without pastors that have only "*narrators.*"[244] Furthermore:

> "Many EC (emerging church) participants de-emphasize preaching a Bible message from a pulpit and opt to use the time for individual worship by setting up stations featuring a variety of activities. One station might feature a table for journaling; another might prompt quiet meditation

---

[242] Gary E. Gilley, "The Kingdom of Emergent Theology—Part I" (*THINK on these things,* Southern View Chapel, Springfield, IL, Sept. 2007) 2. This is a quote of Mark Driscoll reported by Dr. Gilley.

[243] Dan Kimball, *The Emerging Church, Vintage Christianity For New Generations* (Zondervan, Grand Rapids, MI, 2003) 32.

[244] MacArthur, op. cit., 17.

and provide headphones so the worshiper can listen to quiet, soothing music. Other stations might feature art or poetry. *Experiencing* Jesus and *connecting* with a community of worshipers is the way to reach postmodernists, according to many in the EC."[245] (my addition, not my emphasis, HDW).

The emerging church claims a desire to be "non-confrontational." However, surely the leaders of these 'communities' realize their theology, worship style, ecumenism, and renewed "sacramentalism" is confrontational to any person who is a careful student of God's Words (2 Tim. 2:15). The New Testament instructions to the church are drastically different from these so-called postmodern churches. In reality, they are nothing more than social gatherings to soothe the guilt of sin by *experiences* and by *connecting* with others who are Biblically illiterate. They refuse to accept guidance from well-studied Scripture by wise elders in some churches. Authority that begins with precise Words *received* from God is shunned.

> "There is reluctance to emphasize absolutes. A secular writer, commenting on the EC movement and postmodern Christianity, summed things up this way: 'What makes a postmodern ministry so easy to embrace is that it doesn't demonize youth culture—Marilyn Manson, 'South Park,' or gangsta rap, for example—like traditional fundamentalists. Postmodern congregants aren't challenged to reject the outside world."[246]

The "postmodern congregants" are exactly that—congregants, but not a church (Acts 2:42, Col. 3:16).

---

[245] Steve Herzig, "The Emerging Church: What is it?" (*Israel My Glory*, The Friends of Israel Gospel Ministry, Inc., September/October, 2007) 27.
[246] Ibid. 28 (Herzig, "The Emerging Church: What is it?").

The Roots of the Emerging Church

Although the emerging church is a broad-based movement, there is evidence of its roots in earlier centuries.

"Frederick Schleiermacher (1768-1834) of Halle, Germany, **exalted experience and feeling over Bible doctrine**. He used traditional Christian language but reinterpreted it. He emphasized the necessity of knowing Christ through faith, but "faith" **did not refer to believing the Bible as the infallible Word of God but merely to man's own intuition or consciousness**. He did not consider historical biblical truth to be necessary to faith. Thus Schleiermacher could say, "With my intellect I am a philosopher, and **with my feelings quite a devout man; ay, more than that, a Christian**" (quoted by Daniel Edward, "Schleiermacher Interpreted by Himself and the Men of His School," *British and Foreign Evangelical Review*, vol. 25, 1876, p. 609). Schleiermacher barred doctrinal preaching from the pulpit (Iain Murray, *Evangelicalism Divided*, 2000, p. 11). "Schleiermacher is correctly viewed as the chief source of the massive change which has occurred in the historic Protestant denominations during the last two hundred years. ... In his separation of the intellectual content of Christianity (the objective biblical revelation) from Christian 'feeling', Schleiermacher seemed to provide a means whereby the essence of Christianity could remain unaffected, no matter how much of the Bible was rejected. Hostile criticism of Scripture need not therefore be seen as a threat to the 'faith' ... Christianity, it was concluded, could be successful irrespective of whether Scripture were preserved as the Word of God , and this thought was the more appealing as the theological scholarship of the nineteenth century became increasingly destructive" (Iain Murray, *Evangelicalism Divided*). Schleiermacher paved the way for the New Evangelical view that men can be genuine Christians and "love the Lord," even though they reject biblical doctrine. For this reason, Billy Graham can have sweet fellowship with modernistic unbelievers and Roman Catholic bishops and popes."²⁴⁷

The roots of apostasy have spread to encompass the rising tide of the worldwide postmodern emerging church movement. The movement is having a great influence on many institutions. Dr. Gary Gilley reports:

> "Today, while the emergent community is barely a decade old it has permeated churches, Bible colleges, seminaries, and parachurch organizations throughout the world."²⁴⁸

These changes signal a complete abandonment of "Truth" and a substitution of the postmodernist concept of reality, absolute relativism, and (un)certainty in order to not offend a "seeker" who might attend. One of their most significant postulates is the elimination of the theological doctrine of divine omniscience. This will put the nail in the coffin of the living-dead postmodern church. This is one of the tenets of process theology,²⁴⁹ a theological disaster.

---

²⁴⁷ David Cloud, "Part I, New Evangelicalism" (Way of Life Literature, Port Huron, MI, Fundamental Baptist Information Service, 2001) http://www.wayoflife.org/fbns/fundamen1.htm , accessed 11/09/07.
²⁴⁸ Gilley, op. cit., 2 ("The Kingdom of Emergent Theology").
²⁴⁹ Jon Tal Murphee, Divine Paradoxes, A Finite View of an Infinite God. (Christian Publications, Inc. Camp Hill, PA, 1998) 8. Also see this web site (http://en.wikipedia.org/wiki/Process_theology). "Process theology (also known as neoclassical theology) is a school of thought influenced by the metaphysical process philosophy of Alfred North Whitehead (1861–1947). While there are process theologies that are similar, but unrelated to the work of Whitehead (such as Pierre Teilhard de Chardin) the term is generally applied to the Whiteheadian school. Process theology is unrelated to the Process Church. The concepts of process theology include:
- God is not omnipotent in the sense of being coercive. The divine has a power of persuasion rather than coercion. Process theologians interpret the classical doctrine of omnipotence as involving force, and suggest

Open and Process Theology

Another significant theological assertion by many postmodernists besides process theology is open theology. Open theology is essentially compatible with most aspects of process theology. The only difference is an Armenian-like emphasis on free-will by open theology, but the bottom line of both theologies is the removal of God's omniscience. Open theology proclaims man's free will has influence on God's knowledge because **(1)** if God gave man free-will, then he does not know what the future will precisely hold, **(2)** if God does not know the future, classical

---

  instead a forbearance in divine power. "Persuasion" in the causal sense means that God does not exert unilateral control.
- Reality is not made up of material substances that endure through time, but serially-ordered events, which are experiential in nature. These events have both a physical and mental aspect. All experience (male, female, atomic, and botanical) is important and contributes to the ongoing and interrelated process of reality.
- The universe is characterized by process and change carried out by the agents of free will. Self-determination characterizes everything in the universe, not just human beings. God cannot totally control any series of events or any individual, but God influences the creaturely exercise of this universal free will by offering possibilities. To say it another way, God has a will in everything, but not everything that occurs is God's will."
- God contains the universe but is not identical with it (panentheism, not pantheism). Some also call this "theocosmocentrism" to emphasize that God has always been related to some world or another.
- Because God interacts with the changing universe, God is changeable (that is to say, God is affected by the actions that take place in the universe) over the course of time. However, the abstract elements of God (goodness, wisdom, etc.) remain eternally solid.

Charles Hartshorne believes that people do not experience subjective (or personal) immortality, but they do have objective immortality because their experiences live on forever in God, who contains all that was. Others believe that people do have subjective experience after bodily death.

Dipolar theism, is the idea that God has both a changing aspect (God's existence as a Living God) and an unchanging aspect (God's eternal essence)."

(orthodox) theology is wrong. It harbors the same old claim that classical theology is rooted in scholasticism of the Greeks and other influences by denying that Scripture came first and therefore influenced various cultures and their myths. An example of this would be the Babylonian fable of Semiramis and her virgin-born son, which is claimed to have influenced the writers of the Bible.[250]

Finally, the postmodern churches are espousing dipolar theology, which teaches that God has characteristics that are conflicting; such as one / many (trinity), merciful / just, spiritual / material, absolute power / persuasiveness, etc. Because they perceive these attributes to be in conflict they maintain that God has only the good in each set of characteristics. This again limits God's omniscience because they say that He can not be omnipotent and persuasive at the same time. These are obviously theories by midget minds. It is "a retrograde form of Christianity."[251] Obviously, grace and mercy, judgment and justice, love and punishment, God and man, and similar characteristics of the substitutionary death of Christ on the Cross are not understood by postmodernist theologians.

Two Streams in the Emerging Church Movement

There are two streams 'emerging' within the postmodern church movement. One is very liberal, and the second claims to be conservative, but is it? The two streams exhibit similarities and differences, but they wind up unified in abandoning the precise doctrines preserved by the

---

[250] This web site lays out in simple language the problem for teachers and pastors concerning open and process theology
(http://www.wrfnet.org/articles/printarticle.asp?ID=726)
[251] Henry, op. cit., 49 (TCOP)

churches throughout the dispensation of the church. Young pastors are leaping before looking. Dr. Gary Gilley reports:

> "at least two basic wings have become discernable. One wing calls itself "**emerging**," claiming to have solid theological credentials, having only adopted methods more in tune with postmodern mindsets. The other wing is termed "**emergent**" and is composed of those who not only are adopting new methodologies but who also challenge the most sacred of doctrines."[252]

The two groups have leaders; each group trying to distance itself from the other. However, Dr. Gilley aptly describes the difficulties in the attempted separation of the two groups from each other. The difficulties always return to a basic misunderstanding of systematic theologically determined doctrines related to: **(1)** the church, its administration and organization, **(2)** separation from theological error, and **(3)** eschatological doctrines long established by very competent students of God's Words.

For example, they merge cultural changes related to 'evolving' ecumenical and universal postmodern ideology into the church. They forget the well-know warnings about universalism and a one-world religion, ruler, and economy.[253]

Separation from doctrinal error is no longer considered a Scriptural admonition at all. What began as a trickle with evangelicalism became a stream with neo-evangelicalism, which has merged into a

---

[252] Gilley, op. cit., 2 ("The Kingdom of Emergent Theology—Part 1).
[253] The so-called universal fatherhood of man is false. Consider:. Jn. 8:42, 44, Mat. 23:9—speaking to the disciples who were believers; ecumenically—Rev. 13, 14:9, etc.—a one world government and religion is coming; joining hands with the "world" and with other religions such as Buddhism, Islam, Hinduism, is the same force bringing all under one banner "*in the last day.*"

flooding river in the postmodern emerging church movement.[254] Separation is completely abandoned except when confronted by widely publicized error that must be addressed, or a church would look extremely foolish if it did not take action (e.g. Jimmy Swaggert, Jim Baker, Ted Haggard debacles).

The third very significant problem is the tendency for postmodernists to believe that the Kingdom of God is their responsibility.[255] They assume their good works will bring about the return of Christ and the kingdom of heaven on earth. However, Dr. Gilley has pointed out the essentially historical demise of similar beliefs that were held by postmillennialists and amillennialists until the mid-twentieth century.

Man is not getting "better," which is obvious from the explosion of blasphemy, wars, fornication, and crime around the world. Furthermore, dispensationalism has already demonstrated:

(1) the failure of man in every dispensation to live-up to God's revealed standard,[256]
(2) the separation of the church from Israel; therefore, the promises are still future for Israel,[257]
(3) the chaos and turmoil of the seventieth week of Daniel (The Great Tribulation lasting seven years) is still future, and
(4) the failure of man's good works to bring about utopia.

---

[254] For example, the Scriptural warnings clearly taught such as Rom. 16:17-18, 1 Thess. 5:21, 2 Tim. 2:17, 2 Cor. 6:17, 2 Jn. 10-11, 2 Thess. 3:6, 14, and many other places.
[255] Gilley, op. cit., 2-9 ("The Kingdom of Emergent Theology—Part 1).
[256] Charles C. Ryrie, *Dispensationalism Today* (Moody Press, Chicago, IL, 1965) 38.
[257] Dwight Pentecost, *Things To Come* (Durham Publishing Company, Grand Rapids, MI, 1958) 88-89.

However, the emerging church movement picks up the old, faulty ideas and clearly:

(1) opposes premillennialism,

(2) champions Replacement Theology, which falsely declares the church replaced Israel in God's plan, and

(3) presents a confused exegesis of the Kingdom of God.

They deny that the Kingdom of God will be brought to earth by the Lord Jesus Christ when He comes at the end of the Tribulation (seventieth week of Daniel) to establish His throne on earth for one thousand years.[258] The "young" postmodern pastors, promoting Christ's return after man corrects and resolves problems on earth, are so anti-Biblical that further comment is not warranted. Certainly, this false belief detracts from God's glory. God alone is capable of bringing about peace because:

> *"The heart is deceitful above all things, and desperately wicked: who can know it?" (Jeremiah 17:9).*

What is Their Source of Authority?

There is an obvious dilemma to all of this concerning the postmodern emerging church: "What is their authority?" There seems to be a gauzy claim of "community," which determines its direction by either a democracy or republic type of decision-making, but by individuals with MANY eclectic secular and religious beliefs. Although they claim the Lord Jesus Christ through experience," they certainly deny His Words, which are the foundation of His precise contract with man. However, every

---

[258] J. Dwight Pentecost, *Things To Come, A Study in Biblical Eschatology* (Academie Books, Grand Rapids, MI, Zondervan Publishing House, 1958) 433ff. The entire book should be read very carefully by the proponents of the emerging church movement to correct their un-Scriptural eschatology.

church is so dramatically different that it is obvious that their 'authority' is as fluid as water.

Renald E. Showers, writing about the emerging church, says:

> "Is the source of authority to be (1) a market-driven philosophy; (2) the opinions of the people in the pews; (3) God, through the revelation He has given in Scripture concerning the church?"[259]

Some other thoughts need to be added to these questions that the emerging church should answer:

(1) which Hebrew/Aramaic/Greek text is to be used as the *received* Words of God—the Masoretic Hebrew Text/Greek Textus Receptus (RT) underlying the KJB or some other text such as the UBS/NA texts, which differ by 8,000 words from the RT in the NT alone and by 20,000 to 30,000 recommended changes in the OT;

(2) which version of the Bible, since there are such widely different techniques used to translate—verbal/formal equivalent or dynamic equivalent;

(3) what determines the doctrines that apply to the individual:
   (a) your constructed "community" doctrines or
   (b) the Words preserved by the nation Israel and the sanctified churches?

Throughout history, men of faith in the Lord Jesus Christ have considered the revealed truth in Scripture as the sole authority for God's assemblies in the Old Testament and the local church. A church is God's assembly. Therefore, the administration and organization of the church comes under His authority. What is the reason so many "emerging

---

[259] Renald E. Showers, "Critical Issues Facing Today's Churches" (*Israel My Glory*, Friends of Israel Gospel Ministry, Westville, NJ, September/October, 2007) 10.

churches" changed their names and concept to a "community?" Is it to match their new definition as a "community" of people that believe diverse doctrines, precepts, ways, judgments, laws, concepts, etc., which are remarkably different from the Bible? Of course, it is! This is the postmodernist's way of escaping God's authority. They realize that if it is not called a church, they can manipulate the organization and administration in order not to be held accountable to Biblical doctrine. God said:

> *"And hath put all things under his [Christ's] feet, and gave him **to be the head over all things to the church**," (Ephesians 1:22)*

Hummmm! The only way the postmodernists can put away this clear statement is to deny that the Bible is Truth, which is the inspired, complete, infallible, inerrant, and perfect *"voice of the wor*ds of God," preserved as He promised. Is it any wonder that the Hebrew Masoretic and Greek Traditional/Received Texts are rejected with every lame excuse and concocted theory possible? The church is a "called out" assembly, which is to be holy unto God through obedience to His Words (Truth, Jn. 17:17) and with the responsibility to "*receive*" and "*keep*" (preserve) His Words (Jn. 14:15, 21-23, 1 Thess. 2:13). There are significant warnings in the Scriptures to those who do not *receive* the truth; for example:

> *"And with all deceivableness of unrighteousness in them that perish; because they **received not** the love of **the truth**, that they might be saved" (2 Thessalonians 2:10). "Now we command you, brethren, in the name of our Lord Jesus Christ, that ye withdraw yourselves from every brother that walketh disorderly, and not after **the tradition** which he **received** of us" (2 Thessalonians 3:6).*

Visual Orientation

Another feature of the postmodern church that must be considered is the change from the preaching/teaching/verbal to the image/sacrament/verbal presentation of Christianity. The postmodernists emphasize the image characteristics of Biblical language and passages such as:

(1) Christ is the "express image" of the invisible Father,
(2) the tabernacle is an image of God's "home" in heaven and of Christ,
(3) the striking imagery of smoke, fire, and thunder at Mount Sinai demonstrated God's power,
(4) general revelation calls upon creation to create a picture of God's glory, abilities, and power,
(5) Jesus is the image of the Word, o [lo<goj, etc., to justify their image-oriented worship. They call upon the second Decalogue *"Thou shalt not make unto thee any graven image, or any likeness of any thing that is in heaven above, or that is in the earth beneath, or that is in the water under the earth:"* (Ex. 20:4) as only a warning not to worship inanimate idols.

However, they fail to identify several important problems when image-communication becomes a significant means to convey a message:

(1) The image may lose preciseness and specificity.
(2) Image presentations such as plays, movies, character acting may become theatrical entertainment rather that WORSHIP.
(3) The inspired Words of Scripture become secondary to the image/media display.

This last feature will further corrupt the message/contract from God to and with man by eliminating very specific, precise, preserved Words. If anyone reading this believes that image/media presentation of the Scripture is only theoretical, then please see the next quote concerning the future plans of the American Bible Societies.

> "Another organization deeply concerned about this media raised generation is the American Bible Society. Lately the Society has been asking the question, "How can the message of the Holy Scriptures be faithfully translated and communicated from one medium to another?" Or to put it another way, is it possible to make a video version of the Bible that has as much authority as a print version of the Bible? This is a rather interesting question, which the Society has answered in the affirmative. Beginning in 1989 the Society launched an experiment to test the limit and possibilities of a screen translation and has since come to the conclusion that 'screen and electronic technologies could transfer and inculturate the very message of the Holy Scriptures and do so with faithfulness and integrity."[260]

Replacement of Orthodox Terminology

A final note of caution is warranted concerning the postmodern emerging church. They are changing the usual words that classical orthodox theology and Scripture use to identify concepts and doctrines. For example, they rarely use the word church. They have replaced it with "community" (of believers). They rarely use the word "truth" or doctrine.

Any one reading their material will soon realize that they have dropped the usual doctrinal words because the words conjure up so many negative feelings, which have developed from the failure(s) of the "church age." Of course, every dispensation has ended in the failure of man. This dispensation is not any different. But should classical doctrinal or identifying words be changed? Are they being changed to try and attract "unsuspecting" seekers into a fellowship? Could this add to and hasten the

---

[260] Arthur W. Hunt III, *The Vanishing Word, The Veneration of Visual Imagery in the Postmodern World* (Crossway Books, Wheaton, IL, 2003) 207.

failure of this age? You decide. Here are some examples without explanation.

Classical Word	Postmodern Word
Church	Community
Pastor	Narrator
Testimony	Web of belief
Spirituality	Activism
Prayer	Quietism
Bible	Book of the community
True	Real
Preaching the Word church	Alphabet community
Scripture	The metaphor-conveyed transcendent reality of Him and His kingdom
Written Bible	Language of Gutenberg book
Evangelical	wholistic
Old Testament Books	Hortatory (urging a course of action) discourse
New Testament Gospels	Peepholes
Context appeals	Nebulous appeals
Born-again	Transformation
Rationality of discourse	Ascendance of image
Bible	Symbolic language book

Does anyone believe that the assault on the preserved inspired Hebrew, Aramaic, and Greek Words behind the King James Bible will not grow exponentially worse? The assault will be enhanced by the conscience being considered the *"voice of the Lord."* Freedom and liberty from the "contract' with God are producing ridiculous and harmful proclamations by churches. For example, these statements were found on the websites of two postmodern churches. First, Mars Hill Church in Seattle, Washington, where Mark Driscoll is pastor:

> **"What We Believe**
> When it comes to doctrine, culture, preferences, traditions, lifestyles, politics, behavior, etc., Mars Hill Church takes a "closed-hand/open-hand" approach. The

closed hand hangs onto the non-negotiable tenets of Christian orthodoxy: sin is the problem, Jesus is the answer, the Bible s true, and Hell is hot.

The open hand, however, allows room for differences when it comes to secondary matters; we liberally allow freedom for conscience and wisdom to guide where the Bible is silent. The open hand fosters unity among the diversity of expressions found in the Mars Hill congregation: Democrats and Republicans, soccer moms and indie rockers, carnivores and vegans, trendy bohemians and Microsoft nerds.

Hence, Mars Hill Church is in favor of good beer (in moderation), great sex (in marriage), and even tattoos (Jesus has one). But our goal must always be love and concern for our friends so that we don't enjoy our freedom at the expense of their faith.

In this way, we are seeking to simultaneously heed the Bible's commands to have sound doctrine (1Timothy 4:16; Titus 1:9, 2:1), to love our Christian brothers and sisters (1 Peter 4:8; 1 John 4:7-21), and to avoid unnecessary divisions (Romans 16:17; 1 Corinthians 1:10, 12:25; Titus 3:10)."[261] (HDW, my emphasis).

The second website for Summit Church, Durham, North Carolina, pastored by J. D. Greear contains the following incorrect beliefs concerning the Bible. In addition, they demonstrate their confusion because they mention their used of the corrupted version, the New Living Translation (NLT)[262]:

"We believe the Bible to be God's Word, a true and fully accurate account of God's love for us. Its purpose is to teach

---

[261] Mars Hills Church, "What We Believe" (http://www.marshillchurch.org/content/WhatWeBelieve).
[262] For example, Summit Church quotes the NLT: "Since you excel in so many ways-you have so much faith, such enthusiasm, and such love for us-now I want you to excel also in this gracious ministry of giving." (2 Cor 8:7) (NLT) at this site: http://www.summitchurch.cc/templates/System/details.asp?id=29456&PID=371893

us how to have a relationship with Him, worship Him and bring Him glory. The Holy Bible was written by men divinely inspired and is God's revelation of Himself to man. It is a perfect treasure of divine instruction. It has God for its author, salvation for its end, and truth, without any mixture of error, for its matter. Therefore, all Scripture is totally true and trustworthy. It reveals the principles by which God judges us, and therefore is, and will remain to the end of the world, the true center of Christian union, and the supreme standard by which all human conduct, creeds, and religious opinions should be tried. All Scripture is a testimony to Christ, who is Himself the focus of divine revelation."[263]

The Bible is God's perfect Words, which tell us of His love, but also of His judgment. The men who wrote the Bible were not inspired, the Words they recorded were.

A Significant Cause For Failure of Postmodernism

One of the most significant reasons postmodernism will fail is the use of false, perverse, dynamic equivalent translations by the seeker-sensitive and emerging churches, which are only man's corruptions and false interpretations promoted and peddled as the Words of God. Therefore, instead of illumination by the Spirit, hunches arise which are light years apart from the proper hermeneutics and exegesis of God's Words. One example should suffice. The example should also demonstrate why the postmodernists are claiming Islam, Hinduism, and other false religions can lead to God. In John 6:47, Gods' words *received* and properly translated say:

---

[263] This quote was combined from two sites from their web pages: http://www.summitchurch.cc/templates/System/details.asp?id=29456&PID=322311&Style= and
http://www.summitchurch.cc/templates/System/details.asp?id=29456&PID=455939&Style=#I

*Verily, verily, I say unto you, He that believeth **on me** hath everlasting life. John 6:47*

If *"on me"* is left out, which it is in many new versions, then you can believe or have faith in the tenets of the Muslims, who claim their heretical religion leads to God. Or, for that matter, someone can have faith in any religious beliefs or god(s) and you will "get to God" or "get to heaven." This is the loud claim of postmodernists—any religion can be true and contain truth, which leads to God. This false belief permeates our society. President George Bush recently offered his belief that Muslims and Hindus worship the same God.

> "In an interview with Al Arabiya reporter Elie Nakouzi, Bush said, 'I believe that all the world, whether they be Muslim, Christian, or any other religion, prays to the same God.'"[264]

Also, to carry it even further, the act of believing itself becomes more important than the object of belief. It is only important that you are a person of "faith" (in anything).

Shocking New Reports

The evidence is accumulating that the postmodern churches are failing. A recent report by Bob Burney at Baptist Press identifies a study conducted by Willow Creek Community Church's executive pastor Greg Hawkins and co-author Cally Parkinson called *"Reveal: Where Are You?"* The book discloses:

---

[264] Pastor Chuck Baldwin, "Can a Christian Pray To Allah?" (October 9, 2007 newsletter, Bible For Today Baptist Church, from an original article that appeared on www.worldnetdaily.com /news/article.sap?ARTICLE_ID=58026).

"that most of what they have been doing for these many years and what they have taught **millions of others to do** is not producing solid disciples of Jesus Christ. Numbers yes, but not disciples."[265]

Burney reports that the significant failures of Willow Creek Pastor Bill Hybels and his ministry staff are on equal par with the failure of Benjamin Spock's child-rearing principles, which turned out "brats."

Hybels' shocking confession admits:

"We made a mistake. What we should have done when people crossed the line of faith and become Christians, we should have started telling people and teaching people that they have to take responsibility to become 'self feeders.' We should have gotten people, taught people, how to read their Bible between services, how to do the spiritual practices much more aggressively on their own."[266]

Programs by the seeker-sensitive and emerging churches receive millions of dollars. For what?

"Just as Spock's "mistake" was no minor error, so the error of the seeker-sensitive movement is monumental in its scope. **The foundation of thousands of American churches is now discovered to be mere sand....The extent of this error defies measurement**."[267]

In spite of reports like these, the emerging churches of today will continue along an obvious failed path. What is wrong with the "old paths?"

---

[265] Bob Burney, "FIRST-PERSON: A shocking confession from Willow Creek Community Church leaders"
(http://www.bpnews.net/bpnews.asp?id=26768) accessed 11/10/07.
[266] Ibid.
[267] Ibid.

*"Thus saith the LORD, Stand ye in the ways, and see, and ask for the old paths, where is the good way, and walk therein, and ye shall find rest for your souls. **But they said, We will not walk therein**" (Jer. 6:16).*

Statistics Support the Harm Postmodernism is Causing

In order to demonstrate the effects of postmodernism and support the tenets of this work, some significant statistics are presented below so that the reader can appreciate the changes taking place in America and around the world. Dr. David Cloud makes the following report that demonstrates one of the primary effects of postmodern philosophy in a Society:

> "According to a new religious survey England is a nation of doubters. Only 28% of those polled said they believed in a personal God, and 42% said they believe that religion has a harmful effect. An amazing 74% of those polled said they pray never or hardly at all ("Religion causes harm, says poll," Sunday Times, Sept. 2, 2007). The YouGov survey was commissioned by John Humphrys, a broadcaster and writer who describes himself as a "doubter" and who authored a sad new book "In God We Doubt." The root problem in England is its apostate and deeply compromised churches. It is a nation of churches and once was a nation of church goers. Its sovereign takes an oath to "maintain the Laws of God and the true profession of the Gospel." The British Crown and Orb are surmounted by crosses, the one on the Orb representing the Sovereign's role as Defender of the Christian Faith. At his or her ordination the British sovereign bears two sceptres signifying the rule of Christ in England, the Sceptre with the Cross in the right hand, and the Sceptre with the Dove (representing the Holy Spirit) in the left hand. The nation thus professes faith in Christ, but because its churches, as a rule, do not preach the new birth and the fear of God, the land has been taken over by the world, the flesh, and the devil. Self is its god; rock & roll is its religion;

humanism is its faith; lady luck is its hope; new age is its spirituality; and political correctness is its conscience."[268]

Dr. Gilley in his book, *This Little Church Stayed Home,* reports:

"A few years ago Barna Research Group documented that two thirds of Americans do not believe in absolute truth (this number recently rose to 78 %.) To claim to believe absolute truth does not exist is a self-contradiction in itself, for that claim must be based on a belief in something that is true—in the case that truth does not exist...But it gets worse, for the same Barna poll showed that 53 percent of evangelical Christians believe there are no absolutes."[269]

Some claim that the narcissistic hedonism of modernism, which has carried over into postmodernism, is crumbling because of the prevalence of AIDS. However, the evidence is just the opposite. Homosexuality, adultery, and fornication of every type are accelerating in the postmodern world.

Dr. Chuck Missler reports the following comments and statistics in a report called "The Vortex," an MP3 download:

"Where is the most dangerous place for an American to be? In their mother's womb. One in four Americans is murdered there. There are 48 million legal abortions since Roe versus Wade in 1973.
- 1.6 million abortions per year
- 4, 883 abortions per day

---

[268] Dr. David Cloud, "New Survey in England Shows a Nation of Doubters" (Fundamental Baptist Information Service, Friday Church News Notes, September 7, 2007, www.wayoflife.org fbns@wayoflife.org). In this same report, the invasion of pagan religions because of postmodernism is exemplified by this statement: "2007 is a sad milestone in U.S. history, for this was the year that a Hindu first offered prayers in the U.S. Senate as well as in the California and Nevada state Senates."
[269] Gary E. Gilley, *This Little Church Stayed Home, A Faithful Church in Deceptive Times* (Evangelical Press USA, Webster, NY, 2006) 35-36.

- 183 abortions per hour
- 3 abortions per minute

Every 20 seconds an unborn child is murdered in the womb of its mother. The Index of leading cultural indicators over the last 30 years demonstrates:
- 560 % increase in violent crime
- 400% increase in illegitimate births
- 400% increase in the divorce rate
- 300% increase in single-parent homes
- 200% increase in teenage suicides
- 75% drop in SAT scores.

These figures are from the Heritage Foundation in 1993 (We know from current news reports that these figures are increasing exponentially). We lead the industrialized world in murder, rape and violent crime. In elementary and secondary education we are near the bottom in achievement scores. There is a coarseness, callousness, cynicism, banality and vulgarity signaling the decivilization of our nation. Each day in America:
- 2,795 teen pregnancies
- 1006 teen abortions
- 4,219 teenagers contract sexually transmitted diseases
- Every 64 seconds a baby is born to a teenage mother.
- Five minutes later, a baby will have been born to a teenager who already has a child.
- 10 hours later 560 babies will have been born to teenagers.
- We murder babies that are socially inconvenient.
- We change marriage partners like fashion statements
- Homosexuality is just an "alternative lifestyle"
- We have abandoned the sanctity of commitment in all our relationships

Thomas Jefferson said in 1781, "I tremble for my country when I reflect that God is just; that His justice cannot sleep forever."[270]

If this does not cause you to weep for our country, I do not know what will. Postmodernism is wrecking havoc on our 'way of life', our churches, our economy, and our relationships. If these stats are adjusted for population growth, they are significantly worse. God is not mocked. There are abundant warnings throughout His Words concerning judgment when His commandments, precepts, laws, statutes, or way of life is abandoned.

The Bottom Line For The Postmodern Movement

Here is the problem. The postmodernist does not realize that his claims as declarations of truth defeat his number one proclamation; that is, there is no truth. Nevertheless, the postmodernists views establish that, for them, the individual is the determiner of truth, of morality, and of guilt, which "is ultimately a vain attempt to try to eliminate morality and guilt from human life."[271] Moreover, the postmodernist is always on a "quest" for truth. The postmodernist always asserts in language similar to the following quote that he is a seeker of truth.

"Brian [a leader in the Emerging Church Movement] does not present himself as one with "all the answers, 'but

---

[270] Dr. Chuck Missler, "The Vortex" (Koinonia House, *Twilight's Last Gleaming? Judgment on the Horizon* http://www.khouse.org/ 2007, MP3 download).
[271] MacArthur, op. cit. 13.

rather as a pilgrim thinker seeking after truth in the midst of missional Christian work.'"[272]

He can seek "after truth," but we have the truth in 66 books of the Bible. We do not have to go on a quest for it, or seek it, or try to find it (Deut. 30:14, Isa. 51:5, Rom. 10:8, Heb. 11:3). We have to accept it by faith—every Word of it.

Similarly, in their search for a 'new' orthodoxy, many are claiming that there is much in vogue in past epochs that is wrong and very much in the new epoch of postmodernism that is wrong. However, one soon discovers in the writings of those who write about these issues that they consistently fail to start with Scripture. They consistently fail to mention the two cardinal propositions, which cannot be laid aside:

1. We must, as required by the God of the Bible, start with **faith in something**. He determines the starting point, and the way to get there. Once we start with faith (in something), rather than questions, we soon encounter the bottom-line of faith, the answer to the dilemmas of man; the answer is an eternal person; He is the First and the Last of all "things" seen and unseen. He proved His authority and His power over time, nature, spiritual, and physical 'things' by the miracles recorded in His revelation. He is Someone that all the world should turn to by **faith** for their **faith**. This sounds like circular thinking, but the first "faith" in the preceding sentence is belief and trust in Him who describes Himself as the First and the Last, the Alpha and the Omega, the Beginning and the End. The second "faith" in the sentence above is the body of doctrine in 'a system of faith.' The first faith depends on the second

---

[272] Brian McLaren, *A Generous Orthodoxy* (Zondervan, Grand Rapids, MI, 2004) 13.

faith, and the second faith is derived from the Words from the Person, who is the object of the first faith. The first faith (He) determines the second faith, which comes by faith, by hearing His Words. The second faith cannot be established by man's exegetical manipulation of His Words, rather, by simply reading the literal statements of the second faith (e.g. the gospel, the Ten Commandments, etc.). The problem the postmodernist generates is encouraging "seekers" (their term, but a better term is "sinners") to start with a myriad of fables, genealogies, questions, doubts, and other distortions of man's construction rather than the simple language that a child can understand in the Bible. This brings us to the second cardinal proposition.

2. **There is only one absolute authority**. If one starts by **faith in** THE Person and in His Words, He makes it abundantly clear by His Apostle to the Gentiles, Paul, that salvation from sin to eternal life in heaven (with Him) occurs in **only One way**; there is only one gospel. No questions are to be asked; no uncertainty declared. He is the way. He is the Boss. There is no other authority. He determines the faith (belief and truth in "What") which saves and He also determines the faith by the precise, preserved, inspired Words that determine the doctrines by which belief and trust comes.

These are two axiomatic principles, which cannot be discarded by proposing man's uncertainty in "the way" or suggesting "other ways" to God. The One is dependant on the Other. The Other is dependent on the One. Either starting point will lead you to Truth. His name is above all names, He is the Word of God; He is the Lord Jesus Christ; He elevates His Words above all His name (Psa. 138:2).

Truth is not up for grabs to be determined by whoever can come up with the neatest or most appealing idea, concept, or philosophy. In addition, Truth is not only a message, or concept, or thoughts, it is specific, special, inspired, preserved Words that will be present *"for ever"* for anyone who sincerely desires to know the Truth. The problem for most these days, however, is not desiring the bottom-line, the Scriptures, but desiring power (influence) or freedom from authority. Once a person gives up the desire for power or authority, then he is on his way to finding "THE WAY." There is a *"still, small voice"* and this *"voice of words of the Lord"* will echo *"for ever."*

CHAPTER 7

CONCLUSION

Postmodernism is leaving individuals bankrupt, confused, and sick. Unfortunately, the philosophy that marks this generation will continue into the near future. The theological consequence is called "post-evangelicalism" and "anti-fundamentalism." Liberalism, modernism, and neo-evangelicalism were anchored in recognition that there is truth, **but** the proponents of these non-Christian beliefs insisted that there must be a *selection* of parts of truth as a guide; not all "truth" can always be a guide as cultures changed. For example, one of the major tenets of liberalism as reflected in neo-evangelicalism is **non-separatism**, even though there is or may be disagreement over major doctrines. The call of modernism was to gather under the Lordship of Christ as the only prerequisite to fellowship and worship together. The call of postmodernism is belief in any religious doctrine the individual desires. This is an inviolable prerequisite to fellowship and worshipping together in the emerging church.

The churches that grew up under the banner of neo-evangelicalism soon gave way to the *seeker-sensitive* church, which has given way to the *emerging* church of postmodernism. It seems that marketing for members and donations to the "cause" may be an additional final bottom line for the postmodern church; the alleged sincerity of its promoters aside. "Anything goes" doctrine or "anything goes" behavior or "anything goes" entertainment will appeal to a broad section of society, which will fill the pews again for a while. As noted above, there are many reports that the *seeker-friendly* churches that thrived on *The Purpose Driven Life* and *The Purpose Driven Church* materials are beginning to "die." In the future, the need to fill the pews and for financial support will compel many to "*run to and fro*" promoting whatever appeals to a hedonistic society. We are already seeing this transformation in the postmodern and emerging church. The future is bleak for the assemblies and for the society held in the clutches of such barbarity.

Anchored To The Rock <u>Or</u> Geared To The Times

Pastor D. A. Waite has a good saying, which characterizes the one foot in the church and one foot in the world church of today: "anchored to the rock, geared to the times." Depending on the "times," anything goes to bring people into the "hungry for money" assemblies of the last days, that operate under the alleged purpose of "winning others to Christ." But, their methods are through "easy believism," inappropriate "missional" claims, acceptance of uncertainty in one and only one gospel, worldly "image" entertainment and music, declaring God's love, but avoiding the reality that He is a God of justice, and evading the serious consequences of rebellion against His precise, inspired Words.

The lethal false doctrines and theology of postmodernism and the emerging church are more dangerous than any previous philosophy, not because they are especially "new," but because the innocent believers with a weak conscience can be influenced so easily through rapid dissemination of inappropriate information in this age. Many people are accepting the freedom from authority offered by postmodernism, which proclaims the individuals right to decide "doctrine."

T. A. McMahon recently wrote the following in "The Berean Call."

> "Although there are far too many examples of apostasy influencing the church today...there is one spurious trend that encompasses nearly all of what [these] verses address [2 Tim. 4:3, 4, Pro. 14:12, 2 Cor. 11:13, 15, 1 Tim. 4:1, Acts 20:29, 30). It's called the Emerging Church Movement (ECM)...The Emergent Church Movement claims to desire—above all things—to show the love and life of Christ to a culture that is distrustful of the Christianity it perceives as oppressive and absolutist. We're assured by ECM writers that "numbers of postmoderns are attracted to Jesus but detest His church" and can therefore be reached by the emerging church approach. It professes to be more amenable to the culture, more viable in its practice of Christianity, and truer to what Jesus had in mind for His church on earth."²⁷³ [HDW, my addition].

T. A. McMahon goes on to quote Isaiah 8:20: *"To the law and to the testimony: if they speak not according to this word, it is because there is no light in them."* He also addresses the issues that postmodernists avoid the most, which are the precise descriptions, narratives, or propositions of the *authoritative* Words of Jesus. He states:

> "The **biblical Jesus** certainly does not accommodate postmodernism, which is one more example of humanity's rebellion against its Creator."²⁷⁴

Moreover, this author would add that there is outright rebellion against His Words, which He promised would be available *"for ever."* That means, the Words will not be hidden, secret, far away, lost, questionable, probable, uncertain, or in heaven only, but *absolutely* here for any who would seek Him with all their heart. They may hear *"the voice of the words of God"* at any moment, any time, and any place without an audible, uncertain, mystical, confusing voice leading them astray.

---

[273] T. A. McMahon, Weaning Evangelicals Off the Word – Part 3" (*The Berean Call,* Vol. XXII, No. 9, Sept., 2007) 3.
[274] Ibid. 4.

People Geared To The Times Are Not Fit For The Battle

Whatever belief is held in opposition to the Words of God and to proper hermeneutics—IT ALL STARTS WITH THE CASTING BEHIND THEM OF THE PRECISE, PRESERVED, INERRANT, INSPIRED, AND INFALLIBLE, WORDS OF A HOLY GOD and proclaiming: *"YEA HATH GOD SAID?"* (Gen. 3:1). Another way to view these issues is that those promoting false texts, pseudo-revelations, scripturally inconsistent doctrine, and exegetical manipulations have fallen into the hands of the enemy. They no longer hear *"the joyful sound."* They have forgotten God's voice said: *My covenant will I not break, nor alter the thing that is gone out of my lips* (Psalms 89:34). Because they delight in words which are *"chaff"* (Jer. 23:28), and follow not His lead *"in the way"* (Psa. 119:1, 139:24), they are no longer fit for the battle against the enemy. They have missed the mark. As a result, *"[God] hast also turned the edge of [their] sword, and hast not made [them] to stand in the battle"* (Psalms 89:43). They have forgotten that God's Words from His mouth give prophecy, knowledge, wisdom and understanding of God, heaven, man, angels, hell, etc. but most importantly understanding of His Son, His work on the Cross, grace, mercy and judgment. *"For the LORD giveth wisdom: out of his mouth cometh knowledge and understanding"* (Proverbs 2:6). God clearly calls for man to hearken and hear his Words; we are not to listen to watered down words, or modern day 'so-called' prophets, whose words do not come true. God clearly says, *"Hearken unto me now therefore, O ye children, and attend to the **words** of **my mouth*** (Proverbs 7:24). It is His voice! His Words from His lips are the Words of the Righteous, which feed us; not the words of man. *"The lips of the righteous feed many: but* *fools die for want of wisdom*" (Proverbs 10:21). O' Lord, when will man learn?

C. H. Spurgeon, Prince of Preachers, went through a time when His faith wavered. He began to rely on his own "brain" and his own "reason." He confessed His waywardness and returned to the anchor of His soul and "*the voice of the words of the Lord.*" He said:

> "There was an evil hour when I once shipped the anchor of my faith; I cut the cable of my belief; I no longer moored myself hard by the coasts of **Revelation**; I allowed my vessel to drift before the wind; I said to reason, "Be thou my captain;" I said to my own brain, "Be thou my rudder;" and I started on my mad voyage. **Thank God, it is all over now**... Thou book of vast authority! thou art a proclamation from the Emperor of Heaven; far be it from me to exercise my reason in contradicting thee. Reason, thy place is to stand and find out what this volume means, not to tell what this book ought to say. Come thou, my reason, my intellect, sit thou down and listen, for **these words are the words of God**...This Bible is a book of authority; it is an authorized book, for God has written it. Oh! Tremble, lest any of you despise it; mark its authority, for it is the Word of God. "[275]

Spurgeon used the Authorized Version, the King James Bible. It is time for the wayward philosophers of the postmodern age and their followers to turn from their own brain and reason, and return to "*the voice of the words of the Lord.*" That voice can be heard in the KJB because the English words are accurately translated from the pure Words of the *Received Texts,* the Hebrew Masoretic Text and the Greek Traditional/Received text. Our prayer is that they will return and declare: "Thank God, it is all over now." May they quit wallowing in the mud of human philosophy! May we:

---

[275] C. H. Spurgeon, op. cit., 102-104 ("The Bible").

"say of The Bible:

"God's cabinet of revealed counsel 't is!
Where weal and woe, are ordered so
That every man may know which shall be his;
Unless his own mistake, false application make.

"It is the index to eternity.
He cannot miss of endless bliss.
That takes this chart to steer by,
Nor can he be mistook that speaketh by this book.

"It is the book of God. What if I should
Say, God of books, let him that looks
Angry at that expression, as too bold,
His thought in silence smother, till he find such another."[276]

We Will Not Surrender One Page Or One Word Of Scripture

Those who are claiming to hear the audible voice of God, claiming to see and hear angels who guide them, claiming "new" revelations, "new" prophecies, "new" theology, denying the Holy Spirit's illumination and enlightenment, and denying the inspiration of every jot and tittle of God's Words are in for a surprise very shortly for they are *"strangers."* The cascade of 'new' versions that have resulted from casting away God's Holy Words will soon be upon the heap to be burned when He shall appear in all His glory in His blood stained garments (Isa. 63:1, 3).

> *"And he was clothed with a vesture dipped in blood: and his name is called The Word of God." (Revelation 19:13)*

It was the Word of God who gave us the **Words** that will endure forever and who said **three** times in the Scripture:

---

[276] Ibid. 111.

*"Heaven and earth shall pass away, but **my words shall not pass away**" (Matthew 24:35, Mk. 13:31, Lk. 21:33, and validated elsewhere, e.g. Mat. 5:17-18, Isa. 40:8, 1 Pe. 1:23-25).*

Dean John William Burgon believed:

"He who surrenders the first page of his Bible, surrenders **all**."[277] "The express Revelation of the Eternal is that whereon Theological Science builds her fabric of imperishable Truth: that fabric which, while other modes change, shift, and at last become superseded, shines out,--yea, and to the very end of Time will shine out,--unconscious of decay, incapable of improvement, far, far beyond the reach of fashion: a thing unchanged, because in its very nature unchangeable!"[278]

And the *"voice of the words of the Lord"* says:

*"Hear, O earth: behold, I will bring evil upon this people, even the fruit of their thoughts, because they have not hearkened unto **my words**, nor to my law, but rejected it" (Jeremiah 6:19).*

*"Behold, ye trust in **lying words**, that cannot profit" (Jeremiah 7:8).*

*"Therefore as the fire devoureth the stubble, and the flame consumeth the chaff, so their root shall be as rottenness, and their blossom shall go up as dust: because they have cast away the law of the LORD of hosts, and despised **the word** of the Holy One of Israel" (Isaiah 5:24).*

"Because my people hath forgotten me, they have burned incense to vanity, and they have caused them to stumble in their ways from the ancient paths, to walk in paths, in a way not cast up"(Jeremiah 18:15).

---

[277] Dean John William Burgon, *Inspiration and Interpretation* (Dean Burgon Society Press, Collingswood, NJ, originally published 1861, 1999) 50.
[278] Ibid. 120 (Burgon, I and I).

> *"To the law and to the testimony: if they speak not according to **this word**, it is because there is no light in them." (Isaiah 8:20).*
>
> *"I will worship toward thy holy temple, and praise thy name for thy lovingkindness and for thy truth: **for thou hast magnified thy word above all thy name**" (Psalms 138:2)* [279]

We have been given through *inspiration* and by *preservation* the inerrant, infallible *"voice of the words of the Lord"* by means of *revelation*, which are *illuminated* by the Holy Spirit. His Words have been called precious, incomparable, awesome, incredible, wonderful, eternal, blessed, holy, perfect, great, precise, healing, glorious, mighty, comforting, beautiful, delightful, powerful, unique, and on and on we could go, by some of the greatest saints in history.

Some individuals will claim that (1) this work and the *"old paths"* are hardhearted and cold. (2) The Words accurately and faithfully translated in the King James Bible are "hard to read." (3) We must adjust to the culture to win some to Christ.

This author asserts that (1) prosperity and hedonism in this present age has engendered an immaturity among most postmodernists, which will soon be challenged. (2) Their need, which is characterized by the oft-repeated refrain, "I just want to have fun," will never be fulfilled by

---

[279] Dr. Thomas Strouse, "Christ's Use of Targums" (Emmanuel Baptist Theological Seminary, Newington, CT). In this article, Dr. Strouse points out that some have criticized the translation of this verse from Hebrew into English by the KJB. However, Dr. Strouse points out that "the Hebrew is quite elementary even for first year Hebrew students, the KJV gives the only possible formal equivalent translation, and the Lord Jesus Christ did indeed submit Himself to the written Hebrew text preserved in His lifetime." page 7. The Lord Himself frequently appealed to the Hebrew Scriptures, saying: "It is written," "In the law," etc. Shouldn't we appeal to the preserved, inerrant, inspired, infallible Words of God?

their idols, vain entertainment, rock and rap music, technology (ipods, etc) and emotionally generated forms of worship.

Their association of the peaceful countenance of a man, who is "settled" on many things of God, with a lack of feelings or enthusiasm, can only be challenged by the information shared with this author by others and by his own experience. Many men and women have related to me the times that they have shed tears as they have studied to understand, as they have prayed for forgiveness for their failures, and as they have pleaded for this generation's return to the "*old paths,*" earnestly appealing to a Holy God who has declared:

> "*Is not my word **like as a fire**? saith the LORD; and **like a hammer** that breaketh the rock in pieces?" Jeremiah 23:29*

If you have not experienced the fire and power of His Words in "*the old paths*" while contemplating them in the quietness of your prayer closet, then perhaps you need to listen to God:

> "*Thus saith the LORD, Stand ye in the ways, and see, and **ask for the old paths**, where is the good way, and walk therein, and ye shall find rest for your souls. But they said, We will not walk therein.*"(Jeremiah 6:16)

May we all share the message of Christ, "*the voice of His words,*" through and by **THE OLD PATHS. The 'new' way is not working.**

AMEN!!

H. D. Williams, M. D., Ph.D.

BIBLIOGRAPHY

Achtemeier, Paul J. *Harper's Bible Dictionary.* San Francisco, CA. Harper & Roe. Society of Biblical Literature: 1st Edition. 1985.

American Tract Society Dictionary, "Conscience" Broken Arrow, OK. *ATSD, A Dictionary of the Holy Bible.* American Tract Society. 1859. SwordSearcher, Ver. 5.1.1.1, 2007.

Armerding, Carl. "The Power of the Word." *Bibliotheca Sacra.* Dallas, TX. Volume 116. Dallas Theological Seminary. 1959. Logos. 2002.

Armstrong, John. Home page, http://www.johnharmstrong.typepad.com/

Sparks, T. Austin. *What Is Man?* Indianapolis, IN. Premium Literature Company. Unknown date. May be ordered from Testimony Book Ministry, Washington, D.C.

Barnes, Albert. *Notes on the Old Testament, Explanatory and Practical.* Broken Arrow, OK. SwordSearcher, Ver. 5.1.1.1. Originally published sometime between 1832-1872. 2007.

Baldwin, Pastor Chuck. "Can a Christian Pray To Allah?" October 9, 2007 newsletter, Bible For Today Baptist Church, from an original article that appeared on www.worldnetdaily.com /news/article.sap?ARTICLE_ID=58026).

Black, Henry Campbell, M A. *Black's Law Dictionary, Definitions of the Terms and Phrases of American and English Jurisprudence, Ancient and Modern.* St. Paul, MN, 5th Editon, West Publishing Company. 1979.

Blackaby, Henry. *Experiencing God.* Nashville, TN. Broadman and Holman Publishers.

Blackaby, Henry and Richard. *Hearing God's Voice.* Nashville, TN. Broadman and Holman Publishers. 2002.

Brandenburg, Kent, Editor. *Thou Shalt Keep Them.* El Sobrante, CA. Pillar and Ground Publishing. 2003.

Bridgeland, John; John J. Dilulio, Jr.; Karen Burke Morrison. "The Silent Epidemic, Perspectives of High School Dropouts, A Report by Civic Enterprises with Peter D. Hart Research Associates." Bill and Melinda Gates Foundation. March. 2006.

Brown, Harold O. J. *Heresies, Heresy and Orthodoxy In The History of the Church.* Peabody, MA. Hendrickson Publishers. 1988.

Browne, D. D, Rt. Rev. Edward Harold. *The Inspiration of Holy Scripture.* New York, NY. S. W. Green Printers. T. Whittaker, 2 Bible House. 1878. originally printed in a series of Theological Essays entitled, "Aids to Faith."

Burgon, Dean John. *The Last Twelve Verses of Mark, Vindicated Against Recent Critical Objections & Established.* Collingswood, NJ. Dean Burgon Society. Originally published 1871, republished 2nd printing, May, 2002.

_____ *The Traditional Text of the Holy Gospels.* Collingswood, NJ. Dean Burgon Society. 1998.

_____ *The Causes of Corruption of the Traditional Text, Vol. II.* Collingswood, NJ. Dean Burgon Society. Originally published 1896, 1998.

_____ *Revision Revised*

_____ *The Traditional Text of the Holy Gospels*

_____ *Inspiration and Interpretation.* Collingswood, NJ. Dean Burgon Society Press. Originally published in 1861. 1999.

Burns, J. Lanier. "Book Reviews." *Bibliotheca Sacra.* Dallas, TX. Dallas Theological Seminary. Volume 154. 1997. Logos, 2002.

Burney, Bob. "FIRST-PERSON: A shocking confession from Willow Creek Community Church leaders." (http://www.bpnews.net/bpnews.asp?id=26768)

Capra, Fritjof. *The Hidden Connections, Integrating the Biological, Cognitive, and Social Dimensions of Life Into A Science of Sustainability.* Doubleday, NY. Random House. 2002.

Carson, D. A. *Becoming Conversant with The Emerging Church, Understanding a Movement and its Implications.* Grand Rapids, MI. Zondervan. 2005.

_____ *The King James Version Debate, A Plea For Realism.* Grand Rapids, MI. Baker Book House. 1979.

Carter, Tom. *Spurgeon at His Best.* Grand Rapids, MI. Baker Book House. 1988.

Chafer, Lewis Sperry. "Revelation." *Bibliotheca Sacra.* Dallas, TX. Vol. 94. Dallas Theological Seminary. 1937. Logos. 2002.

_____ "Anthropology, Part V." Dallas, TX. *Bibliotheca Sacra,* Volume 101. Dallas Theological Seminary. 1944. Logos, 2002.

_____ *Systematic Theology,* Vol. 1. Grand Rapids, MI. Kregel Publications, originally published 1948. 1976.

Cloud, Dr. David. "Charismatic Movement Continuing To Spread Among Southern Baptists." Port Huron, MI. FBIS. Way of Life Literature. 5/11/07.

_____ "CHUCK COLSON AND ROME" Port Huron, MI. Fundamental Baptist Information Service. P.O. Box 610368. 866-295- 4143. fbns@wayoflife.org. First published October 14, 2002. Updated April 18, 2007

_____ "Paradise Gathering: Another Ecumenical Rock & Roll Fest." Port Huron, MI. FBIS. Way of Life Literature. Friday

Church News. 6/09/07.

———"THE ECUMENICAL THRUST OF THE NATIONAL DAY OF PRAYER." Friday Church News Notes. May 11, 2007. www.wayoflife.org

———"500 CHURCHES AND 67 DENOMINATIONS PARTICIPATE IN FRANKLIN GRAHAM NORFOLK FESTIVAL." Friday Church News Notes, May 25, 2007, www.wayoflife.org fbns@wayoflife.org, 866-295-4143

———"What About Ruckman?" Port Huron, MI. Way Of Life Literature. FBIS. April 19, 2004. http://www.wayoflife.org/articles/ruckman.htm.

———"NEW SURVEY IN ENGLAND SHOWS A NATION OF DOUBTERS." www.wayoflife.org. fbns@wayoflife.org. *Fundamental Baptist Information Service.* Friday Church News Notes. September 7, 2007.

———"Charismatic Movement Continuing To Spread Among Southern Baptists." www.wayoflife.org. fbns@wayoflife.org. *Fundamental Baptist Information Service.* Friday Church News Notes. 5/11/07.

———"FAMOUS ATHEIST PUBLISHES BOOK DESCRIBING "CONVERSION." Friday Church News Notes, November 9, 2007, www.wayoflife.org fbns@wayoflife.org.

——— "Part I, New Evangelicalism." Port Huron, MI. Way of Life Literature, Fundamental Baptist Information Service. 2001. http://www.wayoflife.org/fbns/fundamen1.htm.

Cobb, John. http://en.wikipedia.org/wiki/John_B._Cobb.

Comfort, Phil. *Encountering The Manuscripts, An Introduction to New Testament Paleography and Textual Criticism.* Nashville, TN. Broadman and Holman Publishers. 2005.

——— *Essential Guide to Bible Versions.* Wheaton, IL. Tyndale House Publishers, Inc. 2000.

Congdon, Roger Douglass. "The Doctrine of Conscience." *Bibliotheca Sacra.* Dallas, TX. Vol. 102, 103. Dallas Theological Seminary. Logos. 2002.

Dana, H. E. and Julius R. Mantey. *A Manual Grammar of the Greek New Testament.* New York, NY. The Macmillan Co. 1927. © 1955.

Dawkins, Richard. *The Blind Watchmaker.* NY, NY. W. W. Norton & Company. Reissue edition, September 1996.

Dockery, David S., Editor. *The Challenge of Postmodernism: An Evangelical Engagement.* Wheaton, IL. Victor Books, Bridgepoint. 1995.

Ehrman, Bart. *Lost Scriptures, Books that Did Not Make It into the*

New Testament. New York, NY. Oxford University Press. 2003.

_____*Lost Christianities, The Battle for Scripture and the Faiths We Never Knew*. New York, NY. Oxford University Press. 2003.

Edersheim, Alfred. *The Life and Times Of Jesus The Messiah*. Peabody, MA. Henrickson Publishers. Originally published in 1883, republished in 1993.

Erickson, Millard J. *The Postmodern World, Discerning the Times and the Spirit of Our Age*. Wheaton, IL. Crossway Books, a division of Good News Publishers. 2002.

Foucault Michael. Home page. http://www.csun.edu/~hfspc002/foucault.home.html

Franke, John. http://www.biblical.edu/pages/discover/faculty-directory.htm.

Gill, Dr. John. *Exposition of the Old and New Testaments, Exposition of the Whole Bible*. Broken Arrow, OK. WordSearch, Ver. 5.1.1.1. 2007.

Gilley, Gary E., Ph.D., *Is That You Lord? Hearing the Voice of the Lord, A Biblical Perspective*. Webster, NY. Evangelical Press. 2007.

_____ *This Little Church Stayed Home, A Faithful Church in Deceptive Times*. Webster, NY. Evangelical Press USA. 2006.

Grenz, Stanley J. Home page, http://www.stanleyjgrenz.com/index2.shtml.

Grisham, Lowell. "Journeying Toward the Mystery: The Contemplative Practice of Centering Prayer, Step by Step." (http://www.explorefaith.org/prayer/essays/center.html).

Hammett, John S. "AN ECCLESIOLOGICAL ASSESSMENT OF THE EMERGING CHURCH MOVEMENT." http://ateam.blogware.com/AnEcclesiologicalAssessment.Hammett.pdf

Henry, Carl F. H. "Postmodernism, The New Spectra?" Essay in *The Challenge of Postmodernism: An Evangelical Engagement*. Wheaton, IL. Victor Books, Bridgepoint. 1995.

Herzig, Steve. "The Emerging Church: What is it?." *Israel My Glory*. The Friends of Israel Gospel Ministry, Inc. September/October, 2007.

HighBeam. http://www.highbeam.com/doc/1O56-logocentrism.html.

Hodges, Zane. "Post-Evangelicalism Confronts The Postmodern Age, A Review of The Challenge of Postmodernism." *The Journal of the Grace Evangelical Society*. Vol. 9. The Grace Evangelical Society. 1996.

Hunt, III, Arthur W. *The Vanishing Word, The Veneration of Visual Imagery in the Postmodern World*. Wheaton, IL. Crossway

Books. 2003.
Hunt, Dave. *Occult Invasion, The Subtle Seduction of the World and Church.* Eugene, OR. Harvest House Publishers. 1998.
International Standard Bible Encyclopedia. "Bath Kol." Broken Arrow, OK. SwordSearcher, Ver. 5.1.1.1
Ironside, H. A. 1 Corinthians.
Jasmin, Dr. Don. "Essential Books on Dispensationalism." *The Fundamental Digest.* West Branch, MI. Vol. 16, Number 3. June-July, 2007.
Jones, Floyd Nolen, Th.D. Ph.D. *Which Version Is The Bible.* Goodyear, AZ. Kings World Press. 2006.
Kelly, William. *Gospel of Matthew.*
Kelso, James L. "Abraham As Archaeology Knows Him Part II — Abraham the Spiritual Genius." *Bible and Spade,* Vol. 2. Associates for Biblical Research. 1973. Logos. 2005.
Khoo, *Dr.* Jeffery, Dean, Far Eastern Bible College. Singapore. *Burning Bush. Vol. 12, Number 2. July, 2006.*
_____ "FEBC Faculty United on Verbal Plenary Preservation (VPP)." Singapore. *The Burning Bush.* Vol. 13, Nu. 2. July, 2007.
_____ Canon, Texts, and Words: Lost and Found or Preserved and Identified?" Singapore. *The Burning Bush.* Vol. 13, Nu. 2. July, 2007.
Kimball, Dan. *The Emerging Church, Vintage Christianity For New Generations.* Grand Rapids, MI. Zondervan. 2003.
MacArthur, John. *The Truth War, Fighting for Certainty in an Age of Deception.* Nashville, TN. Thomas Nelson. 2007.
Machen, J. Gresham. *Christianity and Liberalism.* Grand Rapids, MI. Wm. B. Eerdmans Publishing Company. 1923.
McCheyne, Robert Murray. "Grieve Not The Holy Spirit." Broken Arrow, OK. *Great Preaching.* SwordSearcher, Ver. 5.1.1.1. 2007.
McLaren, Brian. *A Generous Orthodoxy.* Grand Rapids, MI. Zondervan. 2004.
McMahon, Dr. C. Matthew. "Evangelical Postmodern Diversification." www.apuritansmind.com/HistoricalTheology/McMahonEvangelicalPostmodernDiversification.htm
McMahon, T. A. "Weaning Evangelicals Off the Word – Part 3" *The Berean Call,* Vol. XXII, No. 9, Sept., 2007.
Mader, Max W. "A Famine of the Word of God" http://avoiceinthewilderness.org/snotes/sermon83.html
Martin, Walter. *The Kingdom of the Cults.* Bloomington MI. Ravi Zacharias, General Editor. Bethany House Publishers. 2003.

Missler, Chuck. "The Vortex" Koinonia House, Twilight's Last Gleaming? Judgment on the Horizon http://www.khouse.org. MP3 download. 2007.

Moore, Quintin D. Senior Pastor, The Father's House. "What is a Convergence Church?" (http://www.thekingschurch.net/church.pdf, Dec. 2003

———— "Saving Our Youth." Coeur d'Alene, ID. *K-House eNews.* Aug., 14, 2007.

———— "The Failure of Empiricism," *Epistemology, Part 2.* Koinonia House, http://www.khouse.org/articles/2005/563/.

Mohler, Jr., R. Albert. "The Integrity of the Evangelical Tradition and the Challenge of the Postmodern Paradigm" Essay in *The Challenge of Postmodernism: An Evangelical Engagement.* Wheaton, IL. Victor Books, Bridgepoint. 1995.

Moorman, Dr. Jack. *Forever Settled.* Collingswood, NJ. Bible For Today Press. 1999.

———— *Early Manuscripts, Church Fathers, and the Authorized Version.* Collingswood, NJ. Bible For Today Press. 2005.

Murphee, Jon Tal. *Divine Paradoxes, A Finite View of an Infinite God.* Camp Hill, PA. Christian Publications, Inc. 1998.

Nee, Watchman. *Secrets of Spiritual Power.* Sunneytown, PA. Whitaker House. 1999.

Oden, Thomas C. "The Death of Modernity and Postmodern Evangelical Spirituality" Wheaton, IL. Essay by Dr. Oden in *The Challenge of Postmodernism: An Evangelical Engagement.* Victor Books, Bridgepoint. 1995.

Office of Juvenile Justice and Delinquency Prevention. "The Proliferation of Youth Gangs." U.S. Department of Justice, National Criminal Justice Reference Service. http://www.ncjrs.gov/html/ojjdp/2000_9_2/intro.html). (This page recently removed. Search this site for youth gang activity. http://www.ncjrs.gov/whatsncjrs.html.

Osborn, Professor H. S., LL.D. *A Classic Book of Biblical History and Geography.* SwordSearcher, Ver. 5.1.1.1, Originally published, 1890, 2007

Pentecost, Dwight. *Things To Come.* Grand Rapids, MI. Durham Publishing Company. 1958.

Phillips, John. *Exploring Romans, An Expository Commentary.* Grand Rapids, MI. Kregel Publications. 2002.

Rea, Walter. "Seventh Day Adventist, They Alone View Ellen G. White as Inspired." http://www.bible.ca/7-WhiteInspire.htm

Roberts, Alexander ; Donaldson, James ; Coxe, A. Cleveland. "Clement of Alexandria, 'The Stromata,'" (Miscellanies). Oak

Harbor, CA. *The Ante-Nicene Fathers Vol. I, II : Translations of the Writings of the Fathers Down to A.D. 325*. Book I. II, III, VII, Chapter XVI. Logos Research Systems, 1997.

_____ Irenaeus, *Against Heresies. The Ante-Nicene Fathers Vol. I : Translations of the Writings of the Fathers Down to A.D. 325*. Oak Harbor, CA. Logos Research Systems. 1997.

_____ Introductory Note to *The Pastor of Hermas. The Ante-Nicene Fathers Vol. I : Translations of the Writings of the Fathers Down to A.D. 325*. Oak Harbor, CA. Logos Research Systems. 1997.

Robertson's Word Pictures. SwordSearcher, Ver. 5.1.1.1. 2007.

Rorty, Richard. "Pragmatism is a Philosophical Therapy. It Helps You Stop Asking the Unhelpful Questions." (http://www.believermag.com/issues/200306/?read=interview_rorty

Ryken, Leland. "The Bible as Literature, Part 1: Words of Delight: The Bible as Literature." Dallas, TX. *Bibliosacra Theca*. Vol. 147. Dallas Theological Seminary. 1990. Logos. 2002.

Ryrie, Charles. *Dispensationalism Today*. Chicago, IL. Moody Press. 1965.

Sanders, J. Oswald. *Problems of Christian Discipleship, A Spiritual Clinic*. Chicago, IL. Moody Press. Fifth printing paper back edition, 1961.

_____ *A Spiritual Clinic*. Chicago, IL. Moody Press. 5th printing and edition. 1961.

_____ *A Spiritual Guide*, as quoted by Roy B. Zuck, "The Doctrine of the Conscience" (*Bibliotheca Sacra*, Vol. 126, Dallas Theological Seminary, 1969

Sheffield, Bill. *The Beginnings Under Attack*. Springfield, MO. 21st Century Press. 2003.

Shelstrate, Mike. "Rampant Hedonism, The Destruction of America." Rense.Com, http://www.rense.com/general34/ramg.htm

Showers, Renald E. "Critical Issues Facing Today's Churches." Westville, NJ. *Israel My Glory*. Friends of Israel Gospel Ministry. September/October, 2007.

Solomon, Charles R. *The Ins And Out of Rejection*. Sevierville, TN. Solomon Publications. 1991.

Sparks, T. Austin. *What Is Man?* Indianapolis, IN. Premium Literature Company, unknown date, may be ordered from Testimony Book Ministry, Washington, D.C.

Spurgeon, C. H. "The Bible—Sermon 15." *The Spurgeon Sermon Collection*. The Master Christian Library. Ages Software. 2000.

Strouse, Dr. Thomas. "Christ's Use of Targums" Newington, CT. Emmanuel Baptist Theological Seminary. Dr. Strouse is Dean.

_____ "The Translation Model Predicted by Scripture"

(http://www.emmanuel-newington.org/seminary/resources/KJV_Model.pdf).
Stubb, J. Aall Ottesen. *Verbal Inspiration.* Decorah, Iowa. Lutheran Publishing House. 1915.
Torrey, R. A. *Master Christian Library.* Rio, WI. Ages Software, Ver. 8.
Vance, Laurence M., Ph.D. "The Holman Christian Standard Bible (HCSB), The Southern Baptist Bible."
Waite, Pastor D. A., Th.D., Ph.D. *Defending the King James Bible, A Fourfold Superiority: Texts, Translators, Technique, Theology, God's Words Kept Intact in English.* Collingswood, NJ. 2002.
_____*Romans: Preaching Verse by Verse.* Collingswood, NJ. 2005.
_____ *The Heresies of Westcott and Hort, As Seen In Their Own Writings.* Collingswood, NJ. Bible For Today Press. 2004.
Wallace, Dr. Roy. *Studies in Systematic Theology.* Shreveport, LA. LinWel. 2001.
Walvoord, John F. "The Work of the Holy Spirit in the Old Testament." Dallas, TX *Bibliotheca Sacra*, Vol. 97. Dallas Theological Seminary. 1940. Logos, 2002.
Walvoord, John F. "The Work of the Holy Spirit in the Old Testament." Dallas, TX. *Bibliotheca Sacra.* Vol. 97. Dallas Theological Seminary. 1940. Logos. 2002.
Webster, John Webster, "The Cambridge Companion to Karl Barth." http//assets.cambridge.org/052158/4760/sample/0521584760WS.pdf.
John Wesley, "The Witness of The Spirit-Discourse." *Great Preaching.* Swordsearcher. Ver. 5.1.1.1
Williams, H. D., M.D., Ph.D. *Word-For-Word Translating of the Received Texts, Verbal Plenary Translating.* Collingswood, NJ. Bible For Today Press. 2007.
_____ *The Lie That Changed The Modern World.* Collingswood, NJ. The Bible For Today Press. 2004.
_____ "Postmodernism Versus Scripture." Collingswood, NJ. *Dean Burgon Society News.* Number 80. Dean Burgon Society. April-July. 2007.
Williams, James B., General Editor, Randolph Shaylor, Managing Editor. *God's Words In Our Hands, The Bible Preserved For Us.* Greenville, SC. Ambassador Emerald International. 2003.
Zuck, Roy B. "The Doctrine of the Conscience." Dallas, TX. *Bibliotheca Sacra.* Vol. 126. Dallas Theological Seminary. 1969. Logos. 2002.

Internet Sites

www.deanburgonsociety.org

www.biblefortoday.org

www.emmanuel-newington.org/seminary/resources/

www.wrfnet.org/articles/printarticle.asp?ID=726

www.svchapel.org/Assets/Docs/DoctrinalStatement.pdf.

www.zionist.com/2007/03/22/more-palestinian-children-sacrificed-to-allah.

http://findarticles.com/p/articles/mi_qa3985/is_200109/ai_n8955222

www.ncjrs.gov/html/ojjdp/2000_9_2/intro.html

www.svchapel.org/Resources/BookReviews/book_reviews.asp?ID=300

www.svchapel.org/Resources/BookReviews/book_reviews.asp?ID=195

www.svchapel.org/Resources/articles/read_articles.asp?ID=54

www.bible-researcher.com/canon.html and www.bible-researcher.com/canon3.html

www.columbia.edu/cu/augustine/arch/sbrandt/canon.htm

www.telegraph.co.uk/news/main.jhtml?xml=/news/2007/07/11/ntablet111.xml

www.marshillchurch.org/content/WhatWeBelieve

www.summitchurch.cc/templates/System/details.asp?id=29456&PID=371893

www.summitchurch.cc/templates/System/details.asp?id=29456&PID=322311&Style=

www.summitchurch.cc/templates/System/details.asp?id=29456&PID=455939&Style=#I

ATTACHMENTS

COMPARISON CHARTS

MODERNISM VERSUS POSTMODERNISM VERSUS CHRISTIAN THINKING

I. MODERNISM
(1700's-the latter 20th century)

Philosophy of Scientific Rationalism

A. Persons find meaning through personal growth and achievement.
B. Esteem knowledge and excellence.
C. Seek to understand the order of reality and operate within those boundaries.
D. Argues that there must be reason and intellectual honesty to create rules of fair play and to facilitate the potential for healthy coexistence.
E. Turn outward and suggest the best decisions are based on reason and science. People need to have emotion and will controlled by rules and law.
F. Assign value to knowledge for its own sake and maintains it is always valuable whether to the individual or society.
G. Respect individuals although they may not always be right. Fickleness towards heroes is not seen.
H. Pedantic, factual, linear lectures are effective communications and have influence toward insight, knowledge, and discovery.
I. Spirituality is a corporate and individual experience.
J. Faith is centered on the Being in whom faith is based, or faith is solidly based on mankind's ability through science and rationalism known as the religion of "Humanism".

II. POSTMODERNISM
(late 20th century until ?)

Philosophy Extreme Selfism and Uncertainty

A.   Contend that all striving is worthless and in vain since there is no meaning to be gained and no absolute truth to be understood.
B.   Set their sights on comfortable survival and self-satisfaction.
C.   Claim there is no grand design, that all is based on chance, and people therefore need not recognize the limitations and boundaries that circumscribe the world of the moderns.
D.   Claim the universe is decentralized and there is no ultimate authority beyond oneself. Moral anarchy rules the day. (This means consistent chaos and selfishness.)
E.   Turn inward and suggest that the best decisions are based on human will and emotion. They rely on self.
F.   Do not assign value to knowledge for its own sake. Value of knowledge is when the information has practical applications and is personally meaningful.
G.   Someone earns their respect and credibility day by day, and few retain that level of acceptance for long. There are no heroes. Only 'people' doing their jobs. (Firemen, movie stars, rock bands, etc. do not retain loyalty, fame, or celebrity very long these days.)
H.   Conversation is king and communication is predicated on perceiving it as "being genuine." The goal of communication is participation, acceptance, and belonging.
I.   Spirituality is important, but wholly personal.
J.   Faith is based on the person who possesses the faith, not the Being. Faith is syncretic—that is a personally pleasing mixture of whatever spiritual elements exist in the known world, resulting in an eclectic brew of beliefs and practices. Their faith may be given a label as Christianity, but probably bears no resemblance.

III. CHRISTIANITY VERSUS POSTMODERNISM

CHRISTIANITY

A.	Exhorts people to find meaning in life through the practice of loving God and loving one's neighbor.
B.	Recognizes the existence of moral absolutes. Absolutes are determined by God and conveyed through the Bible, "*the voice of the words of the Lord.*"
C.	Acknowledges the existence of one true God, who created everything, exists eternally, and is holy, omniscient, omnipotent, and omnipresent.
D.	Believes the death and resurrection of Jesus is the central episode of human history because it enables humans to be reconciled with God and have an eternal relationship with Him.
E.	Places faith in God and the principles and teachings He delivered through the Bible.[280]

POSTMODERNISM

A.	Suggests there is no real meaning to be achieved, so self-love becomes a reasonable, primary focus.
B.	Implores each individual to determine what is right and wrong for themselves, given the conditions, their feelings and their past experiences. There is no such thing as sin. Therefore there is no need for a savior or for salvation.
C.	Encourages people to define their own understanding of 'God', based on experience and perceptions, without the restraints that religious texts and traditions impose upon the human mind.
D.	Accepts Christian salvation as valid—<u>along with any of several dozen approaches</u> to understanding eternal outcomes.
E.	Would rather rely upon themselves as the ultimate source of meaning, purpose, and value. They live for the moment and have little anxiety about the future; the entire notion of eternal salvation is of little interest to them.*

---

[280] This chart is made possible by the information in George Barna's book, *Real Teens,* 2001.

A LOOK AT MAJOR WORLDVIEW SHIFTS[281]

(From Dan Kimball's book, *The Emerging Church*)

	Ancient World 2500 B.C.- 500 A.D.	Medieval World 500-1500	Modern World 1500-2000+	Postmodern World 2000+-?
Epistemology	Regional worldview. Time period of first historic civilizations. Deities were considered regional and territorial	Judeo-Christian, God-centered worldview.	During the Enlightenment epistemology shifts to a man-centered trust in 'reason' to discover truth.	Self-determined pluralistic view of culture and religion. Conflicting truths and beliefs are accepted.
Understanding	Power and faith were in the kings, empires and local deities.	Power and faith were in the church	Power and faith were in human reasoning, science, and logic, which also helped explain and interpret God.	Power and faith is in personal experience.
Communication	Oral communication and limited local historical records.	Manuscript and oral communication.	Printing press transforms communication.	Internet and media accelerate an instant global communication revolution.

---

[281] This chart is practically a reproduction of a chart in the book, *"The Emerging Church"* by Dan Kimball.

Authority	Authority was in the revelation given through the oracles, poets, kings, and prophets	Authority was in the Bible but only to be understood as taught through the church. The Bible was not in the hands of the people	Authority was in reason, science, and logic and for Christians was in the reasonable interpretation of the Bible.	Suspicion of authority. The Bible is open to many interpretations and is but one of many religious writings.
Theme	"What is man, that thou art mindful of him?" —Psalm 8:4	"I believe in order that I may understand." —Anselm (1033-1099)	"Knowledge is power." —Francis Bacon "I think, therefore I am." —Descartes (1596-1650)	"If it makes you happy, it can't be that bad." —Sheryl Crow "Every viewpoint is a view from a viewpoint."

IRENAEUS (120-192 A.D.)

This author has read conflicting reports about Irenaeus for years. He is reported to have believed in transubstantiation, in Mary as co-redemptionist, in the Shepherd of Hermas as Scripture, etc. However, there are several points that I have discovered over the years that makes me believe:

1. His writings were corrupted by the Roman Catholic Church (RCC) to support their false doctrines.
2. When I reviewed his testimonies very carefully, he clearly accused the heretics of making Mary sinless, of perverting the ordinance of the Lord's Supper with transubstantiation, etc. and he specifically named their heretical doctrines.
3. His original writings were in Greek. We have only a few pages of the originals. Most of what we have is a Latin translation, which makes me suspicious immediately because of the probable corruption of his history by the RCC.
4. Once, I reviewed very carefully the quote where he is alleged to have supported the Shepherd of Hermas as Scripture. One could easily make a case for an "insertion" into the text at that point. It occurs only once in Irenaeus' writings and he never makes another reference to it. As you know, the RCC is reported to desire placing the Shepherd of Hermas into the Canon of Scripture, and removing the book of Revelation because of its identification of the RCC as the Harlot.
5. He is accused of claiming the Lord lived to an "old age." However, he was a VERY sarcastic writer against the Gnostics, and he may very well have been "cutting" the Gnostics and heretics. Many translators relate the difficulty of his writing and the meaning in the passage where this is found.
6. The RCC church is guilty of drumming up accusations against sanctified churches and corrupting history repeatedly. For example, the Waldensian history is often corrupted; their records were burned by the Jesuits and the RCC. I suspect they have done the same to Irenaeus as much as possible to support their heresies.
7. His quotes contain CT readings but he often quoted the heretics who corrupted the received Traditional Text Words. Furthermore, his quotes cannot be made to conform exactly to the CT; so, he may have been quoting from memory in light of the difficulty to access uncials, scrolls, and codices.

INDEX

Aaron, 94
Abbreviations, 7, 13
abortions, 266, 267
Abraham, 184, 287
absolute, 20, 27, 30, 31, 48, 52, 57, 73, 76, 79, 119, 171, 215, 217, 228, 233, 237, 238, 239, 240, 242, 244, 246, 250, 252, 266, 270, 300
Adam, 184
Against Heresies, 108, 109, 166, 169, 170, 177, 289
agent, 67
AIDS, 266
Alexandrian-type text, 167
Alexandrinus, 13, 161
allegorical, 204
American Bible Societies, 259
American Tract Society, 132, 133, 283
Ananias, 89
anchored, 273, 274
Ancient Hebrews, 9, 114
Anderson (Walter Truett), 235
Anger, 8, 88
angry, 88
Ante-Nicene, 8, 107, 166, 168, 170, 177, 183, 288, 289
anthropomorphism, 102
Antichrist, 59
apographs, 79, 193
Apollinarianism, 17, 219
apostasy, 57, 250, 275
Arianism, 219
Armenian-like, 251
Armerding (Carl), 98, 283
assurance, 6, 68, 88, 89, 111, 113, 117, 153, 154, 158, 167, 236
atomic bomb, 59, 221, 222
Augustine, 121, 198, 199
Authorized Version, 48, 187, 188, 210, 211, 277
autographs, 76, 162, 193, 237
axiomatic principles, 270
babes, 39, 89, 151, 152
Baptist Press, 263

Barna, 237, 266, 301
Barnes (Albert), 51, 74, 105, 106, 146, 149, 283
Barth (Karl), 233, 240, 241, 242, 290
Berean Call, 274, 275, 287
Beza, 17, 161, 187
Bibliography, 7, 11, 283
Bill Hybels, 264
Blackaby, 47, 60, 106, 116, 117, 118, 283
Blight, 7, 35
blind watchmaker, 9, 174, 285
book of the community, 245
both/and, 27, 218
Brian McLaren's, 119
Brown (Harold O. J.), 73, 167, 168, 283
Browne, 40, 202, 207, 283
Buddhism, 18, 48, 80, 217, 226, 253
Bunyan (John), 125
Burgon (Dean John W.), 5, 75, 77, 79, 115, 121, 122, 137, 183, 193, 211, 221, 279, 284, 290, 309
Burney (Bob), 263, 264, 284
Byzantine Text, 167
Calvin (John), 121, 149
Cambridge, 117, 118, 242, 290
candle, 67, 138
canon, 65, 75, 96, 103, 114, 160, 189, 191, 192, 205, 208, 291
Capra (Fritjof), 227, 228, 284
cardinal doctrines, 78
cardinal propositions, 269
Carson (D. A.), 21, 236, 237, 238, 244, 246
cave, 41, 42, 95
cessation, 69, 100, 114, 189
Chafer (Lewis Sperry), 25, 71, 74, 131, 132, 144, 145, 170, 172, 180, 182, 204, 284
Charismatic, 17, 18, 72, 169, 284, 285
charismatics, 39, 60, 117, 134, 189
charlatans, 89
Charles Ryrie, 69
China Inland Mission, 63

Chirrona (Mark), 59
Chopra, M.D. (Deepok), 226, 227
Chrysostom, 120
Clement of Alexandria, 107, 288
Cloud, 72, 74, 119, 179, 186, 188, 284, 197, 198, 250, 265, 266
Cobb (John), 232, 233, 285
Collate, 17
Comfort (Philip), 75, 163, 164, 238, 285
Comforter, 90
community, 17, 260, 264, 284
compass, 150
confessionalism, 18
Congdon (Douglas), 71, 121, 128, 133, 134, 135, 137, 138, 139, 145, 285
congregants, 248
contemplative Prayer, 18
contract, 57, 58, 60, 83, 84, 85, 87, 110, 160, 161, 162, 171, 243, 255, 258, 260, 267
contradictory views, 215
convergence (Convergent) Church, 18, 19, 21, 56, 287
convergent, 21, 56
Convergent Church, 18
Cook (Joseph), 134, 144
corporate disasters, 243
Couch (Mal), 76, 77, 78
covenant, 58, 60, 84, 85, 91, 171, 172, 276
covenant theology, 54
creation, 8, 22, 26, 62, 97, 98, 131, 172, 173, 174, 175, 176, 177, 180, 258
Damascus, 89, 92
Dana (H. E.), 285, 192
Daniel, 101, 102, 159, 171, 249
Darwin, 174, 175, 218, 221, 240
Darwinian, 178
date, 77, 136, 188, 189, 220, 222, 237, 283, 289
dates, 221, 222
David Cloud, 72, 74, 119, 179, 186, 188, 197, 198, 250, 265, 266
Davy (William), 121
Dawkins (Richard), 175, 178, 285

Decalogue, 111, 258
deconstructionism, 19, 24, 56, 58, 62, 64, 84, 232, 234, 244
deconstructionist, 56
dedication, 7
deductive logic, 26
Deere (Jack), 60, 113
definitions, 7, 17
deformation, 8, 58
depression, 8, 88
Derrida (Jacques), 27, 232
Descartes (René), 21, 23, 223, 303
destruction, 39, 44, 53, 194, 218, 289
Diabolus, 125
dialectical materialism, 19
dimensions, 23, 91
dipolar theology, 37, 252
direct communion, 61
dispensation(s), 31, 36, 37, 45, 54, 65, 68, 69, 90, 95, 100, 101, 103, 104, 133, 180, 181, 183, 253, 254, 259, 287, 289,
Dispensationalism, 48, 69, 254, 287, 289
Docetism, 20, 219
Dockery (David), 214, 215, 220, 224, 225, 231, 232, 285
doctrine(s), 22, 23, 24, 26, 35, 36, 38, 44, 48, 49, 50, 55, 56, 57, 69, 76, 78, 84, 102, 109, 119, 127, 138, 139, 166, 145, 178, 188, 191, 197, 198, 216, 223, 229, 234, 241, 242, 244, 245, 249, 250, 252, 253, 256, 257, 259, 260, 261, 269, 270, 273, 274, 276, 304
Dogmatism, 20
Dorner (Isaak August), 133
Driscoll, (Mark), 247, 260
Don Jasmin, 48
dynamic equivalent translation(s), 20, 75, 203, 262
ecumenism, 17, 48, 74, 113, 234, 248
Ecumenism, 20
Eddy (Mary Baker Glover), 73
Ehrman, (Bart), 26, 74, 74, 75, 285
either/or, 26, 218
Elijah, 41, 42, 94, 95, 208
emergent, 19, 244, 250, 253

emerging (church), 10, 18, 20, 21, 30, 31, 56, 72, 119, 214, 217, 222, 227, 228, 243, 244, 246, 247, 248, 249, 250, 252, 253, 254, 255, 256, 257, 259, 262, 264, 268, 273, 274, 275, 284, 286, 287, 302
Emerson (Ralph Waldo), 33
Emmanuel, 25, 125, 192, 195, 280, 289
Emmanuel Baptist Theological Seminary, 25, 192, 195, 280, 289
Emmaus, 93
empirical, 30, 179
empiricism, 224
Empiricists, 22
England, 33, 60, 188, 233, 265, 266
enlightenment, 25, 40, 41, 42, 50, 55, 65, 189, 201, 205, 206, 229, 278
Enlightenment, 21, 44, 136, 214, 223, 241, 302
EPIC, 236
epistemologists, 22
epistemology, 21, 22, 214, 223, 233, 287, 302
Erickson (Millard J.), 26, 27, 28, 29, 33, 286
eta, 193
Ethiopian, 57
eunuch, 57, 216
Eusebius, 169
Eutychianism, 22, 219
Evangelicals, 76, 275, 287
exclusivity, 23
existentialism, 23
face to face, 92, 94, 171
famine, 51, 52, 53, 54
Far Eastern Bible College, 77, 115, 190, 287
first love, 67
Flew (Anthony), 178
Floyd Nolen Jones, 76
formal equivalent, verbal translations, 75
fornication, 182, 231, 254, 266
Foucault (Michael), 26, 232, 286
foundation(s), 27, 42, 44, 53, 71, 85, 153, 159, 179, 224, 229, 240, 242, 244, 255, 264, 267, 283

Foundationalism, 23, 233
France, 21, 108, 137
Frederick Schleiermacher, 249
Gad, 101, 207
gangs, 53, 182
Garden (Eden), 44, 50, 65, 89, 111, 165, 171, 184
general revelation, 172, 174, 179, 180, 258
German, 222
giant angels, 59, 202
Gideon, 116
Gilley (Gary E.), 60, 61, 62, 101, 108, 109, 117, 118, 247, 250, 253, 254, 266, 286,
Gnosticism, 22, 73
goad, 146, 147, 148
Gothic, 32, 211
grammata, 193
graphe, 193
Graphe, 10, 192
Graves (J. R.), 136, 144
Great White Throne Judgment, 100
Greek Received Text, 78, 187
Grenz (Stanley), 217, 233, 244, 286
Gruden (Wayne), 60
guilt, 49, 64, 115, 132, 143, 248, 268
Haggard (Ted), 182, 254
Hammett (John), 244, 286
Hebrew Masoretic text, 78, 210
hedonism, 53, 266, 280
hedonistic, 54, 274
Hegel, 224
Hegelian, 20, 23, 24, 28
hermeneutics, 24, 35, 56, 262, 276
Hermeneutics of Suspicion, 24
Herod, 99
High Holy Prayer, 90
HighBeam Research, 27
Hinduism, 18, 48, 80, 81, 181, 217, 226, 253, 262
Hodge (A. A.), 121,
Hodge (A. H.) 138
Hodges (Zane C.), 213
Holman Christian Standard Bible, 64, 290
homosexuals, 27, 81, 231

Hort, 15, 39, 44, 164, 211, 239, 245, 290
Hosler (John O.), 108, 109
humanistic, 20, 23, 30, 36, 48, 81, 181, 200, 201, 220
Humanistic, 8, 10, 80, 81, 231
Hunt III (Arthur W.), 71, 259
Hunt (Dave), 71, 58, 286, 287
Hybels (Bill), 264
hyper-dispensationalists, 54
icons, 58
image, 130, 136, 178, 236, 258, 260, 274
inductive, 23, 26
iniquity, 36, 38, 49, 69, 183
inscripturated, 25, 39, 42, 65, 67, 91, 93, 94, 95, 96, 99, 100, 101, 102, 103, 111, 113, 118, 127, 136, 152, 158, 159, 201, 208
Irenaeus, 108, 109, 160, 166, 167, 168, 169, 170, 177, 289, 304, 305
Ironside (H. A.), 143, 287
Islam, 18, 48, 80, 253, 262
Islamic, 49
Jacob, 92, 162, 184
James (Henry), 224
Jefferson (Thomas J), 268
Jellema (Dick), 232
Jerome, 198, 199, 222
Jerusalem, 48, 102, 179, 199
Job, 9, 97, 101, 111, 112, 140, 170
Jones (Floyd Nolen), 287
jots and tittles, 83, 175, 179
Jude, 37, 38, 50, 101, 127, 151
Kabala, 27
Kant (Immanuel), 33, 224
Karl Barth's, 241, 242
Katrina, 182
Khoo (Jeffery), 77, 116, 190, 287
Kierkegaard, 224
Kimball (Dan), 214, 217, 222, 225, 226, 227, 228, 247, 287, 302
King David, 207
King James Bible, 2, 5, 14, 48, 50, 53, 77, 86, 185, 186, 187, 198, 200, 211, 260, 277, 280, 290, 311, 312
King James Bible translator's, 198
Kingdom of God, 240, 254, 255

KJB, 14, 36, 51, 77, 124, 132, 192, 198, 238, 256, 277, 280
kleptomania, 81
Lactantius, 110
Latin, 13, 14, 15, 123, 163, 211, 304
lectionaries, 17, 163, 211
legalism, 54
liars, 155
liberalism, 218, 219, 273
Liberalism, 26, 218, 230, 240, 273, 287
lips, 83, 87, 103, 111, 112, 160, 276
Locke (John), 21, 223
logic, 26
logocentrism, 27
lower criticism, 244
Luther (Martin), 84, 121
Lyons, 108
MacArthur (John), 216, 223, 224, 247, 268, 287
Machen (Gresham), 218, 219, 220, 230, 287
Maharishi Mahesh Yogi, 226
major divisions, 245
Majority Text, 163
Mansoul, 125
Mars Hill Church, 260, 261
Martensen, 121
Marxism, 28, 63
Marxist, 24
Mary, 58, 73, 225, 304
matter, 61, 72, 78, 91, 107, 117, 167, 176, 182, 187, 196, 200, 201, 207, 227, 242, 249, 262, 263
McCheyne (Robert Murray), 99, 100, 287
McLaren (Brian), 19, 31, 119, 269, 287
McMahon (Matthew), 239, 241, 287
McMahon (T. A.), 274, 275
message, 25, 39, 48, 71, 83, 84, 85, 86, 87, 88, 95, 99, 159, 174, 175, 195, 219, 220, 237, 247, 258, 259, 271, 281, 311
metanarratives, 27, 30, 84
metaphor, 8, 39, 65, 89, 90, 172, 173, 235, 260

Missler (Chuck), 21, 237, 266, 268, 287
model for preservation, 194
Moorman (Jack), 48, 210, 211, 288
Mormons, 73
Morning Star, 31
Moses, 73, 83, 85, 91, 92, 94, 102, 111, 112, 171, 184, 185, 208
Mother Teresa, 227
Murphee (Jon Tal), 288, 250
Muslim, 135, 227, 263
Mysticism, 29, 202
Napier Parkview Baptist Church,, 108
narcissistic, 266
narrator, 29, 260
Nathan, 101, 207
Nebuchadnezzar, 171, 216
negative, 141, 142, 225, 242, 259
neo-evangelicalism, 29, 218, 219, 253, 273
neo-orthodoxy, 29
Nestle/Aland, 211, 239
neuter, 104, 185
New Ageism, 80
New Covenants, 171
Nietzche,, 224
NIV, 14, 51, 72, 116, 191, 237, 238
NKJV, 51, 72
non-cessationists, 189
non-separatism, 273
Oden (Thomas), 213, 214, 221, 288
omnipotent, 28, 37, 52, 84, 221, 250, 252, 301
omnipresent, 28, 37, 52, 84, 221, 301
omniscient, 28, 37, 84, 202, 221, 301
One Word, 11, 278
open theology, 251
Open theology, 251
Oprah, 227
Origen, 13, 183
Origin of Species, 218, 221
orthodox, 26, 152, 208, 240, 252, 259
orthodox theology, 259
Oswald Sanders, 63, 125, 135
Oxford, 22, 74, 174, 178, 285, 286
paganism, 48, 230
Paganism, 230
Pantheism, 202

paradigm shift, 213, 221, 227
paradoxes, 27
pasa, 192, 193
Pastor of Hermas, 169, 289
Paul, 36, 56, 62, 66, 85, 89, 92, 98, 100, 102, 104, 118, 123, 128, 130, 140, 142, 144, 148, 149, 151, 152, 156, 173, 185, 193, 194, 196, 201, 208, 219, 231, 240, 270, 283
Pentateuch, 91, 184
Peshitta, 211
Peter, 5, 9, 53, 70, 110, 186, 187, 188, 194, 201, 206, 209, 261, 283
Philip, 57, 163, 238
Philo, 22, 123
plenary, 14, 30, 116, 287
pluralism, 30
Polycarp, 108, 166
pornography, 231
Pornography, 105
Porphyry (Malcus), 222
positive, 140, 142
postulates, 10, 229, 233
pragmatism, 30, 232, 234, 289
Preacher, 175
pre-incarnate, 33
premodern, 31
Prince of Preachers, 3, 112, 277
process, 19, 24, 25, 37, 39, 41, 83, 87, 101, 142, 159, 174, 175, 176, 193, 195, 209, 227, 233, 241, 250, 251, 252
process theology, 233, 241, 250, 251, 252
proposition, 137, 222, 270
prosperity, 48
providence, 57, 77, 105, 106, 172, 179, 216
Quaker, 61
Quaker Books, 61
quantum, 177, 227
Rabbis, 114
rape, 267
real estate, 59
rebellion, 8, 69, 87, 88, 239, 274, 275
received, 5, 28, 36, 41, 42, 44, 50, 57, 58, 71, 72, 79, 87, 90, 93, 103, 109, 118, 126, 144, 152, 153, 163,

167, 171, 181, 186, 189, 193, 196, 201, 206, 207, 208, 209, 210, 211, 220, 238, 241, 248, 256, 257, 262, 305, 309, 311
Reformation, 8, 31, 58, 121, 136, 186, 221
regenerated, 50
Regenerated, 9, 146
relativism, 31
Renaissance, 32
Replacement Theology, 255
retrograde, 252
Roman Catholic, 26, 31, 72, 119, 250, 304
Romanists, 24
roots, 127, 138, 249, 250
Rorty (Richard), 232, 289
Ruckman (Peter), 186, 187, 188, 285
Ruckmanites, 9, 186
Ryken (Leland), 62, 84, 289
Ryrie (Charles), 254, 289
sacramentalism, 32, 57, 241, 248
Sanders, 64, 146, 149, 150, 151, 289
Satan, 44, 45, 143, 239
Saul, 89, 93, 144, 149, 207
Schleiermacher (Frederick), 249
seducing, 36, 44, 55
seduction, 55
seeker-sensitive church(es), 246, 247, 262, 264, 273
selfism, 30, 44, 56, 58, 63, 165, 216
Septuagint, 14, 51, 309, 312
seven, 38, 54, 59, 86, 89, 90, 97, 153, 180, 254
Seven, 8, 81, 88, 97
Seventh Day Adventist, 73, 135, 288
seventieth week of Daniel, 254, 255
Shamanism, 80
Shaylor (Randolph), 78, 161, 290
Shedd (W. G. T.), 131
silent epidemic, 53, 283
similitudes, 35
Sinaiticus, 161
Smith (Joseph), 73
Socratic, 19, 24
space, 91, 176, 220
Sparks (T. Austin), 136, 188, 189, 283, 289

speak in tongues, 59, 60
special revelation, 43, 172, 180, 181, 183, 184, 185, 189, 193, 205, 207
specific revelation, 170, 180, 182, 184, 207, 208
Spock (Benjamin), 264
Spurgeon (C. H.), 3, 9, 112, 196, 197, 277, 284, 289
statistics, 265, 266
still small voice, 41, 42, 94, 95
streams, 19, 241, 252
Strouse (Dr. Thomas), 25, 192, 193, 195, 280, 289
Stub (J. Aall Osteen), 222
subjectivism, 22, 28, 30, 32, 44, 60, 202, 220, 234
Summit Church, 261
suneidêsis, 123, 124
Swaggart (Jimmy), 183
Sweet (Leonard), 236
systematic theology, 28, 47, 84, 139
TBN, 59
TCOP, 14, 214, 215, 225, 231, 232, 234, 235, 236, 241, 245, 246, 252
television, 47, 55, 165, 226, 227
tenets, 8, 20, 27, 37, 38, 44, 58, 81, 158, 183, 202, 209, 210, 214, 215, 221, 229, 232, 233, 239, 243, 245, 250, 261, 263, 265, 273
Tertullian, 110, 199
testimony, 59, 69, 85, 91, 107, 124, 133, 158, 173, 198, 200, 209, 231, 262, 275, 280
Textus Receptus, 14, 163, 209, 256
Textus Receptus/Traditional Text, 209
THE OLD PATHS, 1, 2, 281
theophany, 33, 92
theopneustos, 10, 102, 191
thermodynamics, 175, 176
Toronto Movement, 62
Torry (R. A.), 133
traditional, 5, 27, 41, 63, 218, 248, 249
traditionalism, 57, 114
transcendentalism, 33, 190
transfiguration, 92
translation(s), 5, 36, 37, 50, 51, 52, 53, 55, 75, 86, 105, 185, 188, 189,

191, 192, 197, 200, 202, 206, 211, 216, 237, 238, 259, 280, 304, 311, 312
tribulation, 254, 255
Trinity, 59, 67, 68, 103, 159, 171, 181
Trinity Broadcasting Network, 59
tripartite man, 139
UBS Greek text, 211
uncertain, 49, 55, 59, 86, 87, 129, 147, 162, 185, 203, 210, 238, 243, 275
uncertainty, 30, 35, 38, 44, 56, 58, 62, 76, 79, 87, 162, 165, 216, 220, 237, 239, 242, 243, 244, 270, 274
unifying principle, 177
unifying universal principle, 177
Upper Room, 43, 90
Uriah, 102
Vaticanus, 13, 161
verbal plenary translating, 20, 72, 75, 84, 290, 309
virgin, 26, 78, 129, 155, 245, 252
Visual Orientation, 11, 258
vocal apparatus, 83
vocalization, 83, 87
vortex, 266, 268, 287
Waite, Th.D, Ph.D., 5, 48, 68, 147, 163, 211, 274, 290
Wallace, 172, 195, 290
Walvoord (John), 42, 43, 96, 204, 290
Warren (Rick), 247
weak, 18, 63, 64, 68, 128, 129, 141, 142, 146, 150, 151, 185, 206, 274
Westcott, 15, 39, 44, 164, 211, 239, 245, 290
Westminster Confession of Faith, 77
White, 288, 309,
White (Ellen G.), 73
Willow Creek, 263, 264, 284
Willow Creek Community Church's, 263
Winograd (Robert), 5, 6
Williams (H. D.), 1, 2, 5, 39, 45, 75, 80, 84, 221, 281
Williams (James B.), 78, 161
witness, 40, 55, 70, 95, 109, 120, 123, 124, 125, 126, 127, 128, 138, 139, 140, 146, 147, 149, 156, 158, 173, 206, 233

Witness, 9, 40, 123, 125, 290
Word-for-Word, 75
Wycliffe, 31
Zuck (Roy B.), 63, 64, 71, 120, 127, 128, 289, 290

ABOUT THE AUTHOR

Dr. Williams was born in Ft. Pierce, Florida. He was saved at the age of fourteen at his local Baptist church under Pastor J. R. White where he was active in the church youth group. His local church ordained him to preach the gospel. After graduating with honors from high school, he attended Stetson University where he met his wife, Patricia, and they were married in 1961. Starting in the ministerial program at Stetson and switching to pre-med in his junior year, he graduated with honors with a B.A. After Stetson, he taught high school at Eau Gallie, Florida for two years, and then continued his training at the University of Miami Medical School where he graduated with honors. Following his medical training, Dr. Williams and Patricia settled in New Port Richey, Florida where he practiced Family Medicine as a board certified family practitioner. He was active in his community as a hospital board member for twenty years, a chief-of-staff, president of the medical society, an advisory board member and president of Moody Bible Institute's Florida program, a board member of the Health Planning Commission, and a teacher at his local Baptist church. He helped develop and administrate a multi-specialist medical clinic with forty thousand patients and seventeen doctors. His Biblical training was obtained at Stetson University, Moody Bible Institute, and Louisiana Baptist University. After retirement, Dr. Williams has continued serving the Lord Jesus Christ as an associate pastor, a teacher, and as vice-president and representative for the Dean Burgon Society. He received a Ph.D. in Biblical studies at Louisiana Baptist University. He has traveled to many foreign lands where he has represented the Dean Burgon Society, teaching pastors and participating in evangelistic events. He is author of the several books, *The Lie That Changed The Modern World; Word-For-Word Translating of the Received Texts, Verbal Plenary Translating; Hearing the Voice of God, The Septuagint is a Paraphrase,* and *The Attack on the Canon of Scripture* in addition to many articles and booklets. Dr. Williams and his wife, Patricia have two sons and five grandchildren.

BOOKS BY DR. WILLIAMS

WORD-FOR-WORD TRANSLATING OF THE RECEIVED TEXT, VERBAL PLENARY TRANSLATING:

This 264 page perfect bound book may be purchased through www.BibleForToday.org. See below. There is a vital need for a book to inform sincere Bible-believing Christians about the proper techniques of translating the WORDS of God into the receptor languages of the world. No book like this one has ever been written. It is a unique and much-needed book. The very first requirement for any translation of the Bible is to have the proper WORDS of Hebrew, Aramaic, and Greek from which to translate. It is the contention of this book that the original verbally and plenarily inspired Hebrew, Aramaic, and Greek WORDS have been verbally and plenarily preserved in accordance with God's promises. These preserved WORDS are those received-text-WORDS which underlie the King James Bible. This volume emphasizes the requirement of a proper technique to be used in all translations of God's WORDS. It must be done in a verbally and plenarily translation technique. That is, the Hebrew, Aramaic, and Greek WORDS must be conveyed into the receptor languages, not merely the ideas, concepts, thoughts, or message. This technique is absent in all of the other manuals on Bible translation. Dr. Williams is not the usual sort of writer. He combines the meticulous skill of a Doctor of Medicine with the artistry and acumen of a Doctor of Philosophy to produce this grand volume. May translators and sincere Christians of all persuasions and professions use this important book worldwide! The Bible For Today Press, BFT #**3302**
ISBN 1-56848-056-3, Order by PHONE: 1-800-JOHN 10:9, Order by FAX: 856-854-2464, Order by MAIL: Bible For Today, 900 Park Avenue Collingswood, NJ 08108'

THE ATTACK ON THE CANON OF SCRIPTURE, A POLEMIC AGAINST MODERN SCHOLARSHIP

This 264 page perfect bound book will be released in January, 2008. ISBN 978-0-9801689-0-7. This 152 page book demonstrates the newest attack on the Words and books of the Bible by modern day scholarship. The changing methods for assaulting the Scriptures are important for those who are concerned about the relentless attempt to destroy them. In a remarkable polemic against modern scholarship, Dr. Williams outlines the most recent means many are using to undermine confidence in the Words of God received through the priesthood of believers. It will be available at Amazon.com. or at BibleForToday.org, BFT # **3340**.

THE LIE THAT CHANGED THE MODERN WORLD
This book is in hardback format, 440 pages in all. ISBN 1-56848-042-3. It is a factual defense not only of the King James Bible, but also of the Hebrew and Greek Words that underlie the King James Bible. The author is a medical doctor, now retired, who has researched this important topic thoroughly. May the Lord Jesus Christ use and honor this study in the days, weeks, months, and years ahead until our Lord Jesus Christ returns. It should be in every layman's library, every Pastor's library, every church library, every college library, every university library, and in every theological seminary library. It is available through Bible For Today Press, www.biblefortoday.org, BFT # **3125**.

THE PURE WORDS OF GOD
This is a perfect bound 136 page book. ISBN 978-0-9801689-1-4. Dr. Williams' book, *The Pure Words of God,* clarifies the use of the word "pure" when it is used to define the Words of God. Should "pure" be applied to translations, to Traditional/Received Texts, or to critical texts? Once the correct application is explained, Dr. Williams clarifies God's commands to receive and keep His pure Words. It is available through Amazon.com or Bible For Today Press at www.biblefortoday.org, BFT #

Look for other books to be released by Dr. Williams in the near future. One work, **The Apostolic Origin of the Traditional Text** is nearing completion and should be released in mid-2008. Another book, **The Septuagint is a Paraphrase**, will be released in early 2008.

www.ingramcontent.com/pod-product-compliance
Lightning Source LLC
Chambersburg PA
CBHW070633160426
43194CB00009B/1450